Patterned Splendour

The **ISEAS – Yusof Ishak Institute** (formerly Institute of Southeast Asian Studies) is an autonomous organization established in 1968. It is a regional centre dedicated to the study of socio-political, security, and economic trends and developments in Southeast Asia and its wider geostrategic and economic environment. The Institute's research programmes are grouped under Regional Economic Studies (RES), Regional Strategic and Political Studies (RSPS), and Regional Social and Cultural Studies (RSCS). The Institute is also home to the ASEAN Studies Centre (ASC), the Singapore APEC Study Centre, and the Temasek History Research Centre (THRC).

ISEAS Publishing, an established academic press, has issued more than 2,000 books and journals. It is the largest scholarly publisher of research about Southeast Asia from within the region. ISEAS Publishing works with many other academic and trade publishers and distributors to disseminate important research and analyses from and about Southeast Asia to the rest of the world.

Patterned Splendour

Textiles Presented on Javanese Metal and Stone Sculptures
Eighth to the Fifteenth Century

Lesley S Pullen

Drawings by
Yiran Huang

YUSOF ISHAK INSTITUTE

First published in Singapore in 2021 by
ISEAS Publishing
30 Heng Mui Keng Terrace
Singapore 119614

Email: publish@iseas.edu.sg
Website: bookshop.iseas.edu.sg

All rights reserved. No part of this publication may be reproduced, stored in a retrieval system, or transmitted in any form or by any means, electronic, mechanical, photocopying, recording or otherwise, without the prior permission of the ISEAS – Yusof Ishak Institute.

© 2021 ISEAS – Yusof Ishak Institute, Singapore

The responsibility for facts and opinions in this publication rests exclusively with the author and her interpretations do not necessarily reflect the views or the policy of the publisher or its supporters.

ISEAS Library Cataloguing-in-Publication Data

Name(s): Pullen, Lesley S., author.
Title: Patterned splendour : textiles presented on Javanese metal and stone sculptures ; eighth to the fifteenth century / by Lesley S. Pullen ; drawings by Yiran Huang.
Description: Singapore : ISEAS–Yusof Ishak Institute, 2021. | Includes bibliographical references.
Identifiers: ISBN 9789814881845 (paperback) | ISBN 9789814881852 (PDF)
Subjects: LCSH: Sculpture—Indonesia—Java. | Textile design—Indonesia—Java.
Classification: LCC NB1160 P98

Typeset by ISEAS Publishing
Printed in Singapore by Markono Print Media Pte Ltd

Front Cover: The photograph is of the statue of Mañjuśrī Arapacana, 1265 CE from Caṇḍi Jago, in the State Hermitage Museum, St Petersburg. The pattern is a drawing by Yiran Huang of the textile presented on this statue.

Back Cover: The pattern is a drawing by Yiran Huang of the textile presented on the statue of Sudhanakumāra, c.1268-80 from Caṇḍi Jago, in the Museum Nasional Indonesia, Jakarta.

Contents

Foreword by John N. Miksic	vii
Preface	xi
Acknowledgements	xiii
Drawing and Photograph Credits	xvii
List of Maps	xviii
Orthography	xix
1. Background	1
2. Javanese Textile Traditions	21
3. Central and Early East Java: Metal and Stone Sculpture from the Eighth to the Eleventh Century	61
4. Kediri and Singhasāri: Stone Sculpture from the Eleventh to the Fourteenth Century	129
5. Majapahit: Stone Sculpture from the Fourteenth to the Fifteenth Century	223
6. Conclusion	251
Epilogue	261
Appendices	
List of Museums	267
Chinese Terms for Geographical Regions: From Yijing 635–718	268
Chinese Terms for Geographical Regions: From Zhufanzi, Twelfth to the Thirteenth Century	269
Old Javanese Literature	270
Glossary	271
Extended Glossary of Textile Terms	275
Bibliography	283
Index	293
About the Author and Illustrator	308

Foreword

Archaeologists have made some progress in the study of ancient Southeast Asian textiles, but the results of this form of research are likely to remain limited to verifying the types of plants used to make the fibres and dyes, and possibly the weaving techniques employed. It seems likely that we will have to depend on indirect methods for the foreseeable future in our attempts to reconstruct the textiles used in early Southeast Asia. Historical sources contain some data, but these have serious limitations. Most surviving documents only refer to textiles in passing. Many terms used to refer to them are no longer understood. Old Javanese vocabulary concerning textiles is extensive, a sign of their interest in this topic and its importance in society, but there is scant chance that the literal meanings of these words will ever be recovered.

For several years I taught a course on traditional arts of Southeast Asia in the eighteenth through early twentieth centuries, in which I emphasized the importance of textiles in trying to understand the roles of what in the West we call art and artists. No female artists and very few male artists are mentioned in ancient inscriptions. Artists were not a separate category of people in ancient Java; as in early twentieth-century Bali, the making of objects possessing what is now called artistic value was a common activity of children as well as adults, as were performances of music and dance. Artists were not marginal members of society, though some people were certainly recognized as more skilful than others in creating textiles or pottery, both of which were exclusively made by women. The high aesthetic and technical value of Southeast Asia textile production only came to be acknowledged in the West in the mid-nineteenth century. Since that time, scholars have elevated the importance of textiles as a medium of artistic expression in traditional Southeast

Asia from the status of a craft to the cultural equivalent of painting and sculpture.

Textile art in precolonial Southeast Asia had great ceremonial and symbolic value. Locally made textiles commanded high economic value not only within Southeast Asian societies but also in diplomatic gift exchange with China. Textiles were traded in both directions, into and out of Southeast Asia to South and East Asia. Indonesia may have exported large quantities of textiles to Cambodia during that civilization's golden age, as the author suggests, but unfortunately we know very little about regional trade within Southeast Asia during this period. Further study of textile patterns may enable scholars to recover information about this topic. Textiles possess major scholarly value as evidence of long-distance communication. One question for future research arises from the question of whether the medium of transmission of the designs was exclusively through textile trade, or whether some other media such as illuminated manuscripts were also involved.

Javanese sculptors in the thirteenth century devoted considerable attention to depicting the textiles worn by figures sculpted in stone. Temple reliefs in central Java may also have depicted textiles worn by people of that time and place, but textile designs might have been represented in plaster coatings that covered most of the reliefs—only faint traces of which survive. It is not known whether statues in central Java were similarly coated with plaster that was then painted. In India, as in ancient Greece, it was common practice to paint statues of divinities. It is possible that the change to carving detailed textile patterns directly on stone in the thirteenth century was correlated with increased social differentiation, which was denoted by the types of textiles people wore. The same types of textiles, and jewellery, were worn by both men and women, which suggested a relative degree of equality between the sexes. A fourteenth-century Chinese trader named Wang Dayuan wrote detailed descriptions of clothing worn in various ports in Southeast Asia. This gives the impression that clothing was a significant badge of local identity in the region. Wang would have easily appreciated this fact, since textiles played the same role in China.

Dr Pullen's book shows how useful it is to compare the evidence for cultural interaction as exhibited in textile motifs with communication patterns expressed in other media such as sculpture, architecture, language and ceramics. This book provides comparisons with textiles in many others parts of Asia: Nepal, Tibet, India, Sri Lanka, Myanmar, Bhutan, Persia, the Sasanian Empire, Central Asia and China, and proposes a new, more detailed chronology of thirteenth-century Javanese statuary based on textile forms. This is a very useful contribution to the study of the history of Javanese art during the thirteenth century—a violent yet brilliantly artistic period. Like jewellery, textiles display elements of both style and fashion. The idea of fashion has fascinated archaeologists such as A.L. Kroeber and David Clarke since the early twentieth century. Fashions change quickly; archaeologists and art historians can use them to create precise evolutionary sequences, which aid in the development of detailed chronologies.

Dr Pullen's analysis shows that thirteenth-century Indonesian sculptors were not making up designs; they were endeavouring to depict real textiles as faithfully as possible. This is useful in deciding whether to accept the assumption that the Indonesian statuary and reliefs were not depicting imaginary realms but were accurately reflecting the society in which the artists lived. Some relevant questions probably can never be answered. Were the motifs found on textiles symbols of character or status, or were bodies purely frameworks on which to hang textiles for display as symbols? And—something that we cannot deduce from the statuary—how important was colour?

The huge number of detailed illustrations found in this book will be a major permanent resource for other scholars. The assiduous effort by Dr Pullen to document these motifs and to trace their distribution over a broad swath of the globe is a significant and lasting contribution to the study of communication and exchanges of artistic ideas in general. I am very happy that the ISEAS – Yusof Ishak Institute has agreed to publish this volume.

John N. Miksic

Preface

There exist numerous free-standing figurative sculptures produced in Java between the eighth and fifteenth centuries that feature dress displaying detailed textile patterns. This surviving body of sculpture, carved in stone and cast in metal, varying in both size and condition, remain in archaeological sites and museums in Indonesia and worldwide. The equatorial climate of Java has precluded any textiles from this period surviving. This book argues, therefore, that the textiles represented on these sculptures offer a unique insight into the patterned splendour of the textiles in circulation during this period. Hence, this publication will contribute to our knowledge of the textiles in circulation at that time by including the first comprehensive record of this body of sculpture, together with their textile patterns classified into a typology of styles.

Because of the limited number of inscriptions and texts from this period, it has proved necessary to conduct the research for this book by utilizing empirical methods to examine all the sculptures. The discussion of each statue is supported by photographs and original line-drawings of their textile designs. A close analysis of these drawings establishes that during a brief period in the late thirteenth century the textile patterns carved on the sculptures reached their greatest diversity and complexity.

In considering supporting evidence from Persia, India, Central Asia and China, this book explores the origins of the medieval textile patterns depicted on these sculptures. It also provides some analysis of specific motifs, such as those representing esoteric iconography. As this research necessitated a detailed analysis of all the sculptures representing textiles, it also contributes significantly to other related aspects of concurrent apparel and ornamentation. It is my intention that this catalogue of textile patterns be utilized by future students and scholars in the stylistic dating of sculptures from Java between the eighth and fifteenth centuries.

Note that this publication addresses only the repeat patterns presented on free-standing figurative sculpture that evidentially reflect pliant textiles adorning a human form in the round. The publication does not address the repeat patterns evident on stone temples or architectural features within sculptures, where the rigid patterns may be understood to represent decorative surface elements.

Acknowledgements

This monograph is based on my 2017 doctoral thesis submitted to SOAS University of London. The initial inspiration for my doctoral research is to be found in a series of articles published by Jan Wisseman Christie from 1991 to 1999, supplemented by observations by scholars such as Hiram Woodward in 1977. Given the importance of the visual image throughout this monograph, I offer a special acknowledgement to Yiran Huang for her work in interpreting through hand drawings with remarkable exactitude and detail the textile patterns represented on the sculptures. Her numerous line drawings have greatly added to the significance of this publication.

I wish to thank a number of the faculty members from the School of Arts at SOAS University of London. Elizabeth Moore, my supervisor, who nurtured me through my first five years whilst I assembled my material, Christian Luczanits, who accepted me as his student for my final writing-up year, and Stacey Pearson, who remained an active and supportive second supervisor throughout. I also thank several internationally recognized Java scholars in the Netherlands, including Pauline Lungsingh Scheurleer, Marijke Klokke and Veronique Degroot, whose deep understanding of Javanese art history provided me with useful direction. A few exceptional individuals on the ground, such as Eko Bastiawan in East Java, Eka Rusdiawanti in Central Java, and Nigel Bullough aka Hadi Sidomulyo at UTC, Trawas, East Java, have played functional roles as local researchers, translators and guides, and have provided constructive ideas and general support. Pak Lutfi, Professor of History, University Negeri Malang, Pak Dwi Cahyone, University Negeri Malang, and Ibu Asti Suryo Astuti, Director, Danar Hadi Textile Gallery, Surakarta, have all guided me on the uses of terms in Javanese dress styles.

Over the years I have received advice from many art historians on the sculptures, including Robert Brown at LACMA in Los Angeles, Edi Sedyawati in Jakarta, Natasha Reichle at the AAM in San Francisco, John Guy at The Met in New York, and Olga Deshpande at the State Hermitage Museum in St Petersburg. During the course of my research, many textile curators and collectors have shared with me their knowledge of medieval Asian textiles: Jacqueline Simcox in London, Jon Thompson (d. 2020) in Oxford, Regula Schorta and her team at the Abegg-Stiftung in Switzerland, Zhao Feng at the CNSM in Hangzhou, James Watt in New York, James Bennett at AGSA in Adelaide, Ruth Barnes at YUAG in New Haven, and Thomas Murray in San Francisco. Several international scholars encouraged me in my research, including Annabel Gallop, Arlo Griffiths, Lydia Kieven, Edmund McKinnon and Jonathan Zilberg. Several fellow students provided practical support with my fieldwork in Asia, including Ida Chow in China and Julia Pratt in Indonesia.

In pursuit of a better understanding of the specific types of basaltic andesite from which these Javanese sculptures are carved, I thank Andy Beard in the Department of Earth and Planetary Sciences at Birkbeck, University of London. I received early translation services from Gosta Bergholtz, Joan Bulmer and Academic Affairs, and proofreading support for my doctoral thesis from Janet Clemo and John Sutcliffe.

During my final field trip in May 2016, I received assistance from Liliek Adelina and Pak Among at the Vihara Buddhayana in Jakarta. I also shared my image library with and received constructive feedback from John Miksic, Goh Geok Yian, Helene Njoto and Elizabeth Moore in Singapore, from Hadi Sidomulyo, Ismail Lutfi, Dwi Cahyone and Bambang Budi Utomo in East Java, and from Asti Suryo Astuti in Central Java.

When converting my doctoral thesis into this book, I secured the advice of George Michell, a long-time friend and published author. Dr Michell was kind enough to read my thesis and to make decisive formatting suggestions. When I presented my doctoral research at the ISEAS – Yusof Ishak Institute in Singapore in January 2018, Ng Kok Kiong and Catherine Ang from ISEAS Publishing attended my lecture, following which I was invited to submit a book proposal for their consideration. Ng Kok Kiong supported and encouraged me through my publishing journey. In March 2020 ISEAS assigned my manuscript to Stephen Logan as Production Editor who with patience and persistence directed this project through the challenging months of the global COVID-19 pandemic. As a first-time author, my relationship with ISEAS remained collegiate and constructive for which I am most grateful. John Miksic, also a long-time friend and subject authority, volunteered many pointers in aspects of academic writing, all of which proved most useful. Professor Miksic also agreed to contribute the foreword.

I conclude by thanking my husband Diccon for taking the majority of the photographs in the field and for his constant support, endless patience, encouragement and active participation throughout my seven-year doctoral project and during the four years to carry this book to publication. Finally, I dedicate this book to my grown-up children, Lara and James, for their ongoing support and belief in me and to my grandchildren, Sam, Harry and Jessica.

Drawing and Photograph Credits

All drawings were completed by hand by Ms Yiran Huang MA, Royal College of Art, London, and remain the sole copyright © of the author. The commissioned line drawings were completed between 2014 and 2016. Ms Huang graduated from the Royal College of Art in 2015 with a Master of Arts in Visual Communication. The drawings are as far as possible an accurate interpretation of the textile patterns, although in some cases the patterns proved difficult to decipher on account of surface deterioration. Each cloth is drawn to the same proportions and is as true a representation as possible of the patterns depicted on the stone surface. In some instances, the petals on a flower may not be the same all over the pattern, therefore what she has drawn may not exactly replicate other parts of the figure's dress. All photographs, unless otherwise stated, were taken by the author or her husband in the field and remain the sole copyright © of the author, or were provided by the relevant museum. Photos of the two statues in the State Hermitage Museum, St Petersberg are the copyright © of the State Hermitage Museum; they were taken by Alexander Koksharov and Konstantin Sinyavsky. The copyright for the reproduction of images has been sought wherever possible. In cases where this was not possible, common guidelines established for the fair use of images that are intended solely for scholarly and research purposes have been followed.

Maps

1. Trade Routes, 8th to 15th century 4
2. Sculpture locations in Sumatra and Kalimantan, 8th to 14th century 46
3. Sculpture Locations in Central Java, 8th to 9th century 62
4. Sculpture Locations in East Java, 10th to 15th century 130
5. Diaspora of Javanese Statues 262

Orthography

Words in languages other than English—such as Bahasa Indonesia, Javanese, Old Javanese, Dutch or German—are written in italics. Diacritics for all Bahasa Indonesia and Sanskrit words, pinyin transliteration for all Chinese words, and the Indonesian and Malay terms are explained in the glossary.

Sanskrit words and names have been transliterated according to the Indian spelling; for example, Śiva with a *v* and not a *w*, as it is usually written in Javanese and Bahasa Indonesia. *Mudrās* such as *dharmacakramudrā* will be written as one word and not in two or hyphenated as is sometimes done. Durgā Mahiṣāsuramardinī will be written the first time in full and then subsequently as Durgā. The names of Javanese rulers have been spelt with the following convention using the ṛ: Kṛtanagara. The conventional orthography for the term *caṇḍi* is Caṇḍi Singosari to represent the temple, whereas the term Singhasāri represents the historical kingdom; this differentiates the use of the two different spellings.

1. Background

The textile patterns appearing on Javanese free-standing sculptures is a little-known subject. These patterns came to the attention of the author after a visit as a student to the Volkenkunde, Leiden (RV) in 1998. The museum contains large andesite stone statues decorated with many different forms of dress, with each part sporting a different pattern. The carvings are so clear and precise that the sculptor had to be replicating a particular pattern, as it is unlikely he invented the complex designs himself. These patterns then presented an unanswered question: what was the inspiration for this multitude of different textile patterns, and where did it originate? Images of lotus flowers with an abundance of scrolling vines evoke Chinese sensibilities and the following of Buddhism. Perfectly cut rosette flowers appear in many different guises, highlighting the appeal of the *karahana*, the Tang rosette flower motif that appeared to be so popular between the end of the seventh and the first quarter of the eighth centuries. A pattern that seems to have evolved from similar designs is used in Sogdiana and Panjikent in Central Asia. This pattern later developed to be a particularly popular motif in the Malay weaving of *songket*—silk fabric with a supplementary weft of gold threads. Statues from the thirteenth century display a short sleeveless upper-body jacket with a pattern that is quite possibly a template for the *songket* patterns we see today. One statue of Gaṇeśa does not have the typical attributes of the much-loved figure

Figure 1 Stylized *kāla*-heads on the textile of a Singhasāri period Gaṇeśa.

from the Hindu pantheon but instead displays specific esoteric attributes and depictions of skulls and stylized *kāla*-heads (fig. 1) on the textile patterns carved on his trousers. What was the symbolic meaning of these textile patterns? Why were these particular East Javanese sculptures, which dated from the late thirteenth century, carved in such an explosion of designs? What was the inspiration behind the patterns and where did this inspiration come from? To answer these questions, a stylistic evaluation and a study of the textiles portrayed on all the statues is necessary.

The "stylistic evaluation" aids in the study and identification of a sculpture and furthers our understanding of the inspiration behind the textile patterns. It became apparent that the transference from Central to early East Java showed a shift in the stylistic evolution of Mahāyāna Buddhist bronze statues. This fact indicates it is not possible to identify the religious affiliation of Central Javanese statues, or indeed early East Javanese statues, by a stylistic evaluation alone, but that it is also necessary to study the textiles that are portrayed on them. By the second half of the thirteenth century, however, the differences between the earlier stone and bronze statues of Central Java compared to the stone statues from East Java became more clearly defined, and a stylistic evaluation is much easier, since the textile patterns by now differed considerably.

Historical and Geographical Context

Trade Relations and Outside Influences

The casting and creation of bronze statues was one of the leading artistic achievements of the Javanese. Large Hindu and Buddhist images were used as cult images inside the shrines, with the smaller ones to be used at home or dedicated to a temple after a pilgrimage. It was apparent that the small bronze figurines had multiple uses and were more than just souvenirs, but rather objects to be revered—something in which one would consider the deity was present, or to which some of his essences had accrued. As a consequence, some of the statues became portable objects for personal veneration, and they were subsequently carried from their place of origin to other countries. These small portable figurines were created during the time of the Central Javanese kingdom known as

Mataram, between the eighth and tenth centuries. Religious affiliations during this period appeared to change with the rise and fall of the rulers, from Hīnayāna to Mahāyāna Buddhism and the Tantric Vajrayāna forms of Buddhism. Construction of *caṇḍi* grew in Java, a popular term for archaeological monuments dating from the "Indianized" period. These structures could also be termed *cungkub,* meaning the *caṇḍi* was a tomb. They were also monuments, the abode of the gods and a reproduction of their dwelling place, perhaps as a covering or roofed structure raised over a grave (Soekmono 1995, p. 1n2). Built between the eighth and the tenth centuries, they were adorned with stone sculptures, which were placed both inside and outside the *caṇḍi*. On most examples, the textiles of the sculptures remained plain, which is the case with the sculptures seen at Borobudur. Many small icons were cast in bronze, silver and gold, and, in contrast to the sculptures, a significant number of these feature decorations showing textile designs. During the long Kediri period and the following thirteenth and fourteenth centuries in East Java, Pauline Lunsingh Scheurleer has argued that although the casting of bronze figures appeared to cease, there seemed to be a resurgence in the building of *caṇḍi* and a continuation of the making of stone statues.

The icons produced in these now Indianized kingdoms may have been Indian in appearance as a direct consequence of Indian commercial exploitation. The content, however, was entirely local, as the Indonesians decided what to appropriate from India. Within the local societies there appeared to be an emergence of indigenous rulers, most likely as a direct effect of the Indian influence and because of the influence of people involved in the interregional trade. The presence of Brahmins enhanced the status of the community as a whole, particularly in light of their role as ritual specialists in "rites of passage" ceremonies. Perhaps this also had an effect on the locally cast statues. It is clear, however, that the indigenous artisans did not slavishly copy the imported Indian models.

Chinese Trade

Map 1 highlights a number of the trade routes that were extant between the eighth and fifteenth centuries and shows the movement and expansion of Buddhism during this period.

In Java, strong Chinese influences were felt. Evidence for this can be found in the official Song history (960–1279 CE), known as the Song Shi, and in Zhao Rugua's book of 1226 titled *Zhufanzhi*. These sources provide details of the types of products that were traded in and out of the Java Sea region. The *Zhufanzhi* is a vital source of goods traded in the countries of the southern seas, and the *Historical Notes on Indonesia and Malaya* compiled from Chinese Sources also provides important details. One relevant quote refers to an envoy from Java. It is not clear

4   Patterned Splendour

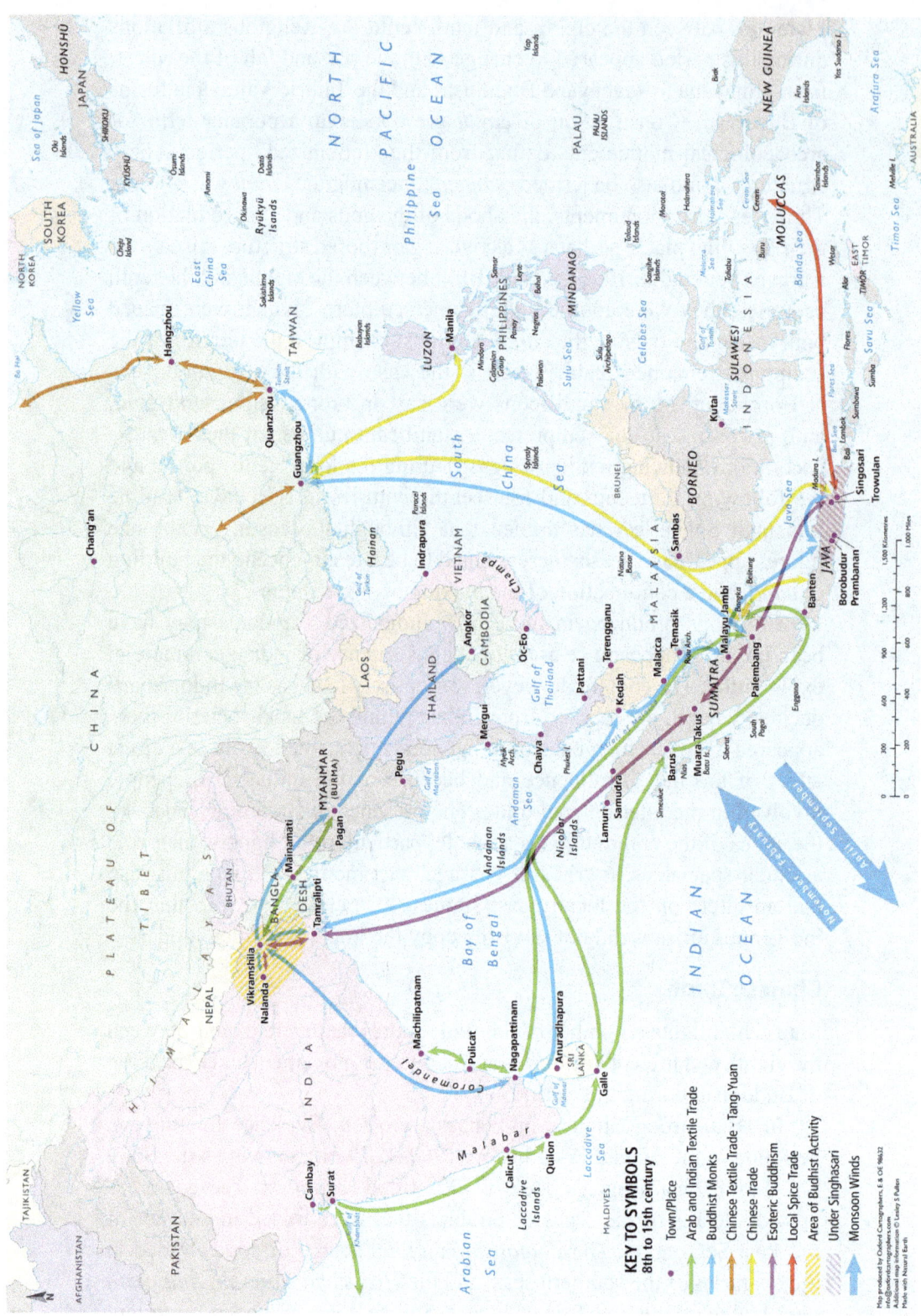

Map 1 Trade Routes, 8th to 15th century.

from which part of Java, but the Javanese were continually fighting Śrivijaya, so given that the year of the visit was 992 CE we can assume the delegation was from Central Java. The gifts sent to the Chinese emperor were described as follows: "the presents sent by the king were ivory, pearls, silk embroidered with flowers and gold, silk of different colours, sandalwood and cotton goods in various colours" (Groeneveldt 1960, pp. 63–78). (There is extended information on Chinese terms for geographical regions in the appendices.)

The detailed description of these items sent to a Song emperor in China indicates that Java was making gold-woven silk cloth or that the Javanese had access to this type of cloth. We know from the *Zhufanzhi* that Malabar in western India had traded items of cotton in all manner of colours to Śrivijaya, and that coloured cotton goods from Gujarat were traded to the Arab countries. Merchants from India and the Arab lands used Śrivijaya and the Malay Peninsula as their main entrepôt for the region. The Arab markets were full of such fabrics as gold and silver damask and soft-gold brocade, which were taken to and bartered in Śrivijaya. The description of the native products of Central Java, however, makes no mention of any silk fabrics, but only "foreign cotton cloth" and spices.

During the Song dynasty, cash was needed for this trade. Chinese merchants were known to smuggle vast quantities of copper coins out of China to use in barter. The copper coins used at the time were for cash transactions, and they were similar to round coins with a square hole in the centre. The coins are known as "Ssu Shu" (or four Shu). In the *Zhufanzhi* (note 40), the term *Sung-shï* is used to describe "strings of copper cash" that were "scattered abroad". As a consequence of this, an edict was issued by the local authorities in 1182 CE making it illegal to export copper coins. The edict had been ignored by the traders and by the local authorities themselves, which led to a total prohibition being issued of the exportation of coins by ocean-going ships to Java. As a result, the Song government urged traders to establish trading stations at the borders, where such products as silk, brocade, chiffon, porcelain and lacquer were exchanged for the aromatics from the Nanhai islands in the southern oceans (Hirth and Rockhill [1911] 1966, pp. 78–81). The quantities of Chinese coins dating from this period found around Kota Cina and Singapore suggest they were used in everyday commerce. One Majapahit text states that Chinese coins became the official currency of the realm in 1330 CE. Wang Duyguan, in his estimation, suggests the markets received "eight thousand Chinese coins every day" (Miksic and Goh 2017, p. 466). The Chinese coins called Gobog and Kepeng on display in the Trowulan Museum in East Java are examples of the kind used in this trade. By overlapping the coins, a simplified version of the pattern of overlapping circles known in Java as *kawung* may be created, and this could have been the inspiration for this ubiquitous pattern. None of the legislation implemented by the Song government had much of an effect on the continuing trade to Java, leading to an almost total draining of copper coinage from China until the end of the Song rule. (Further information on *kawung* and other key textile terms is provided in the extended glossary from p. 275.)

During the thirteenth century, the trading systems of the Indian Ocean region encompassed the Chinese markets of the Song and Yuan dynasties. It is highly likely that this trade influenced some of the textile patterns on the sculptures and possibly the reliefs on the architecture, such as the Chinese-inspired cloud motifs and lotus-plant vegetation carved on the walls of Caṇḍi Kidal, dating to 1269 CE. The indigenous Javanese designs merged with these new Chinese decorative patterns, and this can be seen as a local response to some of the imported objects and art styles.

Continued Chinese influences were revealed by the shipwreck discovered in 1998 between Bangka and Belitung Island off the coast of South Sumatra, which contained the wealthiest shipload of ancient Chinese products ever found. The ship probably sank between 830 and 840 CE. It had collected a considerable cargo from China and was on its way to Java with a large quantity of ceramics, silver ingots and gold. The ship was carrying diplomatic gifts from China to Java, and it would then have probably been destined for Oman. Guy has suggested that another important component of the cargo was likely to have been a significant quantity of Chinese silk (2010, pp. 19–30). It is also likely that some of the patterns depicted on the sculptures display textiles that were not indigenous but which had in many cases originated from India, Persia or indeed China. With the evidence gained of this trade with China, it is apparent some of the patterns on the sculptures reflect Chinese textiles, especially from the Tang and Yuan periods. The patterns, thus, document the continued Indo-Persian trade and beyond to China. At the time, Malay was probably the lingua franca for the region, spreading as far as Madagascar in the western Indian Ocean and throughout the Pacific (Miksic and Goh 2017, p. 40) as a universal language of the traders.

Historical and Religious Implications

The historical and religious implications of these periods of Javanese history are all-encompassing. There appeared to be a mobile network of human agents who carried texts and icons through which Esoteric Buddhist discourses and practices spread far across Asia and into Sumatra and Java. Esoteric Buddhism appears to have shared significant common elements with Tantric Śaivism to such an extent that the two religions participated in the interdependence of discourse in such disparate domains, evident in both ritual and iconography. As a result of this dialogue, the religion of the region represents a combination of two or more elements. Another definition, that of syncretism, the "fusion" of elements or beliefs, might be proposed. But it would appear that Śaivism and Buddhism did not undergo a merger or synthesis of religious doctrine or praxis but rather they maintained their independence as two discrete systems with their separate religious structures (Acri 2015, p. 269). Described as the peaceful coexistence of Buddhism and Śaivism, different paths were taken; however, the same peak was reached in the end, so avoiding the term *syncretism*. The term *esoteric* encompasses Vajrayana and Tantrayana.

Significant royal figures who elected to adopt the religion of Esoteric Buddhism as their official and personal cult may also have supported esoteric rituals to achieve their political ends. The text of the *kakawin Sutasoma*, a Javanese poem written in the fourteenth century, supplies a different opinion of the religious affiliation of Kṛtanāgara, the last of the Singhasāri monarchs, and of his inclinations towards the fusion of Śaivite and Buddhist practices. The *Sutasoma* tells us that King Kṛtanāgara in his last years fervently embraced the Javanese form of Mahāyāna Buddhism, where there was an apparent complete synthesis of religious doctrine that has often been put forward as characteristic of East Javanese religion (Hunter 2007, p. 33).

Prior to the reign of Kṛtanāgara, some monarchs had been described as incarnations of Viṣṇu, including Cambodia's king Jayavarman VII (r. 1181–1220) and Khubilai Khan in China (r. 1260–94). But there were no royal figures that came before Kṛtanāgara—or, indeed, after his death—who described themselves in the way he did. Many times, in inscriptions and in other literary evidence, Kṛtanāgara claimed to be Bhatara Śiva-Buddha, a deity embodying both Śiva and Buddha. There was also never a composite figure of Śiva and Buddha as there was, for example, of Harihara. A good example to illustrate this point is the statue of a deified King Kṛtanāgara as the youthful image of Harihara Ardhanari (fig. 2), with his dual iconography, where he is adorned with a unique dress style and textile pattern.

Buddhism, having died out in India by this period, thrived well into the fifteenth century in the localized situations in Java, now in its local adaption as a form of Esoteric Buddhism. In Sumatra, Esoteric Buddhism continued under King Ādityavarman (r. c.1374–79), who ruled over the upstream highlands of the Batang Hari River and held the authority of Jambi-Malayu on the southeast coast. By the early sixteenth century in East Java, however, the kings and their Hindu-Buddhist religion had collapsed following the arrival of Muslim forces (Reid 2015, p. 88). The idea of the practice of Buddhism in the context of East Java is particularly misleading—it might be better to term it Estoteric Buddhism; however,

Figure 2 Harihara Ardhanari, early 14th century, deification image of a god, possibly King Kṛtanāgara, Majapahit. The State Hermitage Museum, St Petersburg. 1.45m, andesite stone. Inv. No. NQ BD-543.

esoteric practice is as much Śaivite as it is Buddhist. The term Esoteric Buddhism is therefore perhaps a better way of describing this merging or cohesion of Hinduism and Buddhism. Evidence of this particular form of Esoteric Buddhism in Java appears to manifest itself in various ways (Stutterheim 1989, p. 242). But the evidence of Esoteric Buddhism in the Indonesian archipelago is also profoundly syncretic, containing both Hindu and Buddhist elements whose separate identity was further offset by the local Javanese and Balinese genius. The evidence of Esoteric Buddhism is apparent in the details of the textile patterns on the sculptures in the Singhasāri period, along with the one image of Mahākāla found in Sumatra. The use of skull imagery in various forms along with different aspects of their iconography is evident on a number of textile patterns. As a result, it is also apparent that the postulated syncretic nature of Indonesian Esoteric Buddhism is an amalgamation of Indic and indigenous magical features, or as an indigenous amalgamation of varying Indic traditions (Nihom 1994, p. 94). The tantric iconography on the textile patterns on some of the sculptures of the late thirteenth century perhaps highlights King Kṛtanāgara as a practitioner of esoteric rites.

During the Pāla period in northeast India, between the ninth and twelfth centuries, numerous sculptures were created with a particular style and iconography that had an enduring effect on the Hindu and Buddhist art of Java. The rules laid down in the Indian *shilpa-shastras* were reflected on the small statuettes from the Central and early East Javanese period, where many of the sculptures reveal a precise knowledge of Indian religious texts and, indeed, seem at times to have been inspired directly by Indian iconographic treatises. Studying them reveals that Indian styles are not only evident in the iconography of the sculptures but are also very much evident in the textile patterns. Tantric influences, however, do not appear to be represented on the textile patterns of any of the examples of Central or early East Javanese sculptures, except for one sculpture of Agastya dating to the ninth or tenth century. The *seléndang* or sash (fig. 3) draped across the upper body is patterned with the symbols of *vajra*, an aspect for which I cannot account.

I sought to ask how these textile patterns could come about. The most convincing evidence we have to answer this question and upon which to base an argument has been created by the East Javanese artists themselves, who showed a marked tendency to copy (or perhaps appropriated) from Indian and Chinese textile models. The idea that textile patterns and Indian culture arrived from India has been suggested, but that Indonesia did not derive its notions of Indian culture from only one or two parts of the continent, as contacts were made with many regions of the Indian subcontinent (Sen 2009, pp. 67–74; Kulke 2009, pp. 6–14). The influences of Buddhism certainly reached the island of Java through

Figure 3 Agastya, 9th–10th century, detail of the upper body, BPCB–Balai Pelestarian Cagar Budaya, Prambanan. Height unknown, stone. Inv. no. BG 1314.

centres of Buddhist art in Eastern India, and Hinduism arrived from contacts with the Chola in South and Western India. During most of the Hindu-Buddhist period, however, the more significant influence was generally felt from the northeast of India, as the main starting point of Indian artistic inspiration. Many pilgrims from abroad visited the sacred sites of Buddhism such as the monastery and university of Nālandā and Vikramaśīla in Bihar (Bautze-Picron 1993, pp. 277–79) (fig. 4). Indian stylistic ideas and inspiration that were gained by the pilgrims during their stay in Bihar were subsequently absorbed into Javanese art. In many cases these Indian ideas are apparent in the small bronze statuettes of Central and early East Java, and to a lesser extent in the Singhasāri stone statues. Nevertheless, such inspiration was not the only conduit, as it is clear that certain textile patterns seen on the Central Javanese metal statues could have inspired eleventh to twelfth century Tibetan textile patterns, as is evident on bronze statues and depicted on Tibetan manuscript paintings.

Moreover, the life of the Buddhist saint Atīśa (982–1054) in Sumatra highlights the movement and exchange of ideas that was prevalent between Śrivijaya, Java and the Nālandā region. Atīśa stayed at the court of Śrivijaya for twelve years (1013–25), during which time there was

Figure 4 Nālandā Mahavira (University Ruins), 5th–12th century, Ancient Kingdom of Magadha (present day Bihar), North India. Pullen photo.

the beginning of unrest in northeast India with the attack of Mahmūd of Ghanzī. Fortunately the Buddhist University at Nālandā was spared, and as a result there was also an increase of Esoteric Buddhism, at which point in time "classical" Buddhism had virtually disappeared. As Jan Schoterman describes it, "it is not difficult to imagine that Śrivijaya took over the role of northeast India in this period. There one could study classical Buddhism in peace" (Schoterman 2016, p. 115). N.J. Krom describes Atīśa's period in Sumatra as part of "the great role of Buddhist headquarters in the East, which at this time belonged to Sumatra" (Krom 1931, p. 248). In light of the above, the introduction of Buddhism into Tibet occurred at a relatively late date, and as Schoterman has argued, "there were Buddhists in the Indonesian Archipelago long before the introduction of Buddhism in Tibet". It is therefore unlikely that Buddhism in Śrivijaya was influenced by Buddhism from Tibet (Schoterman 2016, p. 115).

Singhasāri Period

After the Central and early East Javanese period, there was a time in the production of sculptures when textile patterns did not appear at all until the thirteenth century. The period of the Kediri kings has left no identifiable archaeological remains of any importance. For East Java, at present three clear dynastic periods have been identified, but there are four 'styles' of sculpture (though not necessarily of textile pattern) that allow them to be placed into either the Kediri, Singosari, Transition or Majapahit periods. During the earliest and longest of these, the Kediri period, and for any of the statues carved prior to 1222 CE, they were mostly small, rather unpolished stone statues of deities from the Śaivite pantheon, and with virtually no evidence of textile patterns. To provide exact parameters for the Kediri style is problematic as there is only one sculpture, or perhaps two, with a textile pattern that fits into this category. The large seated Gaṇeśa known as the Boro Gaṇeśa was dated by inscription to 1239–40 CE. But whilst the dating of this statue is within the Singhasāri period, the style of the sculpture is that of Kediri and categorically not Singosari. The Singosari style became apparent after 31 October 1269 with the issuing of the Charter of Sarwadharma, with the first known inscription of this issued by King Kṛtanāgara (Krom 1926b, p. 464). The types and style of sculptures produced after this period are quite distinctive in comparison to the previous figures. One of the most outstanding features of statues produced during the latter half of the thirteenth century are the depictions of striking textile patterns, where each statue is unique. The concept of a pan-Indian style has now disappeared in favour of an indigenous Javanese-inspired form of dress and of many instances of internationally inspired textile patterns. At least eighty to ninety per cent of stone sculptures dating from this period feature textile patterns, of which no two bear identical designs. Further identification is based on the rather ornate details of jewellery and on the detailed depiction of the various forms of dress, including the wearing of the sleeveless jacket and the conspicuous evidence of a wide band often carved with double lines along the outer edges. The band is shown worn from left to right across the body with a flap folded over on the left shoulder, indicating the wearing of a *seléndang* (fig. 5). This feature, along with the flourish with which the sash is depicted laying across the hips, the accurate depiction of the lotus plant decoration, the realistic carving and the individuality of each figure define a statue as Singosari. The sculptures are few in number and type. All of them reflect both the Śaivite and Buddhist pantheons, and they were often placed together in the same *caṇḍi*. The Singhasāri phase is of major significance, as it will become apparent that a number of the textile patterns resemble those from earlier centuries across Central Asia and China. This indicates that for a few hundred years, Java and Sumatra were part of a cosmopolitan world where ideas and textiles evolved and were subsequently transferred over a long period and distance. An empirical study was made of each sculpture, particularly those characterized by a unique type of pattern and dress. In this instance there is no apparent difference in the type of textile patterns between the religious affiliation or the gender of the statues. Only a small departure from this is evident with the sculptures from Caṇḍi A at Singosari.

Figure 5 Nandīśvara, c.1292, detail of the upper body showing the *seléndang*, Caṇḍi Singosari, Tower Temple, Caṇḍi A, Malang, East Java. Volkenkunde, Leiden. Collection Nationaal Museum van Wereldculturen. Inv. no. RV-1403-1624. 1.7m, andesite stone.

Transition Style

Following on from the Singosari Style, I have introduced the Transition classification to denote a statue that is neither in the Singosari or the Majapahit style. The Transition class is reflected by its upright posture, the lower two hands being held together, the exuberant depiction of the *upavīta* as a long strand of three-pearl to five-pearl chains, the often exaggerated carving of the ornaments, and with no two textile patterns being the same; all the examples of this class were carved after Kṛtanāgara had died and the Singhasāri period had ended. There remain only a few sculptures in this category that are depicted with textile patterns.

It may further our understanding if we employ an interpretation of data relating to style categories based not only on the written sources but on an examination and analysis of the artefacts themselves. Texts, functionality and iconography are all necessary in order to interpret a statue and to place it dynastically. For example, the essential factors in categorizing East Javanese Transition style stone sculptures are the stance of the body, which generally exhibits some movement, that the legs show through the loincloth, the headdress consists of layers, the jewellery is simpler and worn sparingly, and the flanking lotus plants grow from bulbous roots. Surface decoration, however, appears to predominate over form. The lotus plant decoration is used as a "dynastic emblem". This feature perhaps originated from Nālandā, as it is evident in numerous Pāla sculptures. The interpretation of the lotus, however, differs significantly. In 1932, Stutterheim explained the differences in the form the lotus took in all three East Javanese dynastic periods. For sculptures of the Kediri, no depiction of the lotus plant is present. For those of the Singhasāri period, the lotus plant is depicted growing from the corm or root, at either side of the Central figure, and as possessing soft, floppy leaves. By the Majapahit period the plant was depicted growing from a pot at each side of the central figure, and with a rather more stylized appearance. Previous art history books on East Java have tended to use the typology of the lotus plant to place sculptures into a dynastic "box". Some of the Transition sculptures, however, appear with the lotus plant emanating from a smaller rootstock, and with the leaves beginning to show a rigidity of form.

In addition to this crucial form of classification, the posture and physiognomy of the body are also significant in interpreting the style. The very detailed and unique textile patterns and the evidence of skull and *kāla*-head textile patterns are also dynastic classifiers. A regional textile typology develops, as it becomes apparent that during the thirteenth century a distinctive type of textile pattern was being produced that was in complete contrast to those of the Central and early East Javanese period.

Claudine Bautze-Picron discusses the problems of iconographic classification in reference to Pāla statues in the Śaivite and Buddhist pantheons, many of which are interchangeable. She also states that in the countries that saw the production of the Pāla style there are problems of iconography and chronology: "an iconographic classification, within which chronology and style hold their place, would have helped to clarify a situation which is very confused" (1993, p. 285). This approach of an examination of the artefacts will become apparent in the chapters that follow and will highlight the many interconnecting factors that accentuate how the textile patterns might reflect the origins of each statue.

Esoteric Religious Intervention

As an artistic centre, Nālandā had played a major role in the transmission of artistic motifs to Southeast Asia since at least the eighth century, especially to Sumatra and Java (Acri 2016, p. 18), along with the transference of Esoteric Buddhist ideas. This was part of a two-way system that appeared to have had an effect on the textile patterns of the sculptures placed at Caṇḍi Singosari under Kṛtanāgara's rule. David Bade also suggests that the texts that inform us of the reign of Kṛtanāgara had a certain "magical function: to legitimize and to justify the contemporary political scene" (2016, p. 142). Perhaps this was also a result of Esoteric Buddhist ideas.

Bade tell us that King Kṛtanāgara belonged to a Kālacakra tradition of Tantric Buddhism, and that his initiation into this form of Buddhism followed that of Khubilai Khan in Mongol China (2016, p. 141). To better understand why Kṛtanāgara and Khubilai Khan "followed" each other in religious practices, it is worthwhile to consider Bade's explanation:

> The *Yuán Shī* records that Mongol envoys came to Java in 1279, 1280, 1281 and 1286, and that they came back without having obtained submission and royal hostages, and furthermore that a mission to Java in 1289 (?) resulted in the mistreatment of the Mongol envoy. These missions all occurred during Kṛtanāgara's reign in Java and Khubilai's reign as Great Khan, and therefore indicated a prolonged diplomatic relationship between two kings and resistance to Khubilai's demands on the part of Kṛtanāgara. (2016, p. 143)

This perhaps goes some way to explaining the transference of Chinese ideas, motifs and textiles between the two nations at this time.

The strategic location of Bengal saw it become the crossroads between the Indian subcontinent and not only mainland Southeast Asia but also insular Southeast Asia. It became a place of convergence for all types of Buddhist monks. The Buddhist monk Atīśa is credited with a commentary on the *Kālacakratantra* (Miksic 2016, p. 262), and he received teachings on the subject. Magadha, or present-day Bihar state, was considered the source of "esoteric" iconography, which became evident in the lands of Nanhai, the Chinese term for the Southern Seas region. Bengal, on the other hand, was at the convergence of Assam and Yunnan, Pagan and Arakan, Odisha, Bihar, and Nepal and Tibet in the north. It was a place of transition between all parts of Asia. The transference of Buddhism and Buddhist ideas, which converged at Bengal and Bihar, subsequently travelled with the monks to Java. Sumatran monks resided at Nalanda in the ninth century, and at Nagapattinam in the early tenth century. During Yijing's six-month visit to Śrivijaya in 671 CE (Schoterman 2016, p. 114), it is quite possible he noted the unusual way the monks there wore a piece of cloth, possibly a *seléndang*, across one shoulder. This feature is very evident in the sculptures (figs. 27 and 28, pp. 66–67).

It is likely that many of the textiles and imported designs that arrived in Java over time were then subsequently incorporated into the textile designs carved on to the new sculptures at Caṇḍi Singosari. Furthermore, as has been suggested, the Kālacakra cult appeared to have gained a powerful following during the Singhasāri period, especially during the last stages of Kṛtanāgara's reign. A result of this has been the depiction of so-called esoteric iconography in the form of skulls that is apparent on a number of the textile patterns in Java and on one sculpture from Sumatra. Lunsingh Scheurleer has suggested that a skull is a "tantric attribute", and that Gaṇeśa was integrated into Javanese esoteric practices at the time of King Kṛtanāgara. Esoteric Buddhism not only provided strong new magic that reinforced the legitimacy of the ruler in the eyes and minds of his followers, but it also granted him a strong foundation with its international connections and position (Fontein 1990, p. 50; 1998, p. 8).

Majapahit Period

During the fourteenth and fifteenth centuries, throughout the last phase of the East Javanese kingdoms, the statues that were created belonged to the Majapahit style and they were designed to be placed in commemorative *caṇḍi*; that is, *caṇḍi* built in memory of a deceased member of the royal family. During the two hundred years of the Majapahit period, the number of *caṇḍi* built throughout East Java proliferated. Many were constructed of soft brick, and most of these have now disappeared. But the *caṇḍi* that remain, and those that have been partially restored, were built of stone; as was the case with the Singhasāri *caṇḍi* (Kinney 2003, p. 215). The carving of the stone statues, most of which are over a metre and a half in height, has been executed in meticulous and extraordinary detail. Every bead of every chain and every metal plaque of every belt, each representing a gold ornament, has been accurately reproduced. The exaggerated size of these ornaments, as proposed by Marijke Klokke, suggest that the statues represented deceased kings and queens. And "if Javanese kings and queens were thought of as gods after death, it would be logical to represent them as gods" (Klokke 1994, p. 183). Therefore, as gods, they are adorned with elaborate ornaments befitting their status. The differences between the sculptures of the fourteenth century and those of the turn of the fifteenth century are considerable, and the differences between the sculptures destined for strategic *caṇḍi* belonging to a Majapahit monarch and those of minor nobility are also significant. All of the metal ornaments depicted on the sculptures during the preceding centuries in Java attest to the long history of the production of gold jewellery by the Javanese.

The Majapahit period statues vary in size and stone quality, from a refined and carefully carved statue with a smooth surface depicting a *sinjang kawung*, to small, roughly carved andesite statues with a plain *sinjang* and no textile patterns. The smaller, lower-quality statues appear in far greater numbers than the larger decorated pieces illustrated in this book. The figures depicted by both kinds of statues are dressed in a *sinjang*. The term *sinjang* is the Old Javanese word for a long cloth, and *kawung* refers to the pattern of connecting or interlocking circles on this cloth. As we proceed, the information on dress available in Old Javanese sources and in *kakawin* and *kidung* literature will provide many descriptions of textile terminology that will further our identification and understanding of the patterns on these stone statues.

Summary and Argument

This book sets out to address the subject of the detailed patterns that appear on a body of free-standing figurative sculptures from Java dating from the eighth to the fifteenth century. It is divided into six chapters. This chapter has introduced the historical and geographical background and explained the power and patronage of the ruling elite at the time. Chapter 2 will address literary sources on Javanese textile traditions from *kidung* and *kakawin* poetry and analyse the textiles that survive, comparing the layout and construction of the present-day fabrics alongside the stone examples. Other texts that inform us in considerable detail about textile terminology are the many hundreds of *sīma* charters that have survived, the majority of which date from the mid-ninth to the mid-fourteenth century. These remain as a valuable source of the economic and social history of Java. The *sīma* charters are best described as a record of the transfer of tax and labour rights by the ruler. Chapter 3 will present a select group of metal and stone statues dating from the Central and early East Java period of the eighth to the eleventh century. Chapter 4 will cover the Kediri and Singhasāri period of the eleventh to the thirteenth century. And chapter 5 will present the Majapahit in the mid-fourteenth to the early fifteenth century. A comparative chart of the drawings taken from the complete set of sculptures is presented at the end of each chapter. Chapter 6 concludes with a round-up of the material presented and proposes theories to account for the many and varied textiles represented—which reflect the international trade of textiles at the time—and for how the Javanese assimilated these patterns to be able to produce something unique in the form of these statues. The epilogue includes a map illustrating the current locations of these sculptures; it also tells the stories of how some of them came to be there.

The textiles represented in the dress of these figures over this seven-hundred-year period document the local response to successive arrivals of textiles via trade. This response occurred throughout the entire Hindu-Buddhist period, but it was during the Singhasāri period in East Java, in the last quarter of the thirteenth century, that the changes in textile patterns were most clearly evident. Indeed, the evidence first suggests that the diverse mix of textile patterns created on the dress of the sculptures reflected a local response to different imported textile patterns taken from Pagan Buddhist paintings, designs from Gupta architecture, and possibly from imported ceramics. Included in the analysis are a select group of stone statues and small bronze and gold statuettes and plaques originating from Central and early East Java dating between the eighth and mid-eleventh centuries. After this is an analysis of a few stone statues from the Kediri period of the mid-eleventh through early thirteenth centuries. This is followed by the Singhasāri period (1222–92), during which the importation and local production of textiles appears to have reached a peak, as is apparent on the statues. Conversely, by the Majapahit period, from 1293 to the fifteenth century, the textile patterns lack innovation and began to show a certain degree of duplication of patterns.

Four sculptures from Sumatra exhibiting textile patterns date between the eleventh and the fourteenth centuries. The design on one of these Sumatran sculptures highlights the evidence of certain Chinese textiles. On another, there is a similarity with patterns seen on Javanese sculptures. This demonstrates how, collectively, these sculptures provide evidence of the extraordinary diversity in textiles and the interconnection that existed between Java and Sumatra at the time.

The statues presented were chosen because of their carved textile patterns. This group is not the definitive collection of all statues in existence, but highlights the wide variety of patterns in circulation at the time. Each statue has been catalogued by their material, date and location, and by reference to their dress, textile patterns and the carved ornaments adorning them. Specific attention has been given to a description of the textile pattern, accompanied by a high-resolution photo of the statue and a line drawing of the textile pattern. The naming of decorative techniques involved in the creation of the patterns can only be suggestions, and are not conclusive.

2. Javanese Textile Traditions

Literary References: Evidence of Statue Production and Textile Terminology

In the Old Javanese language, there is a term *pande*, meaning "skilled worker, or smith" (Zoetmulder 1982). A goldsmith is referred to as *pande-mas*, and bronze or copper are referred to as *tambaga*. Whilst we have the knowledge of these terms, there does not appear to be any reference to the manufacture of bronze statuettes. It is most likely that a bronzesmith would have been a simple craftsman who worked in a small unit of apprentices (Lunsingh Scheurleer and Klokke 1988b, pp. 13–14). It has also been suggested, however, that the images cast in bronze far outnumber those made in gold or silver. This does not necessarily mean there was an imbalance in the numbers of different types of sculptures cast, but only that the gold and silver statues could have been used to pay local taxes and could also have been melted down. On close analysis, the quality of the statues in gold and silver often appears to be of a subtler nature to that of the bronze figures, which are often rougher in execution. The greatest achievement of the bronze caster of the Central Javanese period was in the highest artistic expression achieved in the "introspective spirituality and the nobility of expression, epitomised by the highest ideals of Buddhism, in a convincing manner such as no Indian sculptor ever achieved" (Fontein, Soekmono and Suleiman 1971, p. 41).

The majority of the bronzes were cast using the lost-wax process, whereas a number of the gold plaques were made by repoussé, with hammered patterns from the front. The smooth surface allowed the craftsmen to hammer in tiny details of the textile patterns. The stone statues, on the other hand, are of varying qualities and colours. The stone used in the thirteenth century ranged from an exceptional pale-grey stone to an almost white stone, in which detailed carvings of patterns were possible. In contrast, the stone employed in the earlier ninth and tenth centuries ranged from dark grey to black; it was rough to the touch, making intricate details such as textile patterns challenging to execute. It is quite evident that the availability and quality of stone depended on the location of the workshops in different periods in history. Unfortunately, there does not appear to be any reference in the Old Javanese literature to the processes of the selection of materials or the execution of the statues.

The carving of stone sculptures appears to have proliferated during the East Javanese period, where there was an apparent preference for Śaivite statues over Buddhist ones. By the Majapahit period, statues were being created in the form of deified ancestors as an act of devotion. At this point in time, the elite regarded Śaivism and Buddhism as different forms of the same truth (Robson and Prapanca 1995, p. 3; Fontein 1990, p. 49). Sedyawati has suggested that the craftsmen who made the statues would have had a low status in society. They would have formed part of a class of professionals called *wulu-wulu*, which included woodcarvers, performers and sculptors. She has suggested that craftsmen would have lived in villages and paid taxes. Some of those who were more favoured for their skills would perhaps have lived in the palace compound and would therefore have served the state or royalty (Sedyawati 1990, p. 106). We can perhaps conclude therefore that the palace-based sculptors created the stone sculptures for the Caṇḍi Singosari and Caṇḍi Jago sites, and that they perhaps had access to a different variety of textiles from which to model the designs they worked into their sculptures. It is apparent that to produce a perfect replica of a pattern—for example, one of the animal roundel patterns—would have been almost impossible. A Javanese version was therefore made, with the pattern becoming acculturated and subsequently reflecting the local inspiration of the Javanese sculptor.

In *Kalangwan: A Survey of Old Javanese Literature* (Zoetmulder 1974, preface), Petrus Zoetmulder describes the art of writing poetry in ancient Java, which is a subject of intrinsic interest and represents an important chapter in the cultural history of the Indonesian people. Yet, whilst the *Kalangwan* serves as an important aid in furthering our studies of life in Java during the classical period, our knowledge of the history of this period is mainly derived from charters and inscriptions, often scribed on copper plates or stones known as *prasasti*. The *prasasti* have been preserved as "language monuments".

Many different languages appear in the ancient documents. For example, until the ninth century only a few inscriptions survived in Sanskrit and Old Malay, yet Old Javanese was the language of the earliest Javanese literature and a rich source for the art history of pre-modern Java. Old Javanese often includes words originating from Sanskrit, but despite the influence of foreign terms the Old Javanese language remains essentially Indonesian. Old Javanese poetry known as *kidung* and *kakawin* were composed between the tenth and sixteenth centuries in a Sanskritized form. The *kakawin* are court epics modelled on the *kavya* of South Asia in the form of the *Ramayana* and *Mahābhārata*. They were composed in Indian metres and written in Old Javanese. The *kidung* were written in Middle Javanese. Two of the historical *kidung*—*Kidung Harsawijaya* (KH) and *Kidung Rangga Lawe* (KRL)—deal with the rebellion surrounding the demise of Kṛtanāgara in 1292 and the founding of Majapahit. Scholars have sought to unravel the textual evidence from ancient literature, especially the KH and the KRL, and through the study of Old Javanese literature it is possible to gain a glimpse into the field of *kalangwan*.

The KH holds many descriptions of dress styles and patterns, as does the *Serat Tatatjara* (ST), a text that documents Javanese customs and traditions and which includes numerous accounts and references to dress. One example, for instance, recounts Raden Wijaya, the king of Majapahit, who wore a "*sinjang kawung*". Between the eighth and the twentieth centuries, at the time of the Surakarta kingdom, this pattern was only worn by the servants of the king (Sumaryoto 1993, p. 37). The use of this term as a form of dress for a king during the Majapahit period would indicate the importance at the time of a long cloth with a *kawung* pattern. This might justify, therefore, the appearance of the *sinjang* with a *kawung* motif on so many of the Majapahit sculptures, such as depicted on the statue of a queen as Pārvatī (fig. 6).

Figure 6 A Majapahit statue of a queen as Pārvatī, detail of the *sinjang kawung*. Pullen photo.

Javanese texts produced over the centuries often contain passages referring to prominent characters and the dress or costume they wore. These only provide descriptions of the types of clothing and the patterns on them though, with no information as to the appearance or the style of the materials from which they were made. We can therefore only conjecture as to the dress of the ancient Javanese and "construct a correlation with the patterns we find in the present-day dress" (Sumaryoto 1993, p. 31). For example, one only has to look at a modern couple getting married who have requested to be dressed *jangkêp*; meaning, to be married in a full set of clothes replicating the royal figures from the ancient stone sculptures. Such a tradition highlights the longevity and the continuity of Javanese court dress styles.

The *Nāgarakṛtāgama* (*Nāg.*) is an epic *kakawin* dating from 1365 written by Mpu Prapañca. The original name given to it by its author was the *Deśawarṇana*. Prapañca was the 'Superintendent of Buddhist Affairs' at the court of King Rājasanagara, known informally as Hayam Wuruk. The poem gives a detailed account of contemporary matters and religion in connection with the court during the Majapahit kingdom. It also includes essential first-hand information about King Kṛtanāgara (Zoetmulder 1974). Other texts that inform us in considerable detail, particularly on textile terminology, are the many hundreds of *sīma* charters that have survived, the bulk of which date from the mid-ninth to the mid-fourteenth century. These remain a valuable source of information on the economic and social history of Java. The *sīma* tax-transfer charters are best described as:

> A record of the transfer of tax and labour rights by a ruler or highly placed taxing authority to a specified beneficiary, in most cases the beneficiary was a religious foundation enjoying royal or aristocratic patronage often connected with the veneration of royal ancestor figures whose prestige seems to have underpinned political power. (Christie 1993b, p. 181)

The interpretation of the *sīma* is essential for their significance in the study of Javanese textiles. The level of detail they provide, however, spanning the centuries, varies considerably. For example, in the ninth and early tenth centuries, the charters were dominated by lists of gifts given at ceremonies, such as those detailing the allocation of cloth presented to individuals, members of the royal family and high officials. By the mid-eleventh century, the preoccupation was with sumptuary regulations governing insignia and rank and the accompanying paraphernalia. Restrictions applied to the use of certain types of textiles, and this affords some perspective on the role of those textiles in early Javanese societies. The *sīma* also describe the colours and names of textile patterns and the names and types of professional trades during these periods (Christie 1993a, p. 13). For example, one term mentioned in the *wnang* or "privilege" lists of the eleventh through fourteenth centuries is *bananten*, which appears to describe a type of coloured or patterned cloth that was used as a hanging or furnishing. The list also includes a number of patterns that have names relating to flowers. Another example is the word *navagraha*, denoting a pattern that has been interpreted in a number of ways, such as nine planets or as nine realms that emit waves of living energy. There are two extant pattern types based on the number nine: a series of intersecting motifs suggestive of the Javanese *jilamprang* pattern, and a motif that is quite possibly a Javanese interpretation of the *navagraha* design referred to in the privilege list.

Appearing also in the *sīma* are the terms *menanun* (weave) and *tenun* (weaving). *Tenun* is a term used today to describe a woven cloth, and *menanun* described a weaver or weaving in the eleventh and twelfth centuries. Terms for colour are also often used. For instance, in Old Javanese the expression for drawing with colour is *tulis warna*. And the words *tulis mas* means writing or drawing upon with gold, referring to a technique in use by the late twelfth century to produce textiles decorated with gold-leaf glue work, or *tinulis ing mas*, meaning to draw upon in gold. Jan Wisseman Christie hints at Persian gold-decorated cloth as the possible source for this technique (Christie 1993b, p. 193; 1999, p. 241). In observing the types of patterns on the sculptures of the thirteenth century, a number of the textiles depicted with a pattern could be described as *tulis mas*. The mid-relief in which the patterns are carved and the types of patterns reflected on the sculptures could be replicating *tulis mas*, present-day *prada* or brocaded *songket* textiles, especially evident in the figures from Caṇḍi A at Singosari. Christie suggests that the technique of *tulis warna* of the twelfth and later centuries was the ancestor of the modern batik (1993a, p. 16).

Christie describes the role and status of the recipients at *sīma* ceremonies, which affected both men and women. Male recipients normally received *wdihan*, a cloth for a man's hip wrapper. The terms *yu* and *hlai* refer to the width of the cloth used for adult men, where two pieces would be sewn together along their length and the ends pulled up between the legs. If the two sections were joined together, the result was a *kain*, which was a length of cloth given to women. The *kain* were measured in *blah*, a Javanese term for a piece. These measurements for cloth also reflect the standard lengths depicted on the figures in the reliefs of the Central Javanese temples from the ninth to tenth centuries, where the male figures are portrayed with the cloth drawn up between the legs. The term *kain* is the word still commonly used today to describe a sheet of cloth worn around the hips of a female. The term *vlah* from the Old Khmer language suggests a borrowing from Old Javanese, which in turn perhaps also suggests that Malay traders carried the cotton cloth to trade in ports along the Mekong River. Christie has suggested this might negate the popular belief that there was less direct trade at that time between India and Cambodia than there was between India and the islands of maritime Southeast Asia (1993, pp. 183–84).

Traders in Java were listed in significant numbers in the *sīma*. One example is the term *acadar*, or the *cadar*, meaning a weaver of cloth. The cloth woven by these professional weavers would have been more delicate than the kind of cloth woven in a domestic household. The term *cadar* today can now refer to a type of gauze. In a number of the gift lists, it is linked with the term *tapis* (which means thin, delicate or transparent), and it could be related to silk textiles (ibid., p. 189). Such mentions might also indicate that during the thirteenth century the Javanese were capable of making beautiful fabrics that were good enough to be exported to China. Whether any of these fabrics appear on the sculptures is unknown; however, it is entirely possible that a type of gold woven cloth, perhaps replicating an imported pattern, was the template for some of the patterns on the sculptures, as suggested earlier. There are numerous textiles in existence from the nineteenth and twentieth centuries that clearly show designs of concentric interlocking oval shapes, lotus flower medallions and rosettes—patterns that are very similar to the many variations of the carvings on the statues. These patterns are also clearly reflected in a number of silk textiles seen in the China National Silk Museum dating from the Xixia to the Yuan period.

The *cadar* weavers used a *pacadaran* or *cadar* loom, which would probably have had a discontinuous warp. This type of loom is still in use in parts of Indonesia today. The *cadar* type of loom allows for a part of the loom called the comb or reed to separate the fine cotton or silk warp threads, allowing them to ride on the surface, thereby supplementing the weft and serving as a means to create a pattern element. A reed or comb is required in the production of the type of gold-woven textiles today known as *songket*. The term is derived from the Malay word *menyongket*, meaning "to embroider with silver or gold threads". Strictly speaking it is not embroidery but is instead a woven textile. It is usually worked on a darkish-red silk background, which highlights the complexity of the gold patterning (Selvanayagam 1990, p. xv). It is traditionally made with the *cadar* type of loom. It is therefore possible that gold cloth was in extensive use in Java and Bali from the beginning of the tenth century, as the *cadar* loom was in everyday use. Within the coastal port towns of Java and South Sumatra, where areas of court culture existed, there was a group of professional merchants selling textiles and ready-made garments known as *abasana* (Christie 1993a, p. 14). And whilst it is hard to determine what manner of textile patterns were produced at this time, as there are no extant examples, it is evident from the terminology discussed above that gold-woven cloth was being made in Java from at least the tenth century.

I suggest that many of the patterns on the stone sculptures could represent a textile technique known as *songket*, or a brocade. The argument for this comes from research into Minangkabau textiles in Sumatra. In the Minangkabau region of West Sumatra, the *kain balapak* is a *songket* cloth featuring a dense decoration of gold thread. This cloth was worn during festive occasions as a *seléndang* or *kain*. Suwati Kartiwa describes the origins of *songket* and notes that its patterns have been known from prehistoric times, as similar patterns can be seen on earthenware from West Sumatra. The geometric designs appear as abstract forms of flora and fauna, and some exhibit features of Chinese inspiration. Certain foreign influences that have been felt from the prehistoric period and during the Hindu period manifest in the use of silk, with silver and gold threads being materials that initially were unknown in Indonesia.

The term *kain songket* applies to the technique of weaving patterns on silk with additional threads of gold or silver. The term is derived from *sungkit* or *jungkit*, whereby a few threads of the warp would be lifted during weaving and supplementary weft threads inserted to form a pattern (before multicoloured threads were usually employed) (Kartiwa 1979, pp. 57–69). The decision to use *songket* as the preferred term for the patterning on many of the Singosari sculptures is based on the abstract flora and fauna motifs described by Kartiwa and on the information gained from the texts discussed earlier.

The technique of weaving ikat was known in the Indo-Persian sphere from at least the sixth century. In this technique a cloth is patterned using a resist method of tying the pattern in the warp or the weft. The first visual evidence of ikat is depicted on the elite textiles featured on the mural paintings at Ajanta. Figures are depicted in these paintings wearing short *dhotīs* patterned with the ikat technique (Guy and Thakar 2015, p. 13); the technique can be identified by the horizontal bands across the textiles. The *sīma* charters record that both red and blue dyes, known as *wungkudu* and indigo, were used for warp ikat textile weaving. The gift lists, particularly those for the ninth and tenth centuries, appear to include only minimal references to textile patterns. They do mention, however, the quality, the place of origin, the colour, whether they bore a floral or vegetal motif, the price and the use for the material. There was a preponderance of different kinds of cotton in red and blue. One piece of white cloth that was designated as having come from India was described with patterns that appear quite commonly on the small statues, such as scattered flowers, circles and dots across a plain ground (Christie 1993a, pp. 12–14). There appeared to be a ready supply of pre-patterned and pre-dyed yarns, and it seems most households would produce the majority of cloth they would need, at least for ceremonial occasions. Ikat was executed on a body-tension loom, and was probably known from the Central Javanese period. Such a loom is illustrated on a stone carving of a girl, who is depicted seated in an open pavilion, weaving cloth of a diamond-shaped pattern (Christie 1993b, p. 187). The carving is on the base of a stone pillar that is now housed at the Trowulan Museum.

A *kakawin* poem of the twelfth or thirteenth century places various weaving terms in the context of an average household. The most noteworthy member of the semi-professional *miśra* category was the *mangapus,* a processor, or a person classed with dye-workers. The term *mangapus* may hold the key to our understanding of the production of patterned or decorated cloth used in most Javanese households at the time. The word *apus* in Old Javanese means a tie, a band, bond or thread, and it is a synonym for the word ikat (*ikĕt*). It is a term that is used infrequently in the Javanese charters, but it also appears in Balinese inscriptions of the same period (Christie 1993b, p. 186). It might be pertinent to note that there is no evidence of paint on any of the sculptures.

Trade and Textiles – South and Southeast Asia Relations

There was a considerable variety of influences in the thirteenth century, as is evident from the diversity of textile patterns. These range from the Indo-Persian world through to the Liao, Southern Song and the Yuan periods in China and Mainland Southeast Asia. In contrast, a number of East Javanese stone textile patterns were influenced by locally woven textiles; textiles that would subsequently have been used as trade items to China. By the mid-fourteenth to the early fifteenth century, however, the international influences appear to have disappeared, and the sculptures uniformly display a similar type of dress with a *sinjang kawung* pattern, which probably reflects a Javanese-made cloth. The description reinforces this argument by John Guy of Java as part of a globally interconnected world with a single ocean:

> Extensive regional trade in indigenous Southeast Asian textiles underlines the complexity of the traditional trading system. A degree of regional specialization and the emergence of an element of cash-cropping in local economies … resulted in considerable regional movement of textiles. (1998, p. 75)

This regional movement of textiles had also been aptly described a few hundred years earlier by Chau Ju-Kua in the *Zhufanzhi* (Hirth and Rockhill 1965), and also by Marco Polo who describes Java thus:

Java is of surpassing wealth, producing all ... kinds of spices,... frequented by vast amounts of shipping, and by merchants who buy and sell costly goods from which they reap great profit. Indeed, the treasure of this island is so great as to be past telling. (1875, pp. 272–74).

The description in the *Zhufanzhi*, written in the last decade of the thirteenth century, helps to focus our attention on the importance of Java with respect to international trade in the region. It is also helpful to consider the ways other nations could have interacted with Java by studying the movement of textile patterns across Central Asia, India, China and Tibet. These patterns, and the impact they had on Java, could have been the result of unconscious borrowings—a convergence of past ideas that reached Java indirectly over time. But it is also possible that this transference of ideas could have been the result of a proactive adoption of ideas. Nicolaas Johannes Krom has suggested that "weaving is a metaphor for the creation of the world both in Southeast Asia and in India" (1926, p. 361), and this statement perhaps highlights the importance, symbolism and significance that cloth held for the people of Java.

The oceans between China, Southeast Asia, India, West Asia and the coast of Africa are often described as the "single ocean". This statement is derived from the fact of the sizeable neutral zone of water that meant treasures from distant shores always arrived on the coasts of Sumatra and Śrivijaya and the trading ports in Java. It led to lively commercial exchange that encouraged communication and left its mark on the history of Southeast Asia. The developments and change that took place on the Indian subcontinent reached the Indonesian islands reasonably quickly, and this subsequently led to the rise of the Hindu devotional cults. Parts of the reliefs at Borobudur, for example, were interpreted as a Mahāyāna Buddhist text, a *sūtra* that reached Java and other parts of Southeast Asia. The reliefs are based on six Buddhist texts: the *Mahakarmavibhangga*, *Jatakas*, *Avadanas*, *Lalitavistara*, *Gandavyuha* and *Bhadracari* (Miksic 1990).

The extensive cross communication over this single ocean raises the possibility of Indian influences on the history and culture of the region. Oliver Wolters suggests that the rulers and urban elite were to take the introduction of foreign ideas and modernity in their stride, which led the elite to not only expect a continuous flow of foreign goods but also ongoing arrivals of Indian literature, which they appear to have absorbed into their traditions (1999, pp. 44–47). This apparent absorption of foreign literature and merchandise—not only from India but also from further west and from China in the East—appeared to have aided in the creation of an elite society that was open to all the ideas that came its way.

The members of this elite could then belong to a new "whole", and the inclusion of Indian materials and ideas allowed the rulers to believe that their centres and the materials created within them were unique. Because the foreign materials appeared to be incorporated into many local cultures, the range of material the local rulers adopted was then perhaps subsequently adapted. This resulted in the foreign material apparently disappearing entirely and being subsumed within indigenous designs (Wolters 1999, p. 57).

Such an occurrence becomes clearly apparent in studying the small bronze and gold statuettes and the Śaivite and Buddhist stone sculptures, all of which depict iconography that reflect their Indian roots. There are some notable exceptions, however. Example of such include the ninth-century seated stone Gaṇeśa (fig. 37, p. 75) at the NMI and the stone *dvārapāla* (fig. 40, p. 78) at the Museum Sonobudoyo, both of which were carved with a variation on a type of flower with pointed petals. A variation on this pattern is also carved in shallow relief on the *seléndang* and on the *dhotī* of a seated stone figure of an Avalokiteśvara from Bihar, which is dated to the tenth or eleventh century and remains in the National Museum, New Delhi.

In contrast to this, in studying the statues from the thirteenth to the fourteenth century, a new "whole" becomes apparent—whilst the religious aspects of the Indian traditions may be visible, what we see now is an amalgamation of styles that reflect a local Javanese interpretation of different textiles. By this period there would already have been a considerable number of Muslims among the officials and dignitaries within the Majapahit court. The introduction of the *wali-sanga*, or nine preachers, was attributed to the Islamization of the island (De Casparis and Mabbett 1994, p. 330). This change in the religious cohesion of the period may have had an impact on the particular use of the *kawung* pattern (and its use of the number nine) on the statues of the Majapahit period. This represented a departure from the modes of the previous centuries, where so many of the designs reflected fabrics with Buddhist or animal patterns. Further study of the patterns on these figures, therefore, can only improve our knowledge of the history of the region. In the past it appears the legitimacy granted to kings by divine right enabled them to create expensive statues of the highest quality, and which often depicted the patterns that would have appeared on the textiles of this period. At this time there appeared to be a move away from the esoteric form of Śaivism and Buddhism to that of a cult of deifying royal figures, which appeared to be homogeneous in the guise of either Śiva, Pārvatī or Harihara. By the end of the Majapahit period, deified statues of royal figures, in which a king and a god appear presented together in one statue, were followed by new forms in East Java. These then appear as depictions of the heroes of the *Mahābhārata*, such as Bhīma and Kertolo (Kinney 2003, p. 41). Numerous statues of Bhima appear at Caṇḍi Sukuh in Central Java dating from the fifteenth century. These new statue forms appear as semi-divine beings, and they represent an end to the Majapahit period (ibid., p. 273).

Indian Textiles

The exact nature of the types of textiles traded from the Indo-Persian sphere to Southeast Asia are unknown. What is known, however, is that Indian cotton appeared to be in massive demand in Java, and that it was imported over a long period. The Yuan also appeared to need cloth from India such as white cotton for use in the uniforms of soldiers fighting in the hot southern regions. The white fabric came to be known in the Ming period as *kanipha*, in Thailand as *bafta* and in Malaysia as *kain*. The Indian merchants transported the material via Southeast Asia on the way to China. In Śrivijaya, for example, the Southeast Asian merchants who traded in the port of Palembang would re-export the cloth along with other commodities. The history of the Song dynasty mentions envoys, probably arriving from Sumatra, who brought with them Indian textiles. These details from the Song appear to be the first mention of Indian textiles exported to Southeast Asia (Devare 2009, p. 180). Such imported Indian pieces of cotton often subsequently came to be the templates for the production of Javanese textiles.

Perhaps what also arrived from India was a cloth garment known as a *dhotī*, which was then adapted as a local form of dress. This was the lower body garment worn by both men and women, known from texts dating back to the second century BCE up to the twelfth century. The

Figure 7 Śiva, 9th century, Gemuruh, near Wonosobo, Central Java. Museum Nasional Indonesia. 24 cm, cast gold. Inv. no. 497a/4569.

dhotī was originally worn short, tied tightly around the legs and caught up and tucked in at the rear of the dress. In the following centuries, the *dhotī* was worn both long and short. For example, the style of a *dhotī* is clearly evident wrapping the limbs of the small gold Śiva in figure 7. Another examples of a garment that could have arrived from India is the *sarong or sarung*, the Malay word describing a cloth wrapped around the hips. In ancient times this was also called a *sari*. The sari that is known today, however, is not the same as the *sari* of old. Today, the sarong represents a *kain* sewn into a tube skirt. But in classical Java all the sculptures were depicted with a *kain* as a sheet cloth wrapped around the body, as we can see in the small gold Pārvatī in figure 8.

Much of the material examined in this chapter emphasizes the importance of the ancient Javanese literature *kalangwan*, such as *kidung* and *kakawin* poems, as a source of dress and textile patterns, especially from the KH and the ST. It also highlights the knowledge of economic and social history gained from the *sīma* charters. As a result of this knowledge, the types of garments shown on the Javanese sculptures are revealed to us. Having looked at the historical sources and the texts that refer to the textile terms and patterns, suggestions can be made about the sculptures themselves, taking into account international influences and local developments. We know from the *sīma* and the Javanese market lists of the eleventh and twelfth centuries that the Javanese were producing their own skeins of coloured silk. We also know from inscriptions that a great variety of textiles were being made in Java from the tenth century onwards. But very little is known of the types of textiles that were available prior to this period. From the texts, we know that what came from India was mostly white cotton, with some patterns described as flowers and circles with dots scattered across a plain ground.

Figure 8 Pārvatī, 9th century, Gemuruh, near Wonosobo, Central Java. Museum Nasional Indonesia. 21 cm, gold. Inv. no. 519a/4570.

As Christie has noted, this description closely resembles some of the patterns on the Indian statuary of the Central Javanese period. She also refers to the earliest reference of Javanese silk arriving in China, when a Cham mission to the Chinese court carried a Javanese "*ge-man*" silk. Unfortunately, we know nothing further about this textile. Later, Javanese missions carried coloured silks to China, some of which were of local Javanese origin and some that were classified by the Chinese as brocades and damasks, which probably referred to *kain songket*, *kain limar* and embroidery work (Christie 1998a, p. 21). The dominant type of loom in use in maritime Southeast Asia was the Austronesian body-tension or back-strap loom. It remained the dominant loom type in Indonesia until recent centuries (Christie 1998b, p. 17). Market lists from the period mention the use of a loom reed or *suri*. This feature, as described earlier, allowed the warp threads to be separated to enable the weaving of supplementary weft threads that would float over the warp. It has been suggested that this type of loom, known as the *cadar* loom in Java, was imported by South Indians from Persia. Whilst the Javanese looms were unlike the South Indian or Persian looms, the use of the loom reed may have been inspired or introduced by this contact (Christie 1998a, p. 22). This type of loom is needed to create plaids, *songket* and *limar* fabrics, which would indicate that by this time in the tenth century the Javanese would have been able to weave more sophisticated silks and to produce a finer and more luxurious cloth. This information is important and clearly points to the ability of the Javanese to weave silk textiles in complex forms such as brocade or *songket*.

It is not easy to find any counter-argument to the suggestion that some of the stone patterns represent a brocade or *songket*, as there is otherwise no viable explanation. One could perhaps suggest these patterns reflect a *patola* from Western India or maybe a cotton chintz, a painted resist and mordant dyed fabric from Western or East India. But whilst these cotton and double ikat textiles do reflect some of the same kind of patterning seen on the sculptures, I would advocate that they were not the templates for the designs on the thirteenth-century sculptures. These groups of Indian textiles were not really known about or traded at this early date. Also, the carvings in mid-relief are more likely to reflect a textile made with a supplementary thread in gold or a coloured silk thread, or perhaps a pattern stamped or embossed with gold.

Chinese Textiles

During the "free-trade" period of the following Yuan, it is apparent that Sino-Muslim traders were increasingly active in the waters of Southeast Asia, as indicated in map 1 (p. 4).

A textile technique known as "cloth of gold", or *nasīj*, which originated from Central Asia, was traded from China. Luxury silk and gold textiles such as *nasīj* were used as part exchange in a prosperous trade that developed (Watt 1997, p. 127; 2010, p. 7), especially during the Mongol period. Thomas Allsen describes *nasīj* as derived from the Arabic word *nasaja*, "to weave", with the generic meaning of "woven stuff" or "textile". In the Mongolian era it was shortened to *nasīj*, literally meaning "cloth of gold and silk". This term could also refer to a brocade, a textile to which are added ornamental threads, usually in the weft—in the case of *nasīj*, the ornamental threads were of gold. In the sources from the thirteenth and fourteenth centuries, the term most often referred to cloth woven of silk with gold thread, such as the glittering and sumptuous textiles known as the "Tartar cloths" of the medieval period, and is associated with the Mongols (Allsen 1997, pp. 3–4).

Allsen has described how the use of *nasīj* was extensive, with merchants arriving at the Mongol court with a steady supply of elegant clothing, especially garments of gold brocade. Chinese records from circa 1250 show that from Cathay and other countries further south came "cloths of silk and gold and cotton materials which they wear in the summer" (ibid., p. 29). This information is repeated in the *Zhufanzhi*, where it states that the port town of Jambi imported silk brocade (we do not know if this meant *nasīj*), damask and tie-dyed clothes during the Śrivijaya period. The Malay kingdom known as Langkasuka (a name no longer in use), an ancient state on the northeast coast of Malaya, was considered by the Arabs as part of "China", a land beyond the east coast of Malaya and thought of as the extreme limit of China (Wheatley 1961, p. 258). This region of peninsular Malaysia and the southeast coast of Thailand were known for the production of *songket*. The history of the Liang dynasty (506–566 CE) states that the Langkasuka kingdom was founded at the end of the first century CE between the south of Pattani in Thailand and north of Kedah on the Malay east coast. Chinese reports describe the king as dressed in "rose coloured cloth with gold flowers" (Lunsingh Scheurleer 2008, pp. 33–34). This textile could well have been a *songket* of some kind, as the red colour is indicative of traditional Malay *songket* woven with supplementary gold or silver threads.

During the Chola period, Indian merchants, the Chinese, and Arab sailors appeared to know that Java imported tie-dyed cloths and brocades via Borneo. It appears the Chinese were well aware that there were two different levels to the Malay market; consequently, they allocated the higher-value silks as critical products for the wealthier Southeast Asian ports. Examples of the kind of silk fabrics traded included damasks and brocades. Brocades and damasks are a rich woven fabric with a raised pattern, typically with gold or silver thread, and would have been woven on a Jacquard loom. In ancient times the kind of loom needed to weave a brocade containing an animal pattern set within roundels would have been a drawloom (Zhao 2015, p. 472). The drawloom is a loom with a flexible patterning device that allows warp yarns to be lifted independently in any combination. There is evidence for the existence of the drawloom during the Tang period, but it certainly existed during the Song dynasty (Buckley and Boudout 2015, p. 41). There would also have been sarcenets, which is a coarse silk fabric often used for linings, made with a silk warp and hemp weft (Yoshinobu 1970, pp. 112–21), and which was known mainly from the Middle East. In the import lists of the late Song period, what appears are silk and cotton traded by both merchants and peddlers in the international market. The Chinese, however, also exported silks. During the "free-trade" period of the Yuan dynasty that followed, it appeared that Sino-Muslim traders were increasingly active in the waters of Southeast Asia.

Figure 9a Prajñāpāramitā, detail of the border pattern of her *kain*. Muara Jambi site museum.

Figure 9b Indian *patola* double ikat silk textile, *jilamprang* pattern. Private collection.

Specific textual references have been recorded regarding the types of cloth traded at the diplomatic level, such as refined silks, which were highly valued. This was a result of a shift in trading patterns. Many foreign merchants gathered together in the Chinese ports, and Chinese merchants likewise began to form small communities in the ports on the north coast of Java and in Śrivijaya (Stuart-Fox 2003, pp. 50–51). By the early thirteenth century, there appears to have been a tremendous increase in the range of silk products exported to the Malay region. During the year 1219, as stated in the *Song Huiyao Jigao*, it was recommended that silk be used as a means of exchange rather than the precious metals previously used. The three types of silks mentioned were plain dyed silk cloth, printed and patterned silks, and silks with patterns gained through dyeing (Heng 2009, p. 169). The Prajñāpāramitā from Sumatra (fig. 131, p. 183) exhibits a very detailed pattern on the sash that is depicted laying across her hips. The patterns closely resemble *sulaman* or embroidery. A.N.J.Th. van der Hoop describes how *sulaman* originated from China and was used on silks from Palembang, where the art demonstrates a mix of Chinese, Javanese and Siamese influences (Hoop 1949, p. 236). The border pattern on the figure's *kain* appears to clearly represent a stylized version of the *tumpal* (fig. 9a), the isosceles triangular pattern that appears so often on *patola* and Indian trade cottons (fig. 9b). This statue is a clear example of acculturation, where knowledge of a particular pattern was interpreted into a local Sumatran style. As a result, the statue represents first-hand evidence of the use in the region of Chinese and Siamese textile patterns in the late thirteenth century.

Central Asian Patterns

The examples of patterns preserved in Sasanian and Sogdian murals lead us to conjecture how the textile patterns appearing on the Javanese sculptures might have looked. For example, although the figures of Pārvatī (fig. 10a) and Mañjuśrī Arapacana (fig. 10b) are dressed in the Javanese style, the patterns appear "foreign", possibly of Indo-Persian origin. The end years of the Sasanian Empire, around 671 CE, were contiguous with the beginning of the Tang period in 619 CE. At the time, Sasanian silks were imported into China and were often replicated. As a consequence, additional textiles were produced that appeared bearing an amalgamation of Chinese and Iranian motifs (Allsen 1997, p. 11). Examples of some of the patterns created include confronted animals or single animals such as ducks, lions, peacocks and deer, usually set within or without a pearl roundel. Both of these empires had established a clothing code and a set of sumptuary laws on the most exquisite silks. Interaction continued between Central Asia and China long after the fall of the Sasanian dynasty. It would appear that Indo-Persian courtly images enjoyed wide prestige spanning the region from Constantinople in the west to Xian in China to the east. The ornamental patterns that were attributed to a Persian style can be seen as being symbolically powerful.

A further example comes from work completed in the Russian North Caucasus region in a site known by its Turkic name, Kubachi. Zvezdana Dode's work at Kubachi reflects precisely what this book aims to portray. She states:

Figure 10a Detail of the textile pattern on Pārvatī, Caṇḍi Singosari. Pullen photo.

> Textiles are a very important part of historical evidence. They also play an important art-historical source for ornamental patterns found in other forms of decorative arts. Costly and beautiful imported silks have always been a source of inspiration for local artists who copied images from foreign textiles onto items of their own art tradition. (Dode 2014, p. 127)

Dode asks, "how did artistic motifs spread?" In her research carried out on the Kubachi reliefs, she assumed that fabrics and perhaps other objects of material art would have played a key role in cultural exchange between different regions of the world. She suggests that the stone carvers at Kubachi did not directly copy the textile ornaments, which is what I propose also took place in Java. The patterns on the Singosari sculptures appear to have been created as a local interpretation of foreign imported textiles. Dode describes one example of special interest, which is also reflected here. There are close parallels between the ornamental patterns on the stone reliefs and the silk fabrics. For example, a direct correspondence can be made between the images of a deer on a Yuan dynasty silk lampas textile with those on two Kubachi reliefs. The reliefs in the north Caucasus are dated to the Mongol period, around the last quarter of the thirteenth to the early fourteenth century. Carved on the sculpture of Pārvatī (fig.10a) is a textile pattern of a duck and other animals within roundels, one of which is possibly a deer. Here we can see the same kind of relationship described by Dode between textiles and another medium. She concludes by articulating that "emblems and symbols of significance originated from the heart of the Mongol empire, where cultural influences extended in all directions towards the periphery" (ibid., pp. 128–39). The periphery of the Mongol empire included Java as one of its trading partners. From Dode's article, where she recorded the Kubachi reliefs, we can deduce that what we see in the East Java statues parallels in some instances these reliefs—a reflection of Indo-Sasanian/Mongol designs where there has been some direct borrowing and subsequent imitation.

Figure 10b Detail of the textile pattern on Mañjuśrī Arapacana, State Hermitage Museum, St Petersburg. Pullen photo.

Stone Sculpture Textile Patterns

Some of the sculptures made during the Singhasāri period exhibit exceptional textile patterns. One, for example, is Brahmā, who is carved with the *sinjang* showing a series of rosettes and vegetal patterns. The rosettes are typical of the flowers woven into nineteenth to twentieth century Malay and Palembang *songket limar*. This pattern is also evident on the Dikpāla Nairṛti and on the Brahmā (fig. 11). The pattern also appears in a very similar schematic layout on Indian cotton textiles that are block-printed with resist and mordant dye in blue and red. Knowledge of this pattern reaches even further back; for example, it appears on eleventh-century wall paintings of a king at Pagan, and on the textile pattern depicted on a harp player among the seventh-century Sasanian rock reliefs at Taq-i-Bustan (fig. 12). Mathew Canepa describes the Taq-i-Bustan rock reliefs as containing multiple images of its patron the king. The reliefs not only preserve royal activities but also royal fashion and textile ornament, including the clothing of the courtiers, servants and musicians, where great pains were taken to record with precision the textile patterns. A sixth-century robe found in Constantinople is portrayed with birds in roundels, a pattern not known in Rome but one that closely matches textiles from Persia. Such ornamentation could be perceived as exotic and define the patron as part of the social elite. The similarity of some of the ornament designs at Taq-i-Bustan with the two sculptures of Pārvatī and Mañjuśrī is uncanny. The depiction of a *Simurgh/senmurv*, an Iranian mythical animal, along with a large rosette placed within roundels is also uncannily similar to the patterns, not only on these statues but also on Mañjuśrī, where the pattern

Figure 11 Nairṛti and Brahmā, detail of the textile pattern.

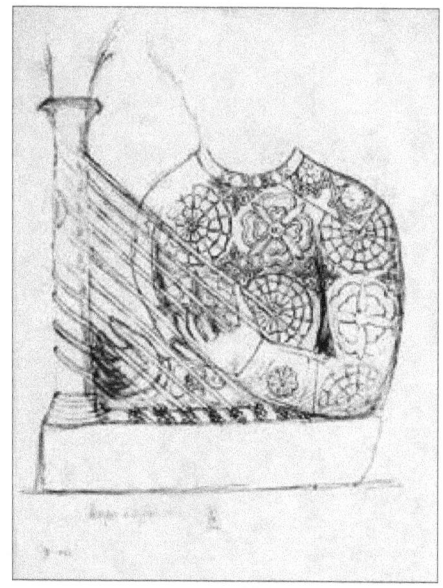

Figure 12 Harper in right boat (drawing), Taq-i-Bustan (Iran). 21.6cm x 27 cm. Sassanian Rock Reliefs, the Ernst Herzfeld papers. Freer Gallery of Art and Arthur M. Sackler Gallery Archives. Smithsonian Institution, Washington, D.C. Inv. no. FSA A.6 05.0931.

depicts roundels with ducks and deer. Canepa suggests "ornamental motifs could often migrate from silk to other types of textiles or even to architectural settings" (2014, pp. 2–11). This point made by Canepa, along with the earlier one by Dode, highlights the continued cross-cultural exchange between the Sasanian world and China.

The two sculptures of Mañjuśrī and Pārvatī are carved with textile patterns that do not fit into any design category known today in Java, Sumatra or the Malay Peninsula. The only pattern visible on Pārvatī can be read as a motif of a duck in a roundel. In the remaining roundels, the head and legs of different animals are just discernible. The Mañjuśrī, in contrast, is carved with a perfect pattern of juxtaposed circles in which the motifs represent three different imaginary animals, the pseudo-*Simurgh*, *makara* and griffin. It also includes two different roundels of vegetal designs, including a pattern using the leaf of the lotus vine—described as a "recalcitrant spiral" (Hoop 1949, p. 272)—which can also be seen carved on the walls of Caṇḍi Kalasan and is depicted in roundels at Caṇḍi Kidal. Some of the roundel patterns are also somewhat reminiscent of Chinese cloud designs. Pervasive influences of Sasanian designs remained throughout the Asian continent long after the decline of the Sasanian Empire, as evidenced in some of the textile patterns

Figure 13 Nandīśvara, *c.*1292, detail of the jacket side-by-side with a twentieth-century *songket* textile from Palembang, South Sumatra. Private collection. Pullen photo.

from the Singhasāri period; many of which remain inexplicable. Hiram Woodward details a stone pattern carved on the walls of Caṇḍi Sewu that he attributes as a Chinese silk. He describes it as made up of roundels containing images of animals such as lions and deer, alternating roundels filled with large rosettes, and with foliate Greek crosses in between. Despite the eighth-century dating for this pattern of Central Java, it is interesting to note that nothing like it is evident on the sculptures from the Central or early East Java period. But, as has been suggested, this pattern is not in fact Chinese, but instead has its roots in Sogdian traditions. The rosettes, however, closely resemble Chinese patterns found in Tang China of the eighth century. Such themes present "tantalizing evidence of the spread of such motifs" (Woodward 1977, pp. 233–37). I propose that the Tang rosette is clearly visible on the patterns of Nairṛti and Brahmā. These designs could also, however, be a larger version of the rosette patterns depicted on the jacket of Nandīśvara (fig. 13). Whatever the source of these patterns, many scholars have concluded that—whether in paint, carved reliefs or stone—they reflect the textiles in circulation at the time.

Figure 14 Durgā Mahiṣāsuramardinī, 13th century, detail of the textile pattern. Pullen photo.

I have earlier alluded to Sasanian connections in order to explain the possible inspiration for some of these patterns. Amy Heller has outlined some possible ideas, to which I concur:

> mural paintings of the textiles in Tibetan monasteries constructed during the late tenth to twelfth centuries indicate the persistent popularity in Tibet of Sasanian roundel motifs enclosing both geometric and animal forms, long after their initial import during the Tibetan empire. (Heller 2006, p. 175).

I turn now to an aspect of clothing on a number of sculptures originating from Caṇḍi A at Singosari. These figures are depicted wearing short, sleeveless upper-body jackets; except for the figure of Agastya, who only wears a *kain*. These jackets are known in Sanskrit as *kavaca*, meaning armour, jacket, mail, shield, amulet or chain. The same word in Dutch is *harnas,* meaning armour, a word that was appropriated by the Javanese to describe this garment. The idea of this short jacket was possibly derived from war jackets worn by the Balinese, as depicted in Balinese paintings. In the twentieth century, Balinese troops wore jackets such as these when they fought against the Dutch.[1] The term *kavaca* hints at the magical protection of this red garment, which is unique to these Singosari sculptures (Stutterheim 1936, p. 308–9).

All of the sculptures at Caṇḍi A are depicted with different textile patterns on their clothing, seeming to reflect the often-used layout of a brocade textile. The patterns are generally carved within bands or chains known as *rantai*, alluding to the possibility that these sculptures represent the earliest examples of brocaded textile patterns. For example, the design on Nandīśvara is clearly a template of a *songket*. As is this early-twentieth-century textile example placed against the torso of Nandīśvara. The lotus flower pattern on the *sinjang* of Durgā (fig. 14) could also be the prototype for a pattern depicted in numerous present-day Malay *songket* designs (fig. 15). The Malay annals, known as the *Sejarah Melayu*, indicate that knowledge of *songket* weaving was introduced from India via the Śrivijaya kingdom of Palembang and Jambi. The textile weavers on the Terengganu coast of peninsular Malaysia believe India was the original source of *songket* weaving (Selvanayagam 1990, p. xviii).

Figure 15 *Songket* textile, Palembang, South Sumatra, detail of a twentieth-century textile. Private collection.

An Amalgamation of Ideas

What became apparent from the specific typologies discussed earlier was the extreme differences between the textile patterns on the sculptures between the Central and early Java period of the ninth and early eleventh centuries and the East Java period of the thirteenth and the subsequent fourteenth and early fifteenth centuries. From the Central and early East Java period, the bronze statues are divided reasonably evenly between Hindu and Buddhist deities, whilst the stone sculptures are all Śaivite. The patterns decorated within narrow bands suggest either an ikat textile or painted resist and mordant dyed Indian cotton, often made up of geometric patterns or a series of patterns that appear to resemble "dots and dashes". These are similar to the ikat textiles seen at Ajanta and to representations of Tibetan textile patterns in the later eleventh to twelfth centuries, as is evident from sculptures and paintings. But despite their later date, it is possible that ikat was known much earlier, as evidenced by the Ajanta paintings. By the beginning of the East Java period, however, the patterns and the size of the sculptures had changed considerably. No longer are there any small bronze figures, but there are large stone statues, most of which represent Śaivite and some Mahāyāna Buddhist deities. These sculptures display a broad range of dress styles and an even greater variety of textile patterns, including some with apparent esoteric iconography. No two patterns are identical, unlike those in Central Java, where many statuettes appear with the same or similar designs. The limited numbers of patterned bronzes would indicate a limited amount and variety of textiles made it to Central Java during this period.

Wolters' theory of "localization" was a way to analyse how local people reacted to the onset of Indian material. How did the materials arrive? How were they perceived? Were they perhaps, "drained of their original significance by a process which I shall refer to as localization. The materials, be they words, sounds of words, books, or artifacts, had to be localized in different ways before they could fit into various local complexes" (1999, p. 55). The Javanese had incorporated all of these ideas that arrived from India; however, the result was in no way Indian, but was purely Javanese. This approach was especially evident by the beginning of the thirteenth century and up to the end of the fourteenth century. During this period there was indeed evidence of Indian culture in the style and iconography of the sculptures, but by now the textile patterns appeared to hold a much closer comparison with locally produced textiles, overlaid with certain foreign influences from Central Asia and specific silk brocade textiles from China.

The textile patterns visible on the Central and early East Java bronzes exhibit a mixture of designs. The purest and most frequent among them are repeated patterns of a series of floral forms, small circles and dots, floral designs surrounded by circles, and simple patterns in wavy horizontal bands. The more complex patterns appear as compound arrangements of horizontal or vertical double bands infilled with geometrical pattern forms and floral motifs. In some cases the patterns were very detailed and densely carved. Further study of other media and the work of earlier scholars on the interpretation of textile patterns and techniques could provide more examples of what the patterns and techniques represented on the stone and bronze statues may be reflecting.

Some scholars have looked at the question of identifying what the technique of production might have been in studying textile patterns on paintings in Buddhist monasteries. For example, Klimburg-Salter in 1994, Flood in 2009 and Guy and Thakar in 2014 all raised such issues. Deborah Klimburg-Salter talks of "honouring the deity with fine textiles". She describes the massive scale of the paintings of the eleventh-century Poo manuscript, which allowed for extraordinary fineness and detailed and complex patterning. The great variety of patterns point to a sophisticated cosmopolitan taste and a broad range of cultural contacts based on the strength of their economies. She also suggests that the fabrics depicted were probably of a lightweight cloth as they lie close to the body. She also makes the assumption that the patterns show specific techniques and were possibly copied from existing textiles. As the painted textiles are not necessarily attributed to local industry, she proposes they originated from Gujarat in western India, which has a long history of resist-dyed textiles (Klimburg-Salter 1994, pp. 158–60).

Finbar Flood, in examining a royal scene at the Dukhang temple in Alchi, describes the dress as having

> a repeated pattern of roundels containing rampant lions, a design that may reflect the impact of contemporary Persian textiles.... [a form of dress that] is widely dispersed in Central Asia and eastern Iran. (Flood 2009, p. 66).

Another example is from the extensive work of Guy and Thakar on the Sumtsek chapel at Alchi. They describe one painting as follows:

> Nowhere in the subcontinent can the dynamic movement and exchange of textiles be better studied than here. The chapel contains a series of wall paintings that embody the most complex visual record of the textiles in circulation in medieval north India.... The monumental clay bodhisattvas serve as a unique inventory of the luxury textiles in circulation at the time. (Guy and Thakar 2015, p. 13)

These three examples provide evidence that, whilst not conclusive, helps us to state the origins and types of textiles reflected on the bronze, gold and stone statues.

Malay Materials and Textile Terms

The *ceplok* textile pattern group includes a design known as *kawung*, which consists of a series of interlocking circles in various forms. This pattern appears to dominate around half of the sculptures. The other dominating pattern type represents a combination of rosette flowers, stylized lotus flowers and geometric patterns set with "chains", or *rantai*, made up of vertical and horizontal bands. There are also two

Figure 16a Arcā Leluhur 1, Bumiayu, Sumatra, 11th–13th century.

Map 2 Sculpture locations in Sumatra and Kalimantan, 8th to 14th century.

pattern types made up of adjoining roundels with various mythical and realistic animal motifs. The last groups consist of textile patterns with skulls, one-eyed *kāla* and stylized confronting *kāla*-head motifs. Within the Majapahit period, the sculptures only exhibit one pattern type, the *kawung* in various depictions, but in a simplified form compared to some of the earlier Singhasāri categories.

There remain two seated sculptures of ancestor figures known as Arcā Leluhur. The female statue shown in figure 16a remains in a small site museum at Caṇḍi Bumiayu, as shown in map 2. The female wears

Figure 16b Arcā Dewa/Leluhur, MNI, 12th century. Pullen photo.

tailored garments of a Javanese or Malay type of dress with a long-sleeved jacket worn over a *kain* to the ankles. The garments on the sculpture originating from Java (fig. 16b) are carved with an overall pattern of a daisy flower. The Sumatra *arcā* appears carved with a pattern that reflects a Persian-inspired motif. Both statues wear a jacket known as a *baju* or *kebaya*. The word *baju* was derived initially from the Persian word *bad ʒu* and subsequently adopted into the Malay language.[2] The term *kebaya*, on the other hand, is probably derived from the Arabic word *kaba* or *abaya*. Sylvia Fraser-Lu instead suggests *kebaya* originates from

Figure 17 Seated male figure, Caṇḍi Jago. Image from Brandes (1904).

the Arabic *habaya*, meaning a long tunic that is open down the front (1988, p. 67n11). In today's Malay language, an upper body garment, whether with or without sleeves, is generally termed a *baju*; a word also used for a blouse, robe, tunic or coat. The term *baju* appears in Javanese texts from the early eleventh century, and in Malay manuscripts from the late fourteenth century. Peter Lee adds the following footnote to a 1420 commentary from Ma Huan, a Chinese traveller who journeyed to Southeast Asia: "in Java women wore an upper garment, a short jacket with coloured cloth … a *baju* with a V-shaped opening and a wrapped skirt, a shoulder cloth or *seléndang*" (Lee 2015, p. 44n36).

Carved in relief at Caṇḍi Jago in East Java is another example of a seated figure wearing a patterned long-sleeved *baju*. In this instance the figure is also depicted wearing *lañciṅan*, which in Old Javanese is commonly translated as trousers (Jákl 2016, p. 185). Today the Indonesian word for trousers is *lancingan*, meaning Java-style trousers. A close inspection of figure 17 reveals a line marking the apparent end of the trouser at the ankles. Klokke suggests the figure is a male ascetic, Mucukunda (2000, p. 25). However, as the figure is seated on a couch, pointing threateningly with his right arm, and with his left arm resting on his thigh, in my opinion this figure is unlikely to be an ascetic, as it is considered rude in cultured Javanese society to point. Besides, an ascetic would be unlikely to be wearing an upper-body garment, yet he does appear however to have the dreadlocks of an ascetic. The figure is overly broad compared to the rest of the relief figures and does not display the *wayang* features of the remainder of the Jago reliefs. (*Wayang kulit* puppets are leather puppets made for the shadow theatre; hence the figures are made in two dimensions and present a flat, sideways appearance. Following this, the term "*wayang*" is often used to describe figures that are presented from a somewhat flat, side profile.) Anne Kinney has said that no elements of the *wayang* appear in Central Javanese art, whereas in East Java they are numerous (2003, p. 40). This relief figure remains a mystery, and it is one of a kind from among all the remaining East Javanese *caṇḍi*.

Figure 18 *Baju surjan lurik*, Museum Sonobudoyo, male jacket with a pattern, 21st century. Pullen photo.

Both the jacket and trousers of the relief carving appear decorated with the pattern in horizontal stripes. By way of comparison, a certain type of jacket with vertical stripes is worn today by palace guards—a jacket known as *baju surjan lurik*; *lurik* referring to the stripes. Despite the stripes being vertical rather than horizontal, the concept of the palace guards' jacket is the same, and this would indicate the figure at Jago is likely to represent a palace guard of some sort. A *lurik* textile is a term used in Central Java to describe narrow stripes, and is one of the most archaic types of *tenun* or weaving. *Lurik* fabric makes up the striped jacket (fig. 18); however, as mentioned, the stripes in this example are in a vertical direction compared to horizontal in the stone carving. Perhaps an alternative interpretation to that of Klokke's that the figure is the ascetic Mucukunda can be made, for the following reasons. In Balinese *gĕringsing wayang kebo* textiles, an ascetic or a priest is depicted with piled hair. At the same time this aspect is indeed visible in the image; it is the sole nod to the relief representing an ascetic. An ascetic would also be bare-chested with the *upavīta* depicted across the torso, as we see in the reliefs at Caṇḍi Jago and at Caṇḍi Panataran from the fourteenth century. An ascetic would not be depicted wearing a form of trousers, but rather a *kain* to the ankles, again as depicted in the reliefs. Lastly, his refined physiognomy, the large ear ornaments and no apparent facial hair are the norm for ascetics in the Indic world. But an ascetic dressed in patterned clothes would not be seated in the "European pose" or presented larger than the rest of the reliefs; that would be the preserve for a person of authority or perhaps a king.

Java has a rich heritage of textiles that has played a key and symbolic role in the culture for centuries. Early texts found in Java and the metal and stone figures attest to the uses of these textiles. The dress styles portrayed on the statuettes and sculptures provide a "key" to identifying the various terms used to describe parts of the dress and the patterns, with the most important of these being the *upavīta, seléndang, kain* or *sinjang*. The terms are used to describe the critical textile patterns recognized from the *kakawin* and *kidung* poetry dating from the tenth to the sixteenth century. From these we know that textiles served many functions beyond the primary use of clothing, from ritual gifts to currency.

The sartorial style on the statues of East Java included draped and tailored garments. Meanwhile, the Central Javanese figurines wear only draped garments, such as a loincloth or *dhotī*, often in a manner more closely related to those of the bronzes from Eastern India from the ninth to the eleventh century. These Central Javanese sculptures were described in the early twentieth century as "Indian Art on Javanese soil". Opinions, however, have changed since then. Some of the small Javanese bronze statues may be regarded as direct replicas of Indian art, but most of them can be seen to be imaginative adaptations and to be Javanese in style. So what then is "Javanese style"? The small statuettes dressed in a long *kain* represent a Javanese style of dress. Should the statue be standing, the cloth falls to the ankles with a few neat folds depicted at the front. If the statue is seated, the folds of the *kain* will be depicted on the top of the lotus cushion, lying in many neat pleats. In some cases the limbs are in evidence beneath the fabric, but as the period moves to the thirteenth and fourteenth centuries, limbs are no longer visible beneath the fabric. The sartorial style has now become entirely Javanese, with the wearing of the long *sinjang*.

There are various ways of distinguishing the techniques used to render the textiles represented on the stone statues and the small metal statuettes. For the stone statues, the type and quality of the andesite stone can vary enormously within Central Java, and this factor plays a significant part in the type of patterning carved into the stone. With regard to the bronzes, the smooth surface in many cases lends itself to complex patterns. This though has not always been the case, as seen in the small Nganjuk figures from early East Java. Often the uneven surfaces of these bronze statues do not show any patina, and the craftsmen have only been able to render simple decorations on the *kain*.

A process of analysing the statues is certainly very helpful. But this process can be very meaningfully complemented by producing drawings to illustrate the details of the patterns. This makes it much easier to assign the patterns into groups and to highlight notable differences between them. Such an approach is necessary to be able to understand the different techniques that were possible in Java during these periods, and from this we can deduce what the textile patterns might have been replicating. For example, Indian painted resist and mordant dyed cotton textiles with overall patterns of small floral designs and circles appear in random repeats, along with textiles woven with an ikat design that appears as dots, dashes and geometric patterns carved within horizontal bands. Another group includes most of the small gold statuettes and plaques, where the flexible, smooth nature of the metal lends itself to a far more excellent depiction of patterns.

Dress, Typologies and Definitions

This section will summarize the analysis and information gathered regarding the dress and textile patterns of the Javanese. A knowledge of Old Javanese literature and texts has been essential for the study of dress and pattern terms, as the descriptions given within the texts link the sculptures to the textile patterns in existence today. In my discussion with *Pak* Dwi of the University of Malang in 2016, he suggested that first one

Figure 19 Wayang Wong dancers. Image from Wit (1912).

should study the sculptures, second the texts, and third the ethnography; that is, the comparative material available today—for instance, the textiles depicted on *wayang kulit* shadow puppets and in old photographs, such as the *wayang wong* performers from 1912 shown in figure 19.

This research approach recommended by Pak Dwi aids in our understanding of the different types of dress depicted on the sculptures. For example, worn across the body of the statues are multiple sashes and belts. The same is also apparent on the standing *wayang wong* dancer in figure 20, seen here wearing a traded *patola* or *cinde* cloth as his sash held out to the side of the body. He is also shown wearing a short sleeveless upper-body garment or jacket that is similar in style to those on the sculptures from Caṇḍi A at Singosari. All these features hint at the longevity of this Hindu-Buddhist style of East Javanese dress, which subsequently was adapted and absorbed into the dress for dancers and royalty to be used only at the Mataram *kraton* of Surakarta. In Javanese culture the court is the centre of political and religious authority. Countless ceremonies were held within the courts, many of which include elements dating back to the Hindu-Buddhist period in Java, and traditions that mark the importance of ancestors. The preservation of these traditions has been central to Javanese life (Miksic 2012, p. 85). If one extrapolates the dress styles from the present-day Javanese court and refers back to those of the thirteenth and fourteenth centuries, it becomes evident where these traditions originated, placing the stone statues as templates of the textile patterns and sartorial items in existence at the time in pre-modern Java.

It is also indisputable that Indian textile patterns, despite their longevity on the international trading markets, were not the only source of inspiration for the patterns on the Javanese sculptures. During the eleventh and twelfth centuries there appeared to be a sharp increase in population growth in Java, which led to an increase in wealth and further overseas contact for a broader range of the Javanese populace. This increase in growth appeared to lead to the development of Javanese social structures, but it also resulted in the development of the types of textiles that grace the statues.

Figure 20 Trade *patola*, 19th century, the same pattern and type of textile as depicted in the Wit photograph. Private collection.

Perhaps this comment from Christie best articulates the point: "the textiles portrayed on the East Javanese statuary were not all meant to represent Indian imports; however. Javanese and Indian aesthetics did diverge to a degree. The Javanese patterns were denser than their Indian counterparts" (1991a, p. 18).

The motifs created on the *sinjang* of the fourteenth-century sculptures almost consistently resemble various forms of the pattern group known as *ceplok*, the symbolism of which refers to the Old Javanese Austronesian (Tarling 1992, p. 311) concept of cosmic magic. Take, for example, the deified statue of King Kertarājasa Jayawardhana as Harihara (fig. 21). In Javanese philosophy, the king equals god in the world; the king and queen therefore are depicted wearing a *sinjang kawung*—a "cloth to protect the world" (Sumaryoto 1993, p. 36). Statues such as this were carved to illustrate the subject had passed through a rite of passage ceremony. As Fraser-Lu has suggested, textiles were significant in all stages of life in Southeast Asia, from birth to death (1988, p. 73). We can postulate then that these statues were created and adorned as though for a rite of passage.

Figure 21 Detail of the lower limbs of King Kertarājasa Jayawardhana as Harihara, early 14th century. Pullen photo.

The study of textile patterns on the sculptures emphasizes that very little changed over the preceding millennia. These sculptures, particularly the figures from the thirteenth and fourteenth centuries, show both a continuity of design and originality in the patterns. If the concept of "archetype textiles" is a viable one, then the idea that a series of patterns evolved over the centuries and that they were remade is entirely possible. It is evident that some of the patterns on the stone sculptures were of "foreign" origin. Generally speaking, apart from a few examples, the sculptures of East Java do not reflect the textile pattern terms described in the Old Javanese literature; instead, they more often reflect unique textile patterns that are not seen on any other sculptures in India, Tibet or indeed other Southeast Asian countries. One cannot view Chinese, Malay, Javanese, Indian and Central Asian cultures as distinct and confined to separate periods in history (Lee 2015, p, 30), as it is apparent hybridization is both an ancient and an ongoing global process. As Flood has said, "people and things have been mixed up for a very long time" (2009). It is this mix that we see in Java in the thirteenth and early fourteenth centuries.

Indigenous and Imported Textiles

Sinjang Kawung

Bernhard Bart, a Swiss architect living in Bukittinggi, Minangkabau, wrote an article on *songket* weaving and stone patterns from Java. He has proved that it is entirely possible to make a *songket* woven cloth with the *kawung* pattern that accurately represents some of the stone patterns of the Majapahit sculptures. This woven brocaded cloth of gold created with a supplementary weft thread produces a rich fabric (Bart 2016, pp. 17–18). During the Majapahit period in East Java and Bali, one of the most popular techniques was the use of gold-leaf glue work known as *tulis mas* or *prada*. The term *sinjang kawung*, which appears many times in the *kakawin*, applied to garments of the king's family and the minor nobility, and could also apply to the patterns on the statues of the deified figures. In the context of the statues, it relates to a luxurious heavy fabric over which are layered many large and long sashes and abundant ornaments. The *sinjang* refers to the long cloth wrapped around the body and worn to the ankles, usually portrayed with a pleated fold at the centre front.

At first it may seem difficult to account for the fact that relatively few Majapahit statues were carved with a *sinjang kawung* textile; however, the statues that did carry this pattern probably reflect a level of royal patronage. There is no evidence to suggest an explanation as to why some statues were carved with textile patterns while a more significant number were left plain. Evidence highlights the prestige given to this dress term, but this indicates that the plain statues would not have possessed the same level of prestige. One exception to this is the deified statue of a queen as Pārvatī (fig. 22) who wears a plain *sinjang*, which I suggest was perhaps unfinished. At any rate, judging from the size of her statue, she was probably made to emulate a significant queen.

Bernet Kempers suggests that the Hindu-Javanese sanctuary is a replica of the cosmos, and he proposes that this is an aspect of ancient Indonesian architecture that needs to be discussed:

> There is a parallelism between the macrocosm and the microcosm which pervades everything. The division which seems to be perceivable in the macrocosm holds good also for the human world. The division of 4 or 4 +1, into 2 or 2 +1, either separately or combined. (Bernet Kempers 1959, p. 20)

This division of the macrocosm and microcosm, Bernet Kempers argues, also holds good for the human world; for example, with the four points of the compass on the outer rim and with one in the centre. A close examination of the *kawung* pattern shows the precise composition of this design, which follows the concept of four outer points and one in the middle. I suggest that this pattern, with its deep-rooted symbolism, was only permitted to be used by the highest authority. This might also indicate why there were so few carved statues of deified kings and queens. Stanley Tambiah suggests that the term *maṇḍala* refers to a "cosmological scheme of various sorts in Tantric Hinduism and Buddhism" (Tambiah 2013, p. 503). A *maṇḍala*, attributed to the design and arrangement of Borobudur and Angkor Wat, reflects both simple and complex satellites around a core or centre. The system of a *maṇḍala* appears frequently at various levels of Hindu-Buddhist thought and practice (Tambiah 2013, p. 503). Examples of the simple geometric design appear in five-unit and nine-unit samples. This is described by Tambiah as a quinary formula called *mantjapat,* or five-four. It can refer to the village structure, to four tracts around a fifth central one, or the five-day rotational cycle of a village market. This *maṇḍala* structure can also refer to the nine-unit design in accounts of a king and his ministers arranged in two concentric circles (ibid., p. 504). The most famous of these complex schemes, however, appear in Hindu-Buddhist polities such as we see in Java. Here the king as the *dharma* or moral law, and as the universal ruler and bodhisattva, was seen as the pivot of the polity and as the link between the upper cosmos and the lower plane of humankind (ibid., p. 505).

Figure 22 Detail of the lower limbs of Pārvatī, Queen Tribhuwana Tunggadewi, late 14th century. Pullen photo.

Another way to look at the origin of the *kawung* pattern is to turn to the cross-section of the areng palm fruit, *Arenga pinnata* (syn. *Arenga saccharifera*) (fig. 23). The internal form of this fruit could well have been the source of the *kawung* pattern in Java (Velduisen-Djajasoebrata 1979, p. 212; Warming and Garwoski 1981, p. 170). It is more likely, however, that this interpretation is referring to the modern age and not to during the Hindu-Buddhist period. When the areng fruit is cut lengthways and divided into two equal parts it results in the *kawung* pattern. A contemporary batik or wax resist design from A.N.J.Th. van der Hoop (fig. 24) shows a *kawung* pattern from 1949. The fourteenth-century stone version of King Kertarājasa is remarkably similar.

The *kawung* pattern in the Hindu-Buddhist period is synonymous with Java, and is seen as a pattern with protective qualities. Nicholas Tarling has stated that "protection was the extreme duty of the kings, who were supposed to carry on their beneficial activity after their life on earth by pervading, as it were, the intentions of their subjects" with the "idea of the deification of kings" (1992, p. 310). The pattern did not appear to have any particular religious connotations, but it was perhaps connected to the spiritual or animist cultures of the past. The pattern of interlocking circles is especially evident carved on walls beside the entrance and on stone window blinds of Khmer temples of twelfth-century Cambodia.

Tambiah shows the division of *mantjapat*, which reflects the Mataram state and a nine-unit system of the kings council (2013, p. 504). We can also see this concept of the *mandalas* as Mount Meru within a cosmological scheme and with the theory for the symbols of the *kawung* pattern in the 4+4+1 scheme. Having argued for the theory of 4+4+1 in the construction and symbolism of the *kawung* pattern, we should consider

Figure 23 Cross-section of the *Arenga pinnata* (syn. *Arenga saccharifera*).

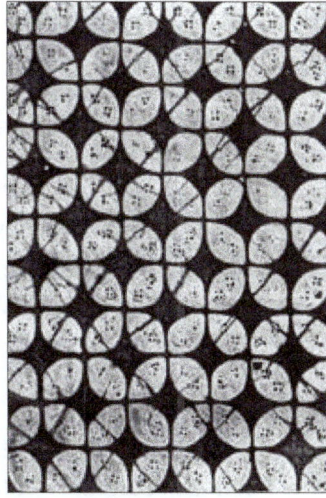

Figure 24 *Batik kawung*, Indonesian Ornamental Motifs. Image from Hoop (1949).

rival theories concerning how the term *batik* has often been incorrectly used. Christie suggests that the term *batik* does not enter the Javanese vocabulary until the seventeenth century. Its predecessor, the term *tulis warna*, or decorated with drawings in colour, however, occurs in the late twelfth through fourteenth centuries. This was a process of free-hand drawing in which a *canting* was used to apply wax to the surface of the cloth (Christie 1993b, pp. 191–92).

The Javanese batik expert K.R.T Hardjonagoro has discussed the philosophy of batik and its place in Javanese textile history. He asked the question, how should we define the term *batik* in Java? As a costume material? As a pattern? Or as part of the *ceplok* pattern group (1979, p. 224)? The *kawung* patterns on the Majapahit stone sculptures have often been described as "batik", for example. Christie argues that the patterns on thirteenth and fourteenth century sculptures are closer in style to "traditional batik patterns" (1991b, p. 17). As a result of these differences, there is a dilemma as to how to describe these patterns. Is the design a *kawung* motif but a batik technique, as Hardjonagoro suggests? But, as we do not know when the wax-resist method known today as batik was truly practised in Java, *batik*, then, remains an incorrect term to describe the *kawung* pattern when referring to the thirteenth and fourteenth centuries. The earliest method of batik as practised in Sunda in West Java and Toraja in Sulawesi was with a method using rice paste and a bamboo nib, which produced a very different and far less refined pattern compared to the cloth we know today. Hardjonagoro also suggests the *kawung* motif is visible on the walls of Hindu-Buddhist temples in Central Java, but we lack any means of identifying the patterning technique. But should the patterns that were produced in stone be considered to be batik? During the Hindu-Buddhist period, the batik technique was not considered as a costume (Hardjonagoro 1979, pp. 244–45). While recognizing it is not possible to prove the technique behind a "stone" pattern one way or the other, it is suggested in the KH that a cloth with a *kawung* motif of some sort was being made at this time and was worn by kings as a *sinjang kawung*. This can be interpreted as a long cloth with a *kawung* pattern woven in the *songket* technique or created as a *prada* textile. Some textiles with specific patterns appear to have protective properties, such as the *sinjang gĕringsing kawung*. The suggestion was that if the king wore the *sinjang kawung*, it enabled him to protect the world. Furthermore, it was thought that if he did not wear this cloth, not only could he not protect the world, he could not be king (Hauser-Schäublin, Nabholz-Kartaschoff and Ramseyer 1991, pp. 120–21). It appears that all the sculptures in the Majapahit period decorated with a textile pattern were meant to represent the deified statue of the deceased ruler. It is apparent in many instances that the statues are shown wearing a textile identified as a *sinjang gĕringsing kawung*. *Kawung* can be produced by various techniques, and the appearance of a *kawung* motif does not prove it was intended to depict a textile decorated by the batik technique.

Navagraha/Nawagrah or Nine-Planet Pattern

Christie describes a selection of the types of cloth granted to recipients of *sīma* charters from the mid-eleventh century until the end of the fourteenth century. During this period, no two charters appeared to be the same, although some charters of the tenth and eleventh centuries were reissued in the fourteenth century. The following terms appear: *navagraha*, or nine-planet pattern; *tinulis ring mas tawar*, garments painted in gold; and *tinulis ing mas*, apparel painted in gold (1991b, pp. 27–28; 1993, pp. 208–9). During the early East Javanese period in the eleventh century, these terms do not appear. It has also become evident that textile patterns with a *navagraha* layout do not appear until the Kediri period, and only on one statue—that of the Boro Gaṇeśa (fig. 25). This leads to the assumption that the *navagraha* pattern is perhaps an early term for the *kawung*, *jilamprang* or *patola* motif. Despite the uncertainty over the terms to be used to refer to textile patterns on stone of the twelfth and thirteenth centuries, by the fourteenth century the kings were wearing a *sinjang kawung*, perhaps also with the *navagraha* pattern, and perhaps painted in gold—*tinulis ing mas*.

Figure 25 Boro Gaṇeśa, 1239–40 CE, detail of the lower body showing textile pattern. Pullen photo.

Summary

The textile traditions of Java are many and varied. This chapter has attempted to encapsulate the variety of dress styles and the textile patterns and designs that possibly found their way to Java during the Central and East Javanese periods. We have considered texts such as the Nāgarakṛtāgama, poetry in the form of *kidung* and *kakawin*, and the *sīma* tax-transfer charters. These sources, along with texts on traditional costumes, have highlighted the types of dress patterns and textile types that were evident in ancient Java. Knowledge of the trading patterns with China and the Indo-Persian world is crucial in analysing the evidence, from which an understanding of many of the Javanese textile designs is possible. Knowledge of the use of *nasīj* in Mongol China and the information about woven gold textiles in Java known as *songket* also illustrate the possibility that many of the patterns on the East Java sculptures represent a woven gold fabric of some kind. The notion of a "single ocean" of trade and ideas across the Indian and Chinese worlds, bringing textiles and patterns to the shores of Java, is a viable one. These patterns were absorbed and interpreted by the local craftsmen and incorporated on the sculptures in Central and East Java. Patterns of roundels with animal designs originated from Indo-Persian designs, which were then incorporated by the Mongols and ended up in East Java, to appear on the two statues of Pārvatī and Mañjuśrī. As a result, these statues highlight the interconnections across the region.

Only from East Java in the Singhasāri period are there any statues wearing jackets. They are believed to give magical protection to the patron of the *caṇḍi*. These stitched, upper-body garments, along with the *baju* and *kain* of the two known ancestor figures, are the only evidence of tailored clothing. The remainder of the statues all wear cloth that is draped fashioned into a *dhotī, kain* or *sinjang*.

Notes

1. Refer to Jákl and Hoogervorst (2017) for further information on this subject.
2. "Most Javanese texts containing Persian loanwords were non-Islamic in content, yet were written at a time when commercial relations with Persians, Gujaratis, Tamils and other 'foreigners' has become commonplace" (Jákl and Hoogervorst 2017, p. 210).

3. Central and Early East Java Metal and Stone Sculpture from the Eighth to the Eleventh Century

Statues originating from the Central Javanese period range in date from the late eighth to the ninth century, and they vary in size from a small bronze statuette at 7.5 centimetres to a monumental stone statue at 3 metres. These, along with a few small bronzes dating from the early East Javanese period in the mid-eleventh century, are the subject of this chapter. These statues were all chosen as examples for their diversity of patterns. Their places of origin are shown in map 3.

The term "Central or early East Java Style" describes a style of sculptures made in Java but showing some similarities to an Indian type of dress. The Indian style is especially evident from Eastern and Southern India in the early years of the Chola of the mid-ninth to the thirteenth century (Huntington and Huntington 1993, p. 509) and of the Pāla dynasties of Eastern India. There are many sculptures that appear to fit more closely with this Indianized style of dress—for example, a small Śiva from Gemuruh and the male figure half of the gold plaque (fig. 26)—a style that is apparent in the apparel but not the textile patterns themselves. The sculptures clearly show the figures wearing a *dhotī,* worn short, pulled up between the legs and tucked in at the rear of the body. Another explicit Indian detail of the dress is the use of the many small metal girdles and belts, chains and sashes. In Java, the chains around the hips are used as girdles, and the broad band or demarcation across the upper body is a sash

61

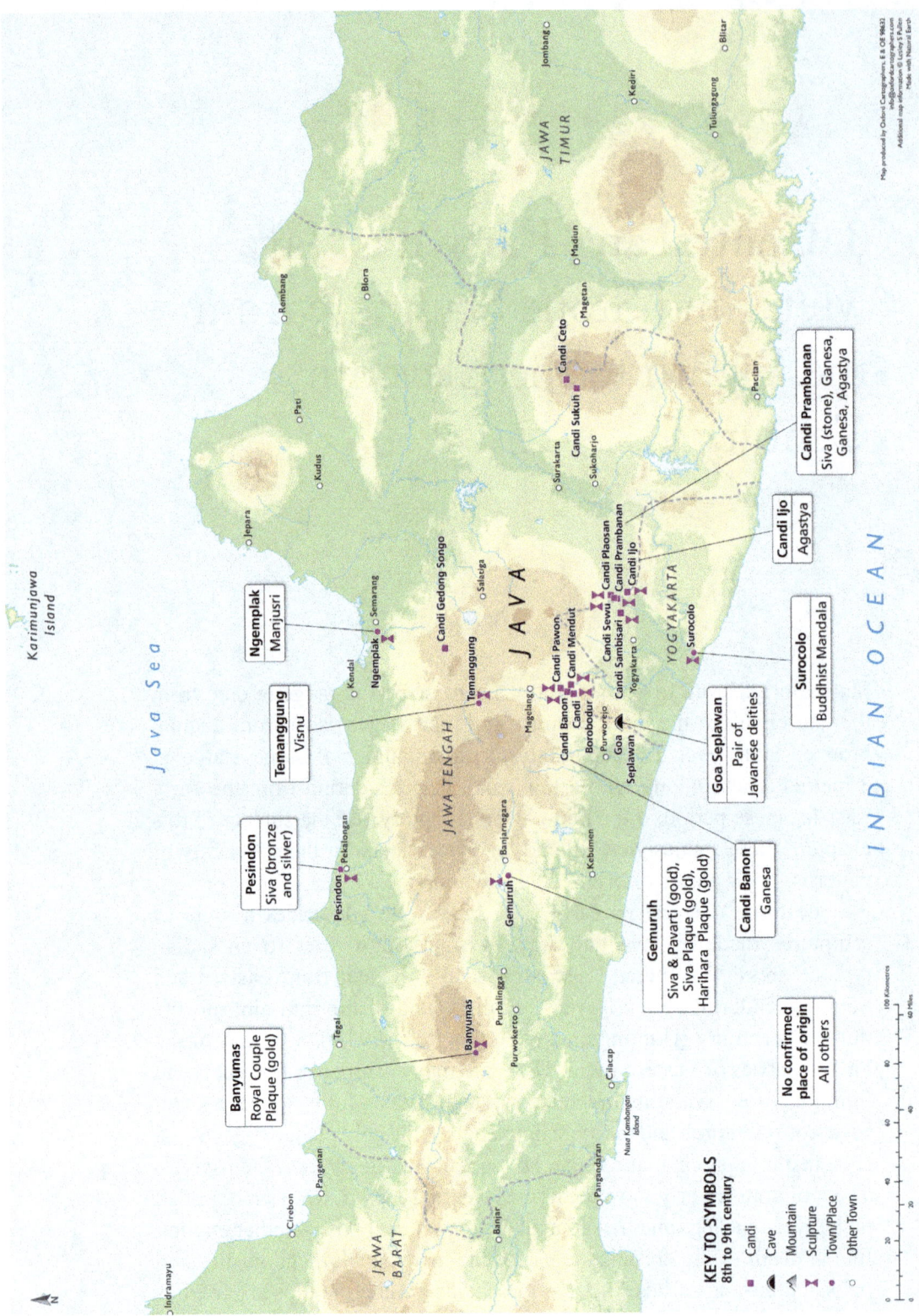

Map 3 Sculpture Locations in Central Java, 8th to 9th century.

Central and Early East Java 63

or *seléndang*. These features are depicted in a somewhat different manner in India. There are obvious similarities, however, between the Indian and Javanese styles. In some instances the *kain* appears to stand proud of the limbs, which is more typical of the Singhasāri period.

The textile patterns are divided into four groups based on their pattern and design type.

Group 1 is made up of four sub-groups covering statues depicting small overall textile patterns in a repeat of flowers, circles and dots. These patterns are reflected in certain Indian painted resist and mordant dyed cotton fabric, which by their very nature indicates the design has a repeat. It is reasonable therefore to suggest that some of the figures in this group are dressed in a textile replicating a painted resist and mordant dyed fabric pattern. Trade in these textiles from Gujarat is known about from as early as 1411 (Barnes 1997a, pp. 63–78). The fact, however, of statues

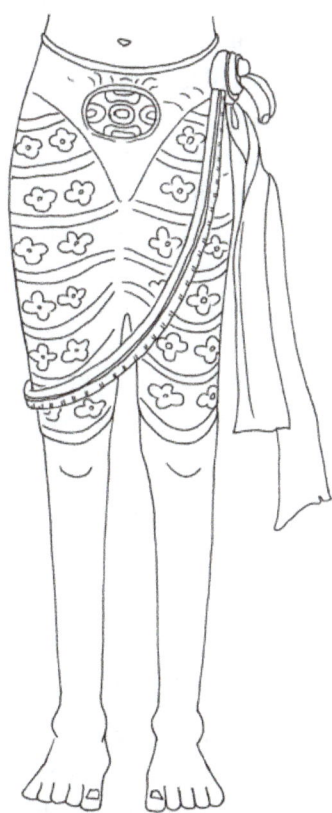

Figure 26 Śiva, 8th–9th century, Gemuruh, near Wonosobo, Central Java. Museum Nasional Indonesia. 21 cm, gold. Inv. no. 519a/4570. Drawing of the textile pattern.

bearing these patterns advocates that they would probably have existed as painted and printed designs much earlier than previously suggested.

Group 2 is made up of three sub-groups that includes complex compound patterns depicting a series of flowers in horizontal and in some cases vertical bands across the *kain*. The layout of the pattern within the bands show a variety of small, four-petal and leaf-shaped flowers, circles and symmetrical designs. Some of these patterns appear quite clearly to imitate Indian designs.

Group 3 consists of only a single sculpture that has a unique and complex "embroidery" pattern.

Group 4 includes two seated ancestor figures. They both wear a long *baju* and *kain* and they exhibit a similar although not identical pattern. One statue is from Java and the other is from Sumatra.

Visual evidence from Indian block-printed textiles as depicted in Jain manuscripts of the fourteenth and fifteenth centuries—such as the *Kalpasutra* in the Prince of Wales Museum and the *Kalacarya Katha* in the British Library—highlight an apparent similarity to many of the patterns in groups 1 to 4. The manuscripts represent a cross-section of possible textile patterns that were, according to Moti Chandra (1973, pp. 177–80), in existence long before the fourteenth century. The details on the dress and textile patterns given in Chandra's publication are an excellent source for the types of dress styles and patterns depicted in Western Indian miniature paintings, on both palm-leaf and paper. These date roughly from 1100 to 1350 and from 1350 to 1450. According to Chandra, there does not appear to be any difference in the designs between these two periods in history. The volume by Chandra is a useful aid in establishing the source of the patterns on the dress of the statuettes covered in this chapter, along with the many patterns in the Newberry Collection of Indo-Egyptian cottons in the Ashmolean Museum.[1]

It is apparent that the Indian influence was felt in Java from different parts of the subcontinent over different periods and many different media. This two-way exchange can only have added to the multiplicity of sources for the Indo-Javanese art created in this period. Fontein, Soekmono and Suleiman suggest some parallels:

> That Indonesian sculpture, despite many obvious parallels with Indian prototypes, almost always has a distinct flavour of its own, should not be attributed solely to the transforming influence of the Javanese "local genius". (1971, p. 33)

The expression "local genius" suggested by Fontein, Soekmono and Suleiman can be taken to reflect the evidence that so many of the Javanese bronzes are decorated with textile patterns compared to the very few among the Indian bronzes. The oft-overused word "influence" in the transmission of these art styles is best regarded as a result of interregional trade. It could be argued that the textiles depicted on earlier sculptures in Central Java appear to parallel those in India more closely than in the later period. Perhaps the evolutionary trajectory of sculptures and temples in East Java was similar, but the appearance has become considerably more Javanese.

The changes that developed in the art—either stylistically or depicted in the iconography—took place in small steps, and this is indeed noticeable with the small and medium-size bronze figures. The shift to East Java produced a series of small bronzes, pointing to a more East Javanese evolution, with statuettes stylistically close to a style known as the Nganjuk style. This style is apparent in the elongated bodies and blobby or spiky ornamentation (Lunsingh Scheurleer and Klokke 1988a, pp. 31–32). Any new classification of these statues would usually be completed by an identification of the material, iconographical forms and of their sacred or secular use, as suggested by Klokke and Lunsingh Scheurleer. In the absence, however, of any data on artists, patrons, time or place of manufacture, or indeed the find location, the only other realistic grouping is by using the textile pattern types.

Group 1: Overall Repeated Textile Patterns

Small Daisy or Rosette flower

Many examples of this simple pattern exist in Central Java.

The unique silver statue of Avalokiteśvara shown in figure 27 is part of the Sambas Treasure held in the British Museum.[2] Sambas is shown in map 2 (p. 46). The statue features a relatively simple overall star motif on the thin *seléndang*. Such a pattern appears frequently in India. The figure of Avalokiteśvara has the long ringlets that are typical of Central Java, as do all the statues in this group bar the last two stone statues of a *dvārapāla* and Agastya.

A small gold Padmapāni (fig. 28) with overly large hands is also part of the Sambas Treasure. His *kain* is carved or perhaps scratched in with a star-shaped motif similar to that on the Avalokiteśvara. He also wears a *seléndang*, which is plain.

The copper Śiva shown in figure 29 is considerably larger. He wears a tiger skin draped around his hips, with its head visible on his right thigh. The patterns on the *kain* are carved with tiny dots in a circle finished with a plain border. The cloth is held at the waist with a belt fastened with a clasp. The patterning of tiny dots is perhaps indicative of *bandhani* or Indian tie-dyed textiles (Barnes 1997a, p. 152), and it is clearly replicated on a number of the block-printed cottons in the Newberry Collection.

66 Patterned Splendour

Figure 27 Avalokitésvara, 8th–9th century, West Borneo. Probably made in Java. From the Sambas Treasure, © Trustees of the British Museum. 18 cm, solid silver. The *ūrnā* is inlaid with gold. Inv. no. BM.1956,0725.6. Drawing of the textile pattern.

Central and Early East Java **67**

Figure 28 Padmapāni, 10th century, West Borneo. Probably made in Java. From the Sambas Treasure, @ Trustees of the British Museum. 9.2 cm, gold figure on a silver base. The *ūrnā* is inlaid with gold. Inv. no.1956,0725.6. Drawing of the textile pattern.

Figure 29 Śiva, 9th century. Tropenmuseum, Amsterdam. Collection Nationaal Museum van Wereldculturen. Inv. no. TM-2960-151. 18.9 cm, copper alloy. Drawing of the textile pattern.

68   Patterned Splendour

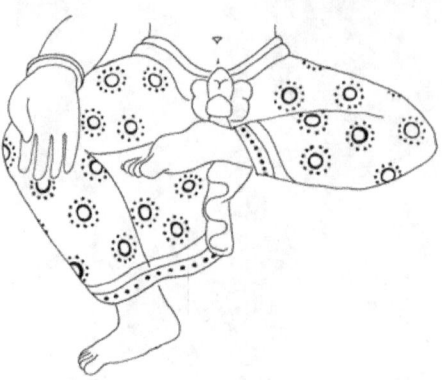

Figure 30 Padmapāni, 8th–9th century, provenance unknown. Museum Nasional Indonesia. 7.5 cm, silver on a wood base (not original). Inv. no. 616/A.56. Drawing of the textile pattern.

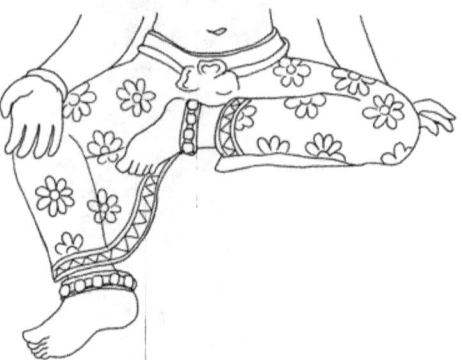

Figure 31 Sita Mañjughosa, Central Javanese period. Balai Arkeologi, Yogyakarta. 29 cm, bronze. Inv. no. unknown. Image from Fontein, Soekmono and Suleiman (1971, p. 150, no. 38). Drawing of the textile pattern.

Central and Early East Java 69

Figure 32 Śiva Mahadeva, 9th century, Śiva Temple, main cella, Loro Jonggrang, Prambanan. Stone. Inv. no. OD 11854, RV-1403-1859. Pullen photo. Detail of the lower legs. Drawing of the textile pattern.

The *seléndang* on the bronze seated Padmapāni shown in figure 30 is carved with a simple series of horizontal bands. The *kain* is folded in a pleat and falls the length of the body. It is carved with a repeated pattern of circles surrounded by dots. The textile is finished with a narrow border consisting of a series of small dots. This pattern could also be a replica of a *bandhani* pattern, referred to as *pelangi* and *tritik* in Java and Bali.

The seated bronze of Mañjuśrī (fig. 31) is known as Sita Mañjughosa, as indicated by the iconographical features of the sword resting on the lotus in the left hand. Here the pattern on the *kain* is made up of a repeated pattern of small, eight-petal daisy flowers finished with a clearly marked border of a line of inverted triangles, possibly reflecting the popular border motif in Java referred to as *tumpal*.

The tiger skin on the large stone standing statue of Śiva (fig. 32) lies on top of the long *kain*. The fineness of the fabric is indicated by the form of the legs being clearly visible beneath the cloth. Two broad sashes with a simple leaf pattern made up of six small oval shapes lie across the hips. These are tied in a large bow that fans stiffly out at the side of the body.

This feature continued into the East Javanese style, where it evolved into a much softer, looped bow. The ends of the sash fall the length of the body and are clearly defined as two pieces of folded cloth. Śiva is depicted with a decorated *kain*—close analysis of the pattern shows a crudely drawn stylized lotus flower surrounded by a four-leafed design carved over the demarked folds of the cloth. Depicted along the lower edge is a roughly cut border pattern made up of double lines. The surface of the face and the upper part of the sculpture is badly exfoliated, and the fingers of the lower-left arm are broken. The statue stands stiffly upright on a lotus platform placed upon a large *yoni* pedestal.

A standing silver statue of Śiva (fig. 33) appears on a small bronze lotus pedestal. The *kain* falls the length of the body; it features a simple continuous pattern of four-petal flowers and is held with a fabric *belt*.

The massive stone statue of Garuda (fig. 34) on view in the Santa Barbara Museum of Art is one of a kind and very unusual. It represents Garuda, the man-bird, as a guardian king. The Garuda remains the state symbol of Indonesia. He is seated cross-legged on a square lotus throne. The sashes from around his waist lie over the cushion, which is a typical Central Javanese feature. He wears the crown of a ruler, but he has flaring hair, which is a characteristic of a guardian figure. His eyes protrude on stalks in a somewhat demonic fashion. He is adorned with the ornaments of a king, with an exaggerated *upavīta* as a thick heavy chain around the torso. Around his hips, tied at each side of the body, is evidence of the bow of the sash lying beneath the chain girdle around the waist. The sash is draped over the long *kain*, which finishes at the ankles with heavy anklets. The pattern on the *kain* represents a simple four-petal flower in a circle, the carving of which, on account of the roughness of the volcanic stone, is not particularly well executed. The feet placed on the cushion, with the soles together in *sitasanamudrā*, is a feature that is apparent with these Gaṇeśa from Central Java (often with the feet not quite touching).

The seated stone Gaṇeśa shown in figure 35 remains outside the Prambanan Museum. He has a clearly defined textile pattern on his trousers comprising a four- or eight-petal rosette with rounded petals. The design is finished with a detailed border pattern around the ankles. Gaṇeśa generally wear loose trousers rather than a *kain*. The patterning on the cloth is indicative of Indian block-printed and resist-dyed cotton, similar to those from the Newberry Collection.

The Gaṇeśa in figure 36 remains outside the Museum Sonobudoyo. His trousers feature a pattern of a four-petal flower interspersed with a pointed four-leaf shape. His trousers are overlaid with a large sash tied in a loose bow at the side of the body, and the two long ends fall on to the lotus cushion. This is not a typical Central Javanese feature, so this Gaṇeśa should be dated to nearer to the tenth or eleventh century.

Central and Early East Java 71

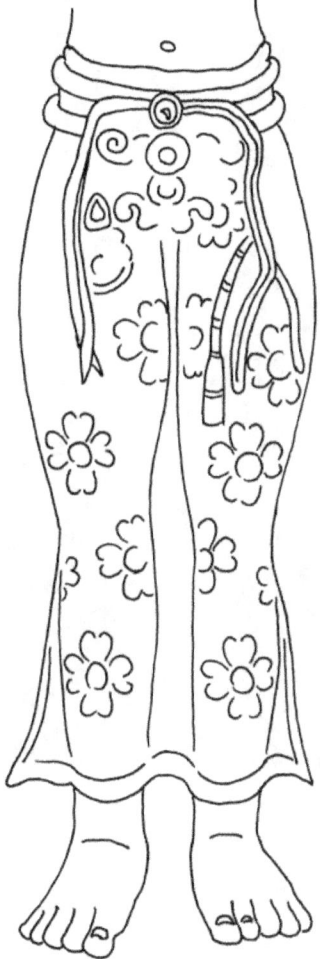

Figure 33 Śiva, 9th century, Pesindon, Kalialang, Ledok, Bagelen (1877; part of a large hoard of gold and silver objects). Museum Nasional Indonesia. 94 cm, bronze and silver. Inv. no. 497. Drawing of the textile pattern.

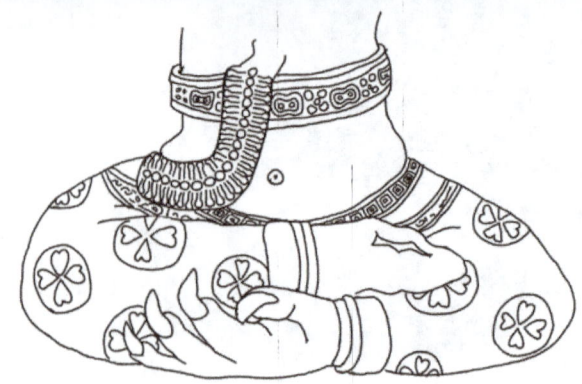

Figure 34 Garuda, the Man-bird as a Guardian King, 9th–10th century, Central Java. 78.7 cm, andesite stone. Inv. no. 2013.18. Santa Barbara Museum of Art, museum purchase with funds provided by an anonymous donor. Drawing of the textile pattern.

Central and Early East Java 73

Figure 35 Gaṇeśa, 8th or 9th century. Museum Caṇḍi Prambanan, Prambanan. Approx. 80–90 cm, stone. Inv. no. unknown. Details of the right hip. Drawing of the textile pattern.

The textile pattern and the remainder of his iconography, however, place him in Central Java.

The Museum Nasional Indonesia (MNI) houses perhaps the finest of the Central Javanese period Gaṇeśa (fig. 37). Here the trousers appear folded on the thighs with a pattern of simple flowers consisting of eight-pointed petals around a central circle. His *kain* is held up by a large, probably metal, belt. This is visible in the drawing.

The stone Gaṇeśa (fig. 38) housed in the Indian Museum in Kolkatta is smaller than the previous statue, and it comes with a fascinating history.[3] The patterned trousers are finished at the ankles, indicated by an undulating line—a particularly unusual pattern for Central Javanese statues. The design is carved in deep relief with concentric roundels containing a stylized lotus motif with between eight and twelve petals. This sophisticated and complex pattern is unique to this one sculpture; the statue should be dated therefore closer to the late tenth century. The sash across the hips is carved in a particularly sophisticated fashion that is unseen in any other statues of Gaṇeśa from Central Java.

Figure 36 Gaṇeśa, 9th–10th century. Museum Sonobudoyo, Yogyakarta. 92 cm, stone. Inv. no. unknown. Details of the right hip. Drawing of the textile pattern.

Central and Early East Java 75

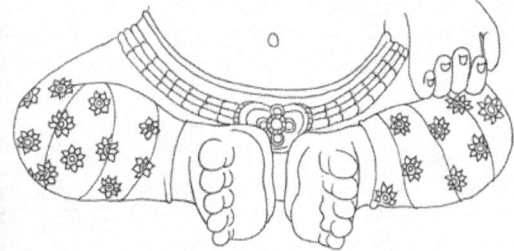

Figure 37 Gaṇeśa, 8th century, Caṇḍi Banon. Museum Nasional Indonesia. 1.48 m, stone. Inv. no. 186b. Details of the right leg. Drawing of the textile pattern.

76 Patterned Splendour

Figure 38 Gaṇeśa, 9th–10th century, Java, Caṇḍi Prambanan. Probably donated by Colonel Colin Mackenzie, who travelled to Java in 1812. Indian Museum, Kolkata. 95 cm, stone. Inv. no. Ja5. Details of the limbs. Drawing of the textile pattern.

The Agastya cult was prevalent in both Central and East Java. A large three-metre statue of Agastya (fig. 39) remains near to but not part of Caṇḍi Ijo—it seems to have been part of a separate complex. A statue of Gaṇeśa (his place of origin is unknown) and the temple for Agastya are in the same vicinity. Ijo is the name for the key site at the top of the plateau; Gupola is the smaller site down by the spring. The attributes of the seer

Agastya are identifiable by his goatee, stout belly and the trident carved at his right side against the stone backing. The left side and his forearms are missing. He wears simple jewellery. The *seléndang* is depicted folded across the body, with the remaining sash folded over on the front of his thighs, which is a typical Central Javanese feature. The long *kain* is covered in large rosettes carved as a repeated pattern across the fabric. It finishes at the ankles, represented by a wavy line and a small border.

Figure 39 Agastya, 8th or 9th century, Caṇḍi Ijo, Gupola Site, Jogjakarta. 3m, stone. Inv. no unknown. Pullen photo. Detail of the limbs. Drawing of the textile pattern.

Figure 40 *Dvārapāla*, 12th–14th century, but probably closer to the 11th century. Museum Sonobudoyo, Yogyakarta. 2.05 m, stone. Inv. no unknown. Details of the rear left hip. Pullen photo. Drawing of the textile pattern.

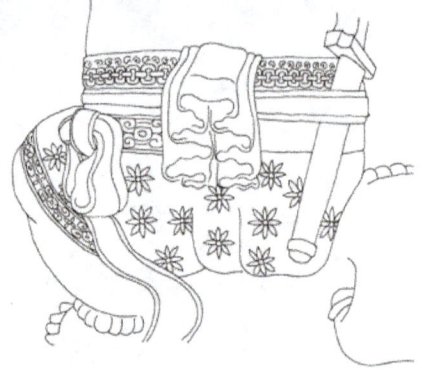

The large stone *dvārapāla*, or guardian figure, shown in figure 40 is carved from a smooth white andesite stone. It remains in the garden of Museum Sonobudoyo. The sculpture is dated to between the twelfth and fourteenth centuries. But, on account of its relatively small size, at only two metres, and with its textile pattern fitting more closely with those from Central Java, it should perhaps be given an earlier date of the eleventh century, nearer the beginning of the East Javanese period. The pattern is a simple continuous design of a daisy flower with pointed petals, finished with a definite "brocaded" pattern along the border. The figure also wears a narrow chain girdle to hold the *dhotī*; the belt is evident at the rear of the body where the cloth has been pulled up between the legs and tucked in the metal belt at the rear. The apparel is unusually detailed for such an early statue, especially for one that remains outside. A typical attribute of guardian figures is that of a raised forefinger—or sometimes two—on the right hand in a threatening gesture known as *tarjanīmudrā*.

Stylized Flowers

The next pattern sub-group consists of only two statues: a gold figure of Viṣṇu and a small gold figure of the Buddha Mahāvairocana.

The Viṣṇu (fig. 41) is finely cast and is dressed in royal attire, as indicated by his elaborate *dhotī*, which is draped most unusually with a section of the cloth over the lower left leg. There is an extraordinary similarity between the style of the dress of this figure with that of a one-metre high Avalokiteśvara made in Tibet by Kashmir artists. The depiction of the *dhotī* and chain girdles on both statues is uncanny. The textile pattern on the Javanese Viṣṇu consists of a four-petal flower made up of four dots and four semi-circles. The *dhotī* is tied with a metal girdle, which is apparent from the carved pattern raised from the body depicting a chain, falling on the front of both legs. The right leg is flexed at the knee and the foot is elevated from the ground as if the figure is taking a step.

The small Buddha Mahāvairocana (fig. 42) is crowned and dressed in royal attire. He appears in deep meditation seated on a lotus cushion upon a low base. His hands are in *bodhyagrīmudrā*, with the right hand holding the thumb of the left hand. The statue is adorned with elaborate jewellery made up of small globules of gold, which are crudely constructed compared to those on the earlier figures. This change in style is evidence of the beginning of the early East Javanese period (Lunsingh Scheurleer and Klokke 1988b, p. 93). The damaged *upavīta* falls to the folded legs, where the *kain* finishes at the ankles with a repeated pattern of four dots and semi-circles. The sash is draped over the right thigh and carved with the same pattern.

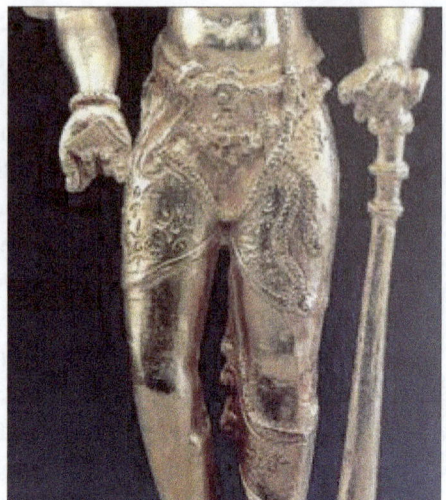

Figure 41 Viṣṇu, Pahingan Temanggung, 8th–9th century. Part of a gold hoard found in 1903. Museum Nasional Indonesia. 18 cm, gold figure and silver base. Inv. no. A2/486. Details of the limbs. Drawing of the textile pattern.

Circles

The next four statues in this sub-group appear with patterns consisting of circles of some kind.

The four-armed and four-headed gold Brahmā (fig. 43) stands on a small lotus pedestal. The *seléndang* is depicted as a broad, decorated band. The *kain,* finished with a wavy line, is decorated with a simple continuous design of circles or dots, with no apparent border pattern. This is indicative of a block print or perhaps a *pelangi* or *tritik* technique. The statue bears no resemblance to any Indian equivalent.

The next figure, however, the seated Mañjuśrī (fig. 44), is cast in the Indian style of bronze statues originating from Pāla in eastern India—the Prajñāpāramitā sutra resting on the lotus rising above his left shoulder is indicative of this form of Mañjuśrī. The statue is adorned with a broad

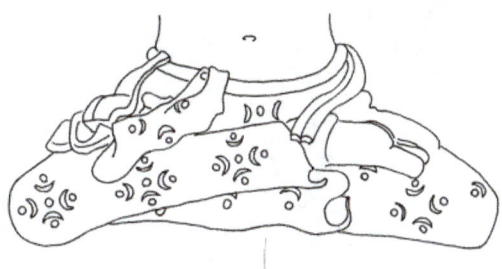

Figure 42 Buddha Mahāvairocana/Vajrasattva, late Central or early East Java, 870–930, provenance unknown. Loan to Rijksmuseum, Amsterdam. Collection Nationaal Museum van Wereldculturen. Inv. no. AK-MAK-313. 8.3 cm, gold. Details of the limbs. Drawing of the textile pattern.

seléndang, and the *dhotī* is clearly shown at the ankles where the thin fabric clings tightly to the legs. The cloth is decorated with a pattern of double horizontal lines in which are carved small circles. As no details of cloth appear in front of the body, it is safe to assume the statue wears a tight-fitting *dhotī* in the Indian style. Klokke and Lunsingh Scheurleer have suggested that this bronze is a local Javanese copy of the bronze Avalokiteśvara from Bangladesh or Orissa (Lunsingh Scheurleer and Klokke 1988b, pp. 69 and 73). The suggestion was made based on the "supple, well-moulded body". Susan Huntington, however, has pointed out key differences in the facial features: the eyes in the Indian examples generally appear larger and stare out, and the figures possess a slightly bulbous nose and fully outlined lips (1994, p. 61), whereas the Javanese figures tend to have more delicate facial features.

Mañjuśrī is depicted wearing what is most likely a type of textile originating from India known as *bandhani* (fig. 45), a tie and dye resist fabric. The pattern on this Mañjuśrī is almost identical to that on a small Indian statuette of a four-armed Avalokiteśvara in the Volkenkunde, Leiden. Despite the fact that the Rijksmuseum figure shows only a small circular pattern, it is likely this type of pattern is imitating a tie-dye, leaving out the dot in the centre of the motif. These small circular

82 Patterned Splendour

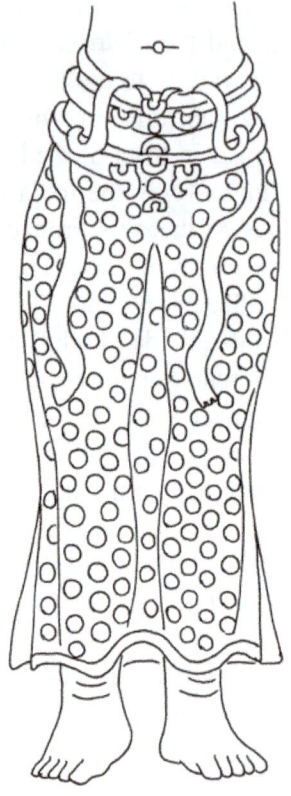

Figure 43 Brahmā, 9th–10th century, Pesindon Village, Kalialang, Ledok, Bagelen, Central Java. 11 cm, gold. Inv. no. A 41/482. Image from Miksic (2007, p. 26). Details of the limbs. Drawing of the textile pattern.

Figure 44 Mañjuśrī, Central Java, 800–850, 21 cm, bronze, lost wax process. On loan from the Royal Association of Friends of Asian Art (purchase MAH van Selst, 1940). Rijksmuseum, Amsterdam. Inv. no. AK-MAK-389, 140. Details of the limbs. Drawing of the textile pattern.

repeated patterns could also however represent a block-printed and resist-dyed cotton, as has been suggested earlier.

The small two-armed bronze Prajñāpāramitā (fig. 46) seated in reflective repose is cast with elaborate jewellery appearing as small globules of bronze, giving it a rather crude "spiky" effect. The *seléndang* is just visible between the breasts. The *kain* is carved with a pattern of a repetitive circular design with a cross and four dots, over which lies a wide sash. The features of this small figure, her face and the casting of the jewellery, the sash and the textile design—but not the pattern—are clearly in the early East Javanese style (Lunsingh Scheurleer and Klokke 1988b, p. 96).

The small bronze figure of the goddess Dhupa (fig. 47) is depicted as a two-armed bodhisattva seated on a lotus cushion. The term *Dhupa* in Indian religions refers to the ritual offering to an image or deity of incense, as practised during a *puja* or religious ceremony. Hence, she is seen here carrying an incense burner in her left hand. Her body is bedecked with jewellery set with stones. She wears the *channavīra*, with the crossed belts dissecting the body. Her distended earlobes are inserted with large earrings. Her *kain* is held with a simple girdle. The *kain* depicts a repeated circular pattern of semicircles and dots. (There are five bronze statuettes in the Samuel Eilenberg Collection that are similar to this one and which also appear to have textile patterns; however, on account of their small size, discerning the details remains a challenge.) Overlaying the *kain* is a narrow sash tied at the right side in a bow. It is difficult to discern whether the sash ends fall to the side of the body, as they are not apparent over the legs. The long slender body, the spiky jewellery, the thin face with a pointed nose, and the slender torso all present as features of the early East Javanese style of bronze figures.

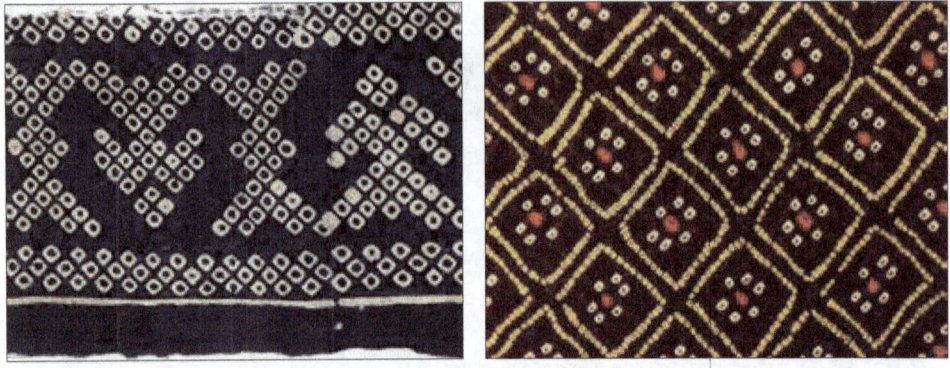

Figure 45 45a Textile fragment imitating *bandhani*, or tie-dye, with geometric patterns and arrow-shapes. EA1990.76. 2nd half of the 10th century–15th century CE. © Ashmolean Museum. **45b** *Bandhini* tie-dye silk textile, early 20th century. Private collection.

Central and Early East Java 85

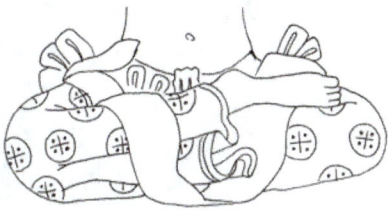

Figure 46 Prajñāpāramitā, late Central or early East Java, 10th–11th century. Volkenkunde, Leiden. Collection Nationaal Museum van Wereldculturen. Inv. no. RV-1403-1697. 12 cm, bronze, lost wax process. Details of the limbs. Drawing of the textile pattern

86 Patterned Splendour

Figure 47 Goddess Dhupa, one of the eight Bodhisattvas Dakinis, early East Java, 10th–11th century, BPCB–Balai Pelestarian Cagar Budaya, Nganjuk, near Kediri, East Java. 11 cm, bronze. Inv No. 5408/C 311. Details of the limbs. Drawing of the textile pattern.

Four-Petal Flowers in Bands

Five statues in bronze, gold and stone exist in this sub-group with a simple floral design.

Figure 48 shows a damaged stone statue of Agastya. He has no head or arms and stands on a small, square base with two kneeling acolytes at either side, which are also damaged and without heads. Agastya is identifiable by his goatee and full belly. He is depicted wearing a short *kain* with a large flower pattern consisting of four long petals set within horizontal bands across the body. The sash is draped across the thighs and folded over in a typical Central Javanese style. A particularly unusual feature is the wide *seléndang* carved with a marked pattern that appears to represent a series of *vajra* set end to end across the cloth.

An extremely unusual pair of Javanese deities cast in gold (fig. 49) has been suggested as perhaps representing a royal couple as deified ancestors (Lunsingh Scheurleer 2013, p. 38, ill. 23). Such a tradition is one that resonates particularly with the Javanese and is a feature that would become apparent in the Majapahit period. The statuettes wear simple but matching jewellery on the upper arms, elbows and wrists and the *channavīra* around the abdomen. They both wear a jewelled *udharabhanda*, or stomach band, and a striking metal girdle around the belly. Their distended ears hold large earrings. The depiction of the *kain* (fig. 50) is unique to these two figures. They both appear to be wearing the *dodot*, a sizeable ceremonial hip wrapper worn only by royalty (Warming and Garwoski 1981, p. 122). The *dodot* on the female covers the lower part of the body to the ankles, and it is worn in the Javanese style with the fullness of the cloth depicted at each side of her body. The male is shown wearing two cloths, as seen from the rear of the body. On the front the *dodot* appears with a pattern, but the legs appear to be bare. On closer inspection the statue can be seen to be cast with a plain cloth, probably representing "trousers" of some kind, hugging the legs, with the ends indicated at the ankles. The pattern consists of horizontal bands with a four-petal flower placed between them. The border pattern on the female figure constitutes an inverted V, perhaps representing the *tumpal* motif that became so popular in Indonesian textiles. The two figures both wear a cloth sash across their thighs. The fabric of the *dodot* appears ruched as if there was a substantial amount of material, which in the case of the female fans out over the top of the sash that is worn low around her hips to hold the *dodot*. The sash is depicted tied in a sizeable stylized bow on the reverse of the body, which somewhat represents a flower.

Statues of Mañjuśrī appear in many different guises. In Java, the figure of Mañjuśrī Kumārabhūta (fig. 51) is particularly popular. Here he is seated in *lalitāsana* on a lotus base placed upon a rectangular throne.

88 Patterned Splendour

Figure 48 Agastya, 9th–10th century, BPCB–Balai Pelestarian Cagar Budaya, Prambanan. 1.6 m, stone. Inv. no. BG 1314. Details of the reverse torso. Drawing of the textile pattern.

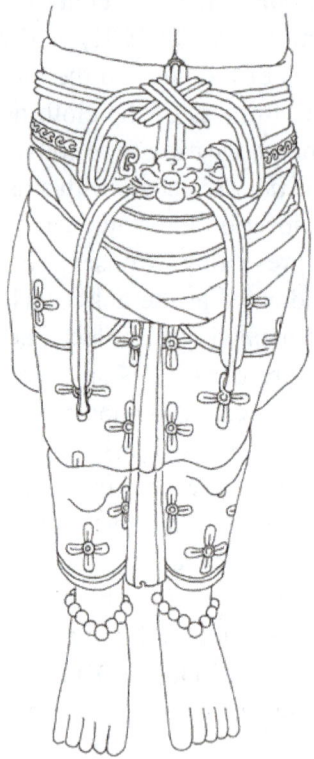

Figure 49 Pair of Javanese deities, 9th–10th century, Middle Javanese, Seplawan Cave, found in 1979. Museum Nasional Indonesia. 11 x 12 cm, gold and silver base. Inv. no. 9011.

90 Patterned Splendour

Figure 50 Pair of Javanese deities. Detail of the lower limbs. Drawing of the pattern on the front and reverse.

Central and Early East Java 91

Figure 51 Mañjuśrī Kumārabhūta, 9th century, origin unknown. Bronze. Private collection. Detail of the lower limbs. Drawing of the textile pattern.

92 Patterned Splendour

The defining features of Mañjuśrī Kumāra are visible in the tiger-claw necklace and the hair in three tight curls known as *śikhādhara*. The jewellery, particularly the ear ornaments, display similarities with the Pāla style of ornamentation.[4] Across the hips is a short *dhotī*, which is evident as the small fold of the cloth is visible under the left ankle on the lotus cushion. It can also be seen at both knees, with a patterned band at the end of the fabric. The pattern on the *dhotī* itself is of a simple four-petal flower within double horizontal bands. Some of the earliest Javanese bronzes could have originated from Southeast Bangladesh in the

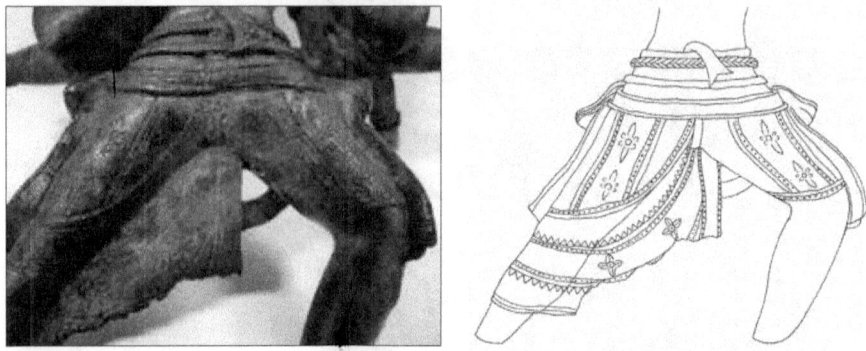

Figure 52 Trailokya-Vijaya, 9th century. 's-Gravenzande Store, Leiden. Collection Nationaal Museum van Wereldculturen. Inv. no. RV-1403-1760. Approx. 10 cm, bronze. Detail of the lower limbs. Drawing of the textile pattern.

Mainamati region, as is evident from this form of Mañjuśrī Kumārabhūta.

The diminutive damaged figure of Trailokya-Vijaya (fig. 52) is a rare statue in Java. The figurine is missing the lower limbs—the feet trample on images of Śiva and Sati—however, the details on the rest of the statue are still intact. Its small size, at ten centimetres, necessitates a magnifying glass to view the details of this finely cast statue. On close inspection it is apparent that the figure wears two cloths: a long plain *kain* that reaches to below the knees, over which is carved a shorter, patterned cloth. The pattern is made up of horizontal bands of circles with small alternating geometric motifs. The *dhotī* is tied in the South Indian style, falling between the legs to the knee on the right leg and to the mid-calf on the left leg. This aspect of the statuette is damaged, as suggested by the incomplete textile pattern. The design is carved with a simple series of vertical stripes interspaced with a small four-petal flower and a zigzag border pattern, perhaps meant to represent the ever-popular *tumpal* triangular motif. Having observed other sculptures of Trailokya-Vijaya, which are generally much more substantial, it is likely this small statue was for personal worship.

The unusual, gold figure of Śiva referred to in chapter 2 (fig. 7, p. 31) is remarkable. At a height of twenty-four centimetres, it has been cast with a slender body and four arms, and it stands with a simple halo behind his head. The figure wears a *dhotī* in the South Indian style pulled tightly up between the legs, as seen in the drawing (fig. 53). It is not possible to see the reverse of the figure, but the cloth was probably tucked in the belt at the rear. The *dhotī* is carved with a simple four-petal flower set within double horizontal bands. This small gold figure stands out amongst the Javanese statues dressed in the "South Indian style" (Bernet Kempers 1959. p, 34, plate 33), but the features remain entirely Javanese. The *dhotī* is tied at the waist with a cloth girdle that twists and falls freely to the left side in an unusual fashion. The statue stands in double *katakaamudrā*, a particularly unusual *mudrā*. A skull appears depicted at the base of the crown, which appears to have held "stones" that are now missing. The figure is wearing simple jewellery, with large earrings in extended earlobes. The *upavīta* is a simple snake cord. This statue of Śiva is a critical example of the high quality of gold castings in the eighth and ninth centuries.

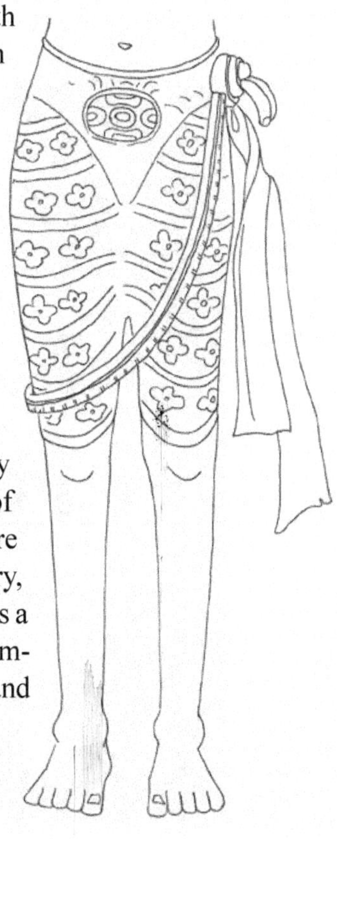

Figure 53 Śiva, 9th century, Gemuruh. Drawing of the textile pattern.

Group 2: Complex Compound Patterns

Flowers in Horizontal Bands

The four statues in this sub-group are of silver and bronze and have been carved with a similar type of floral pattern in bands.

The statue shown in figure 54 is of a silver Mañjuśrī known as Kumārabhūta on account of his youthful appearance and the three tufts of hair that identify him as *śikhādhara* (Bernet Kempers 1959, p. 51, plate 110). Mañjuśrī Kumārabhūta also wears the tiger-claw amulet, another symbol of his youth, which is typically seen on some Pāla statues of Kumārabhūta. In India, the tiger-claw amulet carries strong protective powers. A typical form includes a pair of matching claws, usually mounted with their bases together and inserted into a metal holder. Mañjuśrī is also adorned with crisply defined jewellery, as befits a princely figure. The neckband and heavy silver chain *upavīta* appears in the South Indian style. The *upavīta* is joined with a large metal clasp that matches the clasp of the metal chain girdle. The ears are extended, with large metal earplugs in the Indian style, a style also apparent on many Pāla statues of Mañjuśrī. The *kain* falls to the ankles revealing the limbs beneath a delicate fabric. It is patterned with a design of horizontal bands, circles and a small, alternating floral motif suggestive of a four-petal fleur-de-lis. These unusual crossed markings perhaps represent the

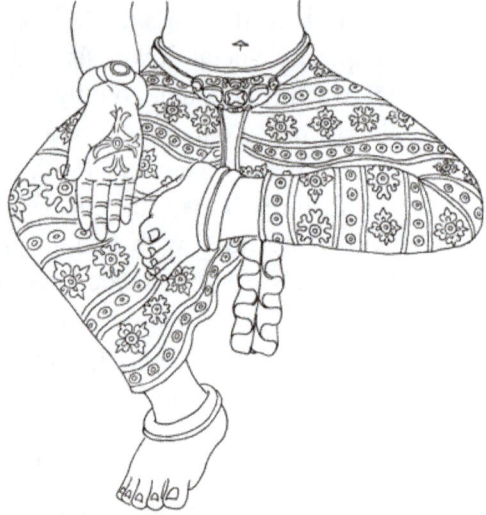

Figure 54 Mañjuśrī Kumārabhūta, early 10th century, Ngemplak Semangan, Semarang, found in 1927. Museum Nasional Indonesia. 28 cm, 92% silver, 8.25 g. Inv. no. 5899/A.1105. Drawing of the textile pattern

vajra in the form of the fleur-de-lis as a lotus flower. From this we can interpret the *vajra* and the fleur-de-lis together as a symbol of attaining Buddhahood. A further Buddhist symbol, marked in his open palm, is that of a *viśvajra* or two crossed *vajras*. A careful analysis of this image suggests it follows the strict iconographical rules of Pāla, Northeast India. Bernet Kempers has suggested that this figure was transported by Buddhist monks or traders into Java at the beginning of the tenth century (1959, p. 52). In theory this is of course entirely possible as the figure

Figure 55 Śiva, 8th–9th century, origin unknown. Metropolitan Museum of Art, New York, gift of Nancy Wiener, 2004. 27.9 cm, gilt bronze. Inv. no. 2004.556. Drawing of the textile pattern.

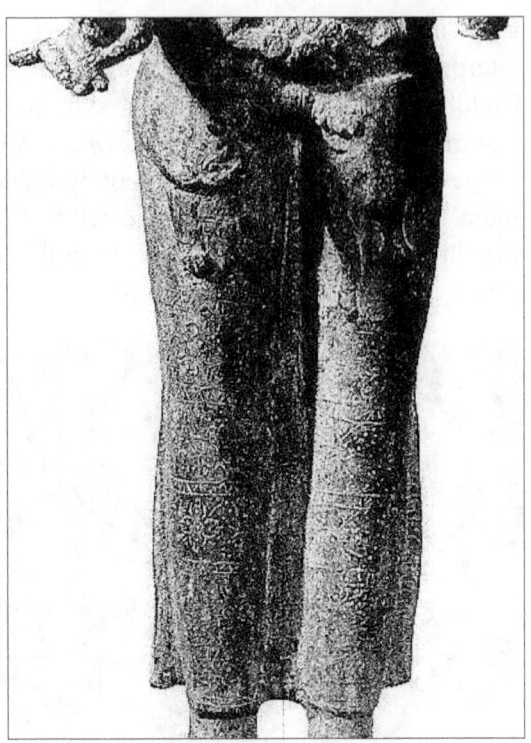
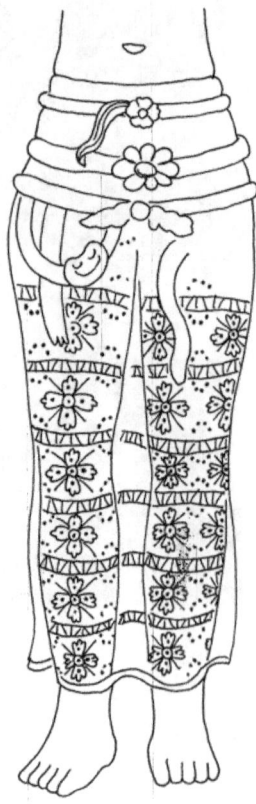

Figure 56 Śiva Mahadeva, a representation of Avalokitéśvara, 9th century, provenance unknown. Museum Sonobudoyo, Jogjakarta. 44 cm, bronze with traces of gilt. Inv. no. unknown. Image from Fontein, Soekmono and Suleiman (1971, p. 82, no. 51) (the sculpture was in storage in 2019). Detail of the lower limbs. Drawing of the textile pattern.

exhibits very little of the Javanese aesthetics we have come to expect for this period; however, there are no known examples in India. There is a suggestion therefore that the sculpture was cast in Java, perhaps by an Indian craftsman. The facial features replicate the local physiognomy rather than Indian features. The statue is a particularly excellent example of Javanese metal casting.

The standing four-armed figure of Śiva shown in figure 55 appears to have been gilded, although the gilding is now considerably worn. The statue remains in the Metropolitan Museum of Art. It is adorned with royal ornaments, evident in the significant drop-shaped Indian-style earrings and metal neck plate. He wears the *seléndang* across his torso, over which lies a broad *upavīta* cast in the guise of a snake, with its head rearing over his left shoulder. His many girdles and sashes are clearly defined and they hold up a long *kain* that reaches to his ankles. Over his hips is the tiger skin of Śiva, with its head on his right thigh. The pattern on the *kain* consists of a stylized four-petal lotus flower within large circles with double outer bands.

The large bronze and gilt figure of a standing Śiva or Avalokiteśvara shown in figure 56 has four arms, displays simple ornamentation and has a marked *seléndang* etched with three lines, with the flap just apparent on the left shoulder. The two pegs at the feet indicate this bronze would have been placed on to a stand, probably replicating a lotus. The *kain* falls as

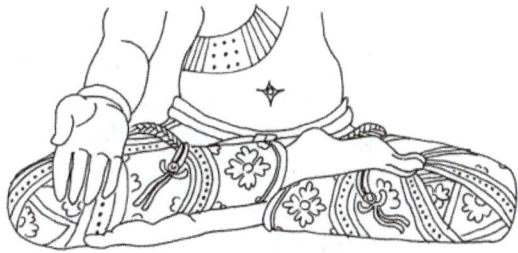

Figure 57 Tārā, 9th century, Bumiayu, Brebes, Central Java. 16 cm, bronze and gold with silver inlay. Museum Nasional Indonesia. Inv. no. 6590. Detail of the lower limbs. Drawing of the textile pattern.

a fine cloth to the ankles. The design on this is made up of a four-petal flower outlined with dots and placed within horizontal bands carved with a geometric border. The fine casting of the facial features, which are in deep meditation, make this a particularly important statue.

Figure 57 is of a seated figure of Tārā cast in dark bronze. Her countenance is also one of deep meditation, with the lips and *ūrṇā* marked in gold. The facial features mark this statue as one of the finest presented here. The *seléndang* is draped across the upper body and is marked with small lines and dots. Over the hips, the *kain* appears as a thin cloth revealing the shape of the body beneath, and it is patterned similarly to the Śiva discussed previously, with a repeat pattern of "fleur-de-lis" or stylized lotus flowers set within double bands incised with small dots. The chain belt is shown draped across the hips over the *kain*, folded at the waist with two simple ties, and with the ends appearing over the lower legs.

Complex Geometric Patterns in Bands

A group of eight icons are in this sub-group, representing a mix of gold plaques and bronze statues. They are remarkable for their distinctive decorative features and in the similarity of the patterns, which are reflected in Indian block-printed and mordant-dyed textiles.

The seated bronze statue of Avalokitésvara (fig. 58) represents another instance of an Indian aesthetic; the facial features, however, make this statue distinctly Javanese. He is adorned with the *upavīta* cast as a chain in the Indian style. The *kain* appears draped to the ankles, finished with pleats at the front and with the cloth revealing the body beneath. For such a small sculpture, at twenty-one centimetres, the intricate pattern crisply depicts a series of horizontal bands filled with circles and small alternating geometric patterns.

The seated image of the goddess Cundā or Mahapratīśara depicted with twelve arms in figure 59 is rather crudely cast in comparison to the sophistication of the previous statue. The goddess wears simple jewellery, large pendula earrings and necklace, and her hair curls falling over her shoulders. The *seléndang* is just visible as a wide band across the body marked with a simple pattern and with the flap evident on the left shoulder. The subtle pattern replicates the one on the *kain* and is similar to that on the previous statue. The design represents a complex compound pattern of horizontal bands decorated with a daisy flower and geometric patterns. The surface of the bronze does not have the smoothness of some of the previous examples.

A remarkable small Avalokitésvara (fig. 60) remains unavailable behind glass, locked in the BPCB office in Prambanan village. Infrequently viewed as it is, this approximately eighteen-centimetre

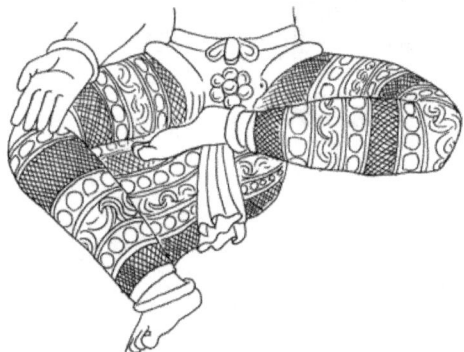

Figure 58 Avalokitésvara, 9th century, original location unknown. Donated to Emperor Franz Joseph by the Javanese painter Raden Saleh. Museum für Völkerkunde, Vienna. 21 cm, bronze. Inv. no. 68.765. Image from Heine-Geldern (1925, p. 19, no. 7). Drawing of the textile pattern.

bronze statue is outstanding in several ways. The figure holds a slight contrapposto to the body, with the right knee slightly bent, which makes the left hip lean to the left. His jewellery and girdles have been cast in a largely Indian manner; however, the sash across his hips has been folded over in the front, which is a feature unique to Central Java and not seen on Indian bronzes. The *kain* falls long to the ankles. The sash falls across the hips and is tied off at the side of the body in a large bow, with the ends falling beside the thighs. The pattern is noteworthy for its intricate detail on so small a statue. It constitutes a complex pattern made up of horizontal bands interspersed with circles and geometric patterns—the patterns continue over the sashes and on the *seléndang* across the torso.

Figure 61 is of a most unusual gold plaque that was cast using the repoussé technique and which depicts a royal couple, male and female, standing side by side. The male figure wears a *dhotī*; but, rather than having the cloth wound around the legs tightly, it has been folded up and partly tucked in at the waistline, following South Indian traditions. Overlaying the *kain* on the female is a fabric sash tucked in at the waist

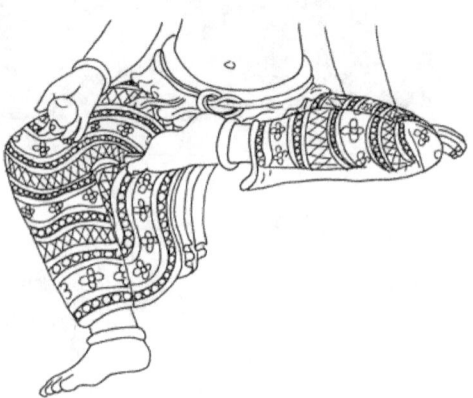

Figure 59 Cundā/Mahāpratisarā, 9th–10th century. Museum Radya Pustaka, Solo. In 2016 the bronze room was closed. 37 cm, bronze, lost wax process. Inv. no. A.528. Detail of the lower limbs and drawing of the textile pattern.

and brought around the hips, a feature not seen in India. The *kain* on the female is held in place with a metal girdle consisting of square plaques. Both male and female wear a crown; the male holds what appears to be a lotus acting as a umbrella or parasol, and neither of the figures are adorned with overly large ear ornaments. These three aspects serve to indicate that the two figures are not divine. The *dhotī* has been decorated with the repoussé technique and incised with decoration, probably from the front. The pattern on the male figure consists of a small stylized four-petal flower within vertical bands. The female is wearing a sophisticated pattern on the *kain*, which falls the length of her body in the indigenous style.

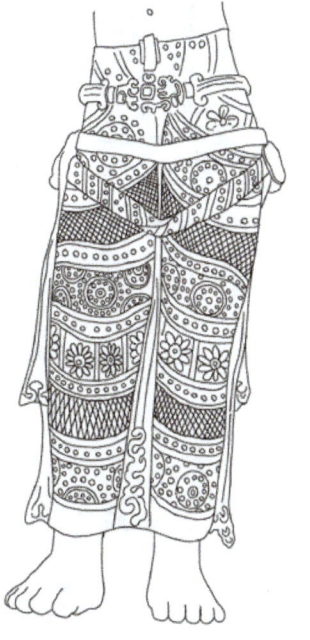

Figure 60 Avalokiteśvara, 9th–10th century, original location unknown. BPCB–Balai Pelestarian Cagar Budaya, Yogyakarta. Access was denied in 2019. Approx. 18 cm, bronze. Inv. no unknown. Detail of the lower limbs. Drawing of the textile pattern.

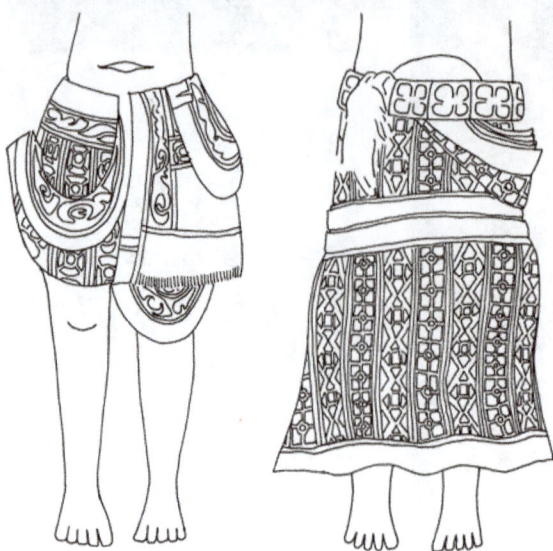

Figure 61 Royal couple plaque, 8th–9th century, Banyumas. Museum Nasional Indonesia. Gold repoussé plaque with a silver/zinc copper alloy border. 20 x 12 cm. Inv. no. 644c/4661. Drawing of the textile pattern

No outline of her legs is visible, which suggests it is meant to indicate a heavier cloth, such as a *kain songket* The *songket* shown in figure 62 from Malaysia is an example of the type of textile and patterning that could be depicted on these small figures. The pattern on the female figure represents an intricate geometric design within broad vertical bands and with a plain border along the lower edge. The pattern is similar to that of her partner's. From the layout of the patterning and the structure of the garment, the fabric could represent a brocade or *songket,* or perhaps cotton that has been bock printed and mordant dyed and overlaid with gold, known as *prada* in Java. The patterning on the *songket* in figure 62 indicates a series of bands with geometric patterning that is identical in structure to that on the plaque.

Helen Jessup has described this plaque as the "image of divine power in the suggestion of the Buddha implicit with a lotus umbrella" (1990, p. 50). The concept of the so-called "lotus umbrella" is also seen, however, as a symbol of royalty. This plaque might have been made as a "portrait"—as indicated by the facial features.

Figure 62 Details of a Malay *kain songket*. Property of Sim Tan, Kuala Lumpur, Malaysia.

The eyes are open and the faces do not appear to share any similarity with any Central Javanese deities.

The small, ten-centimetre bronze Viṣṇu shown in figure 63, missing its lower legs, has a similar style of dress. The surface displays an excellent patina from centuries of handling. Its diminutive size did not stop the smallest of details from being cast on the front of its body. The statue is depicted wearing two cloths. There is a patterned textile to the knees with a design of horizontal bands consisting of circles and small alternating geometric motifs. Under this is a longer, plain *kain*. The sashes and girdles across the waist and hips are particularly finely cast, with the ends of the sashes defined on the thighs. The facial features display some similarities to those of Pāla bronzes. It could be conjectured that the statue had been made somewhere else and carried into Java, or that it was made in Java by an itinerant Indian craftsman, perhaps as a portable form of worship.

In the next sub-group are three gold plaques.

The physiognomy of the four-armed Śiva shown in figure 64 appears somewhat androgynous, with breasts and nipples indicated. The lower right hand holds a trident, and the lower left a water pot. The upper section is decorated with a crescent moon and a sun. The central image is carved standing on a lotus cushion just visible at the lower edge of the plaque. The figure is depicted wearing simple jewellery, including a metal and cloth girdle. The distended earlobes hold large earrings. The *upavīta* appears as a simple cord across the body. The *kain* is tied

104   Patterned Splendour

with a girdle and finishes on the front of both legs. It is patterned with a simple design of incised punched dots within wide plain horizontal bands. The *kain* falls in the style of a typical Javanese sarong, with the fabric hanging stiffly and with no depiction of the limbs beneath. The artist has cleverly depicted the punched design of the textile behind all the girdles. Śiva appears adorned with the usual tiger skin around his hips carved with a realistic animal fur pattern.

The gold plaque of a four-armed Harihara shown in figure 65 is considerably larger than the previous plaque, standing at thirty-six centimetres. It was probably commissioned to be placed in a temple niche, or for a member of the royal family. The right half depicts Śiva holding the *akṣamālā*, prayer beads, and the *kundika*, the water pot. He is accompanied by an anthropomorphic figure of Nandi, his mount, in the lower corner. On the left is an image of Viṣṇu holding a gem and a *bolus*, a

Figure 63 Viṣṇu, 9th century, 's-Gravenzande Store, Leiden. Collection Nationaal Museum van Wereldculturen. Inv. no. 1403-2392. Approx. 10 cm, bronze. Detail of the lower legs. Drawing of the textile pattern.

substance or medication. He is also accompanied by an anthropomorphic image of Garuda, his mount, at the lower edge. The figure has distended ear lobes and wears simple jewellery, including a beaded diadem, the *udharabhanda* or stomach band, and an elaborate metal belt that holds up the *dhotī* worn long to the calves. The centre panel of the *dhotī* has been pulled up between the legs and is probably tucked in at the rear. Across the body is the *upavīta* cast as a simple cord. The surface of the plaque is carved with two different patterns to represent two different deities. Śiva, on the right, displays no pattern, but just the folds of a fine cloth. Viṣṇu, on the left, is shown with a detailed curved pattern along the folds of the cloth. This type of patterning is indicative of a design on the cloth, but because it is so small it remains difficult to decipher. Whilst the plaque is full of the smallest details, in this instance it is difficult to decipher what textile the artist had in mind, beyond that the two halves of the deity differ. I advocate a certain similarity here to plaques from Si Thep, which saw thriving commercial activity and where different imported models

Figure 64 Śiva plaque, 8th–9th century, Pedukuhan Gemuruh, Wonosobo. Museum Nasional Indonesia. 20.5 cm, embossed gold repoussé plaque. Inv. no. A24/517b/4565. Drawing of the textile pattern.

could easily have existed (Brown, pp. 42–44). Both Fontein and Robert Brown have dated this plaque to the eighth or ninth century; however, it could have been earlier, reflecting the interregional trade at the time. No tradition exists in Thailand, or indeed India, of carving textile patterns on gold plaques such as these. It is therefore quite likely this piece is of indigenous origin, but it may incorporate ideas from somewhere else, probably Mainland Southeast Asia.

The gold plaque of Umā as the mother goddess shown in figure 66 is severely damaged. The image holds a rod in her right hand and a scroll or rolled book in her left. She wears simple jewellery. Her ear lobes are long, distended on to her shoulders, and are inserted with large metal earrings. An elaborate thick metal belt holds up the *dhotī*, which is shown folded to above the knees and is probably tucked in at the rear of the body. The textile is carved with a detailed geometric pattern of small four-petal flowers within vertical wavy lines. It is possible that the pattern was drawn or painted on by hand. It is hard to make out, but there may be a thin cloth that falls the length of the body beneath the loincloth. Lying over the hips

Figure 65 Harihara plaque, 8th–9th century, maybe earlier, Gemuruh, Wonosobo. Museum Nasional Indonesia. 36 cm, hammered gold repoussé plaque. Inv. no. A30/517d. Drawing of the textile pattern.

is an unusual twisted fabric belt that is tied off behind the arms with the ends shown flaring out at each side of the body. The *upavīta* is a simple cord across the body. If we look at the art of Si Thep in southern Thailand, there can be seen a similar moulding of the body of the stone sculptures of Viṣṇu from the fourth to the sixth century (Brown 1999, pp. 42–44). However, the gold plaque from Si Thep dated to circa 700 demonstrates a strong contrapposto, indicating little similarity except for the concept of a deity reproduced in a plaque. Moreover, there does not appear to be any known figure in the art of Si Thep with these distinctive features. This figure of a female goddess is therefore probably of indigenous origin.

The textile patterns from the eighth and ninth centuries evoke some similarities with Thai supplementary weft and weft ikat textiles of the present day from the Tai Lue and Lao groups (figs. 67 and 68). The use of narrow bands of patterns on the plaque are similar to the layout of the bands of these Lao and Khmer textiles. And whilst it is unlikely that either of these textile techniques would have been made in the ninth century, it is possible to suggest a similarity in the patterning. It is therefore possible that the textile pattern on this gold plaque could be replicating an ikat or embroidered woven pattern of some kind.

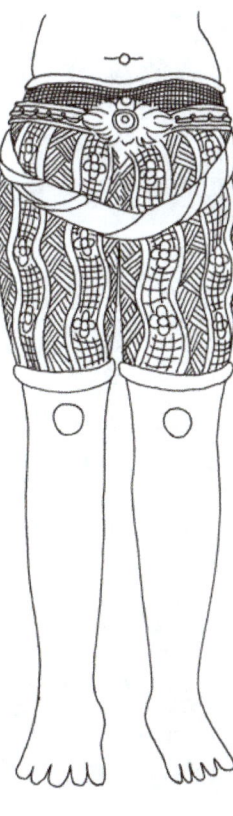

Figure 66 Umā plaque, 9th century, maybe earlier, provenance unknown. Approx. 15 cm, embossed gold repoussé plaque. Museum Nasional Indonesia. Inv. no. unknown. Drawing of the textile pattern.

108 Patterned Splendour

Figure 67 Detail of a Khmer *sampot hol* or weft ikat in silk, 20th century. Private collection.

Figure 68 Details of a Lao Thai *sin mii* or supplementary weft in silk, 20th century. Private collection.

Diagonal Bands Incorporating Flowers

The next sub-group consists of two unusual small bronze figures and a stone Gaṇa.

Standing at seven centimetres and eight centimetres respectively, the divine sow and the divine mare (fig. 69) are part of a Buddhist *maṇḍala* of eighteen statuettes originating from Surocolo in Central Java. They represent part of the early stage of iconographical development of esoteric *maṇḍala*. The statuettes have been divided into three groups. According to Fontein, these two figures are part of a group that would have been placed on a lotus pedestal (1990, pp. 223–29). They appear to be the only two zoomorphic figures within the group, and they are the largest of the statuettes. Both are cast with a pattern on the long *kain*, which is carved

Figure 69 Buddhist maṇḍala in the Nganjuk style, 11th century, Surocolo, Bantul District, near Jogjakarta, found c.1976. 7.9 x 8.2 cm, bronze. Inv. no. unknown. Drawing of the textile pattern.

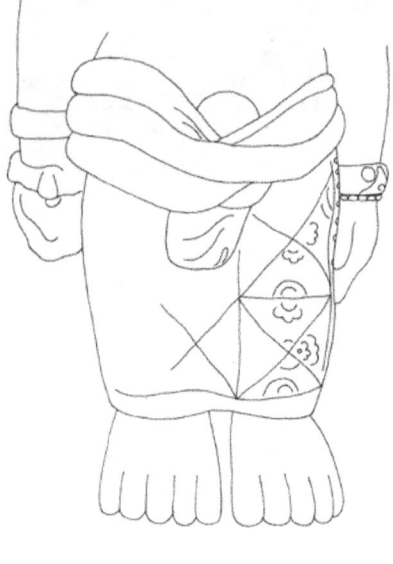

with a pan-Asian motif of linked circles containing a rosette (or lotus)—found as a surface ornament in any number of techniques and media—within a repeated diamond-shaped design. Despite the earlier dating of these small sculptures, the designs on them show parallels to some textiles in the Newberry Collection at the Ashmolean Museum, which are generally believed to be of a later date. Barnes describes numerous patterns displayed on the Indian mordant and resist-dyed textiles found in Egypt as having designs of rosettes with rounded petals and offset within a geometric outline (1997b, p. 63). Such a description matches the

Figure 70 Gaṇa, 9th–11th century, but could be as early as the 8th century. Jawa Tengah Office Museum Ronggorworsito, Semarang. 90 cm, stone. Inv. no. 059/Ar'90–04 00088. Detail of the lower legs. Pullen photo. Drawing of the textile pattern.

layout on these two statuettes. Both of them are adorned with a cloth sash folded over at the front of the body and depicted at the side tied off with a stylized loop. The two-armed image of the female with a boar's head stands astride a lotus cushion. The wide-apart stance of the legs is a highly unusual feature in Javanese sculpture, but it is an element required for esoteric deities, as evident in all the standing Surocolo statuettes. Both are also adorned with a tall, pointed crown with protrusions, and long hair curls on to their shoulders. These two statuettes—as is the case for all the remainder in the group—are decorated with the *channavīra*, or crossed chains. The long, slender body and the somewhat blobby depiction of the chains and the rest of the jewellery again reflects the early East Javanese style of the eleventh and twelfth centuries. Another group of such bronzes are situated in the MNI, behind glass in a poorly lit cabinet. It is entirely possible that some of the small bronzes at the MNI are also decorated with textile patterns, but they are impossible to access. A distinctive feature of this group of statuettes is the somewhat rough surface of the bronze, which appears crudely cast. The figures depict a liveliness, however, that is often not present in the Central Javanese statues.

In complete contrast, but displaying a very similar textile pattern, the squat stone figure of a Gaṇa shown in figure 70 portrays all the features of an attendant of Śiva. A Gaṇa is a rotund dwarf-like figure derived from celestial beings, or *yaksha*, that are adopted in Hinduism as Śiva's faithful attendants, with the Indian god Gaṇeśa as their acknowledged leader. The *kain* on this small squat figure falls straight to his feet, with no depiction of his legs beneath. It has been carved with a pattern of a large, possibly floral, motif set within a triangular framework. A broad cloth girdle is wrapped twice around his copious girth, presumably to hold up his *kain*. His bulging wide-open eyes, bared teeth, overly long arms, substantial ear ornaments and his long hair curls give this squat figure a somewhat demonic appearance. The statue is carved with a large necklet with a central ornament and upper arm bands. There is also a band around his waist, perhaps the *udharabhanda*, which is also set with a decoration, which could be indicating a skull as a tantric symbol. The Ronggorworsito Museum in Semarang dates the statue to the eleventh century, which would place it within the early East Javanese period, but the style fits neither the Central Javanese nor the later East Javanese period. I would instead place him at the very beginning of the Central Javanese period, in the eighth century, judging from the somewhat "lumpy" and unsophisticated appearance and quality of the carving, along with the rather simple pattern on his *kain*. This is merely a suggestion, as more research needs to be completed on this important and unusual figure.

Group 3: Embroidery Patterns

Embroidery patterns in this sub-group are remarkable in Central Java, and they appear on only a select few statues, with no two patterns alike.

A sizeable gold statue of Pārvatī at twenty-one centimetres (fig. 71), paired with one of Śiva (fig. 26, p. 63), remains unique among all of the Javanese sculptures presented in this book. The figure is adorned with jewellery, has large earrings in extended earlobes that fall on to the shoulders, and has a single necklet and matching upper-arm bands that display a motif reflected in the single metal belt. Pārvatī also wears

Figure 71 Pārvatī, 8th–9th century, Gemuruh, near Wonosobo, Central Java. Museum Nasional Indonesia. 21 cm, gold. Inv. no. 519a/4570. Drawing of the textile pattern.

the crossed belts or *channavīra*, portrayed with a large clasp between the breasts. The styling of the cloth and the patterning of the *kain* is extremely rare. The *kain* finishes at the mid-shin level, as would a *tapis* from Lampung in South Sumatra, rather than a longer *kain* from Java, which is typically shown wrapped around the body with a pleat at the front. The shape of the body is not revealed beneath the fabric, which drapes free of the limbs beneath. The pattern can be interpreted in any number of ways; however, I suggest the design represents a continuous floral motif with a stylized "octopus"-shaped theme in vertical bands, which was known to be used by the Lampung people in South Sumatra. On account of the heavy appearance of the fabric, with it not clinging to the legs, and the patterning of the cloth in comparison to the previous sculptures, it is quite possible it represents a brocade or woven fabric, or perhaps an embroidery with silk threads known as silk floss, where the silk is not as tightly twisted as a normal silk thread. This theory is based on similar types of textiles seen today in Lampung. The motif down the central panel is very similar to the "octopus" or "*cumi-cumi*" (fig. 72) theme, a typical pattern for a women's *tapis*. The women's *tapis* evolved in a completely different manner to how it did elsewhere in the Indonesian islands. The design depends primarily on embroidery with gold and silver threads to create detailed patterns. The patterns depicted in horizontal bands are formed with silk floss in a long satin stitch, often replicating animals from the seas, as this stylized octopus would indicate.

Figure 72 Details of a Tapis Inuh and Tapis Paminggir, with cumi-cumi motif along the centre panel of the *tapis*. Private collection.

The *tapis* is worn by women during traditional ceremonies. With Lampung located at the extreme southern tip of Sumatra, the inhabitants were effectively the guardians of the trade routes to and from Southeast Asia. This was definitely the case by the late sixteenth century. The Sunda Strait, however, was not used until the arrival of the Portuguese and the Dutch, when the route across the southern Indian Ocean was discovered, bypassing India completely. Lampung was important, but as a source of spices and other natural products, and not as a destination of merchants. No major port sites have been discovered there. The Dutch, based in Banten on the western tip of Java, controlled the lucrative pepper trade in the Lampung region, with the crop traded to Java (Andaya 1994, p. 434).

Traders from India and China, people from the Arab lands, and the Javanese themselves have travelled to ports in the region of the Strait of Malacca. New materials, techniques, different design elements and ideas for textile patterns were all brought into the region (Gittinger 1979, pp. 79–83). The foreign influences felt by the polity of Śrivijaya were projected to the southern tip of Sumatra from as early as the sixth century, where vast wealth was created by the pepper trade (Holmgren and Spertus 1980, p. 164). The hegemony of the rule from Java in the eighth and ninth centuries could easily have been the influence for these designs, which subsequently reached Central Java and were depicted on this gold deity.

There are many uncanny similarities between this gold statuette and the contemporary *tapis* textiles presented here. Let us assume the two figures of Pārvatī and Śiva (fig. 26, p. 63) could have been cast in Sumatra and transferred over to Java. The style of the statues is somewhat more akin to the slender form of Śrivijaya figures. Their style also reminds us more of South Indian art (Bernet Kempers 1959, p. 34, plate 33) than the more rounded Indianized Central Javanese figures. The very unusual textile pattern is perhaps testimony to the weavers in Sumatra at the time who were able to make such an intricate design. I therefore propose these figures could be dated nearer to the eighth century than their current dating of the ninth century. Let us suppose the two gold statuettes were commissioned as part of the court arts produced during the Śrivijaya period. What the inspiration was, however, behind these two extraordinary figures and their unusual textile patterns is still unknown.

Group 4: Full Dress Patterns

Sculptures that are fully dressed are rare, and only two have been identified that are wearing both a *kain* and a *baju* or jacket. These two statues highlight the use of stitched garments at an early period in the history of Javanese dress.

The dating of the Sumatran female figure (fig. 73) to sometime between the eleventh and early thirteenth centuries places it in the early East Javanese period. The upper body is clothed in a long-sleeved jacket, or *baju*, which comes together at the centre and is held with a belt. The blouse is decorated with a simple triangular motif on the vertical axis made up of four trefoils with a dot in the centre. The *baju* (fig. 74) finishes over the thighs at the side of the body, accompanied by a patterned *kain* to the ankles that is marked with a narrow border. The pattern on the *kain* replicates that on the *baju*, but it appears to be unfinished. The decoration within the circles is unique to this particular sculpture; it is carved with a simple triangular motif on the vertical axis made up of four trefoils with a dot in the centre. The statue is carved with long ear ornaments shaped

Figure 73 Arcā Leluhur 1, 11th–13th century, Bumiayu Temple 1. Site Museum Desa Bumiayu, Kecamatan Tanah Abang, South Sumatra. 62 cm, tuff white volcanic stone. Detail of the lower right leg and upper body. Pullen photo.

like peepul leaves (*ficus religiosa*), a double necklet, upper arm bands, and plain double bracelets and ankle bracelets. A belt is placed over the blouse and clearly recalls metal work of some kind. The *baju* or *vaju* has been described as the most salient of Indo-Persian sartorial items, and is attested in the Old and Middle Javanese literature (Jákl and Hoogervorst 2017, pp. 213–14).

The second seated female ancestor (fig. 75) was found in Java and is dated by the MNI to the twelfth century or later. From a stylistic point of view, however, the textile patterns clearly reflect an earlier date of perhaps the tenth or eleventh century. This statue fits closer with the Kediri period, although realistically it is not possible to place the figure. The description of the dress differs slightly, but it is remarkable to find two sculptures on different islands dressed with patterns in this fashion. The upper body is clothed in a long-sleeved *baju* that comes together at the centre and is held with a belt. The blouse is decorated with a simple eight-petal daisy around a central circle. The large motif is placed symmetrically over the *baju* in a style that is very similar to that of the *dvārapāla* (fig. 40, p. 78) in Museum Sonobudoyo, which has been dated to between the twelfth and fourteenth centuries. The *arcā* figure also wears a patterned *kain*, which finishes above the ankles and is marked with a simple border. The design that appears on the left knee is best deciphered as simple circles.

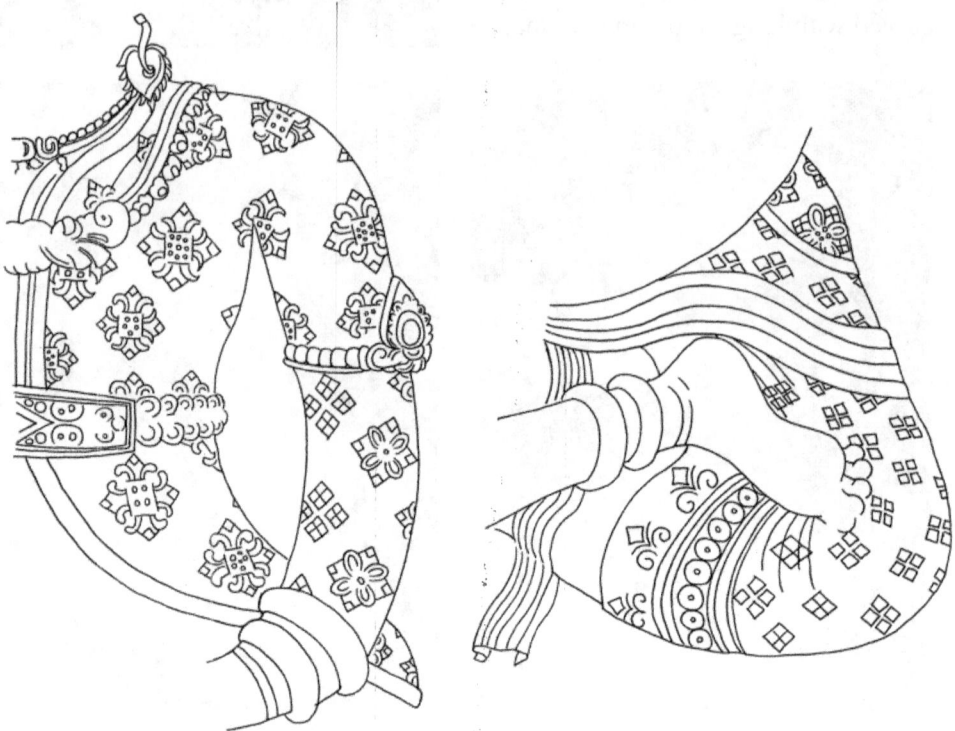

Figure 74 Arcā Leluhur, Bumiayu Temple 1. Drawings of the *baju* and *kain*.

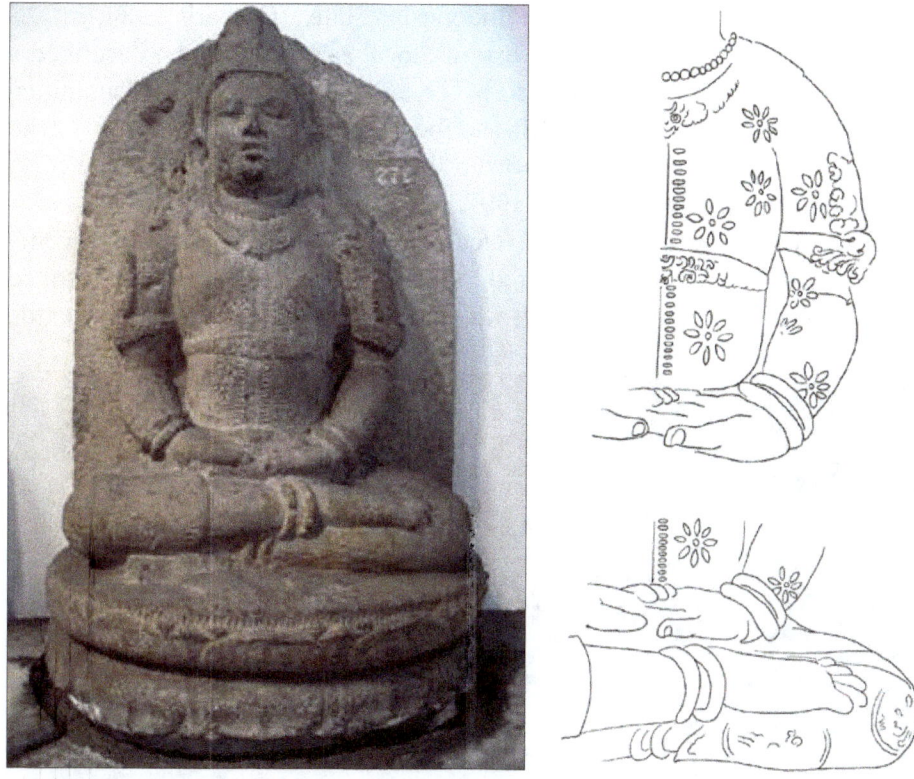

Figure 75 *Arcā Dewa*, approx. dating to 12th century, but maybe earlier 10th–11th century, origin unknown. National Museum Indonesia. 66 cm, stone. Inv. no. 276. Pullen photo. Drawing of the *baju*.

Summary

The Javanese appeared to be willing recipients of ideas from India; ideas that were subsequently absorbed and incorporated. These ideas seemed, however, to be part of a two-way relationship. J.G. de Casparis describes how that among the Indian Nagapattinam bronzes, "a number … apparently show Indonesian influences". He also suggests that "Indonesian influence can be observed in some of the Nālandā bronzes". De Casparis recommends caution though in trying to interpret and analyse the bronzes from these two regions (Casparis 1983, p. 14). Sheldon Pollock describes a "Sanskrit Cosmopolis" that ran from 300 to 1300 CE. The evidence for this appears in Java by way of inscriptions. According to Pollock, "Sanskrit in Java is the first vehicle for literized royal self-expression", and the use of Sanskrit in Java was for the elite only and not everyday use (1996, p. 229). De Casparis describes the period from the tenth century to the first thirty years of the eleventh century "as a brief but important period in international relations in South and Southeast Asia". Relations that are recorded between Śrivijaya and China, East Java and China, and South India and China, but most importantly between the

118   Patterned Splendour

Chola in South India and the Indonesian states (Casparis 1983, p. 12). Wolters provided another theory of "localization" when he described a people that were "ready to absorb", "readily acclimatized" and submitted to "local adaption", the "self-ascribed Southeast Asian Hindus", who abstracted Sanskrit materials from the original context and made them into a "new cultural whole" (1999, p. 173).

From these theories it is clear that during the eighth to eleventh centuries the Javanese appeared to have borrowed ideas, which resulted in transculturation. The result was the rather Indianized types of textile

Figure 76 Green Tara, c.1260, Tibet. Cleveland Museum of Art. 52 x 42 cm, Thangka, opaque watercolour and ink on cotton. Inv. no. 1970.156.

patterns that appeared as early examples of the equivalent to the Indian remnants of block printed cotton and mordant dyed cloth. On close observation, some of the Central and early East Javanese patterns appear also to be reflected in the later period designs on statues of the eleventh and twelfth centuries from Kashmir and Tibet, and in paintings such as the Green Tara (fig. 76) from the Cleveland Museum of Art (CMA). The Javanese had come to develop a regional artistic style that incorporated many ideas learnt from manuscripts, and from the connections that were later made between Tibet, India, Sri Lanka, Java and Śrivijaya. These connections were felt through a renewed focus on Esoteric Buddhism, which was probably triggered by royal patronage between the tenth and twelfth centuries and by a network of connections between South Asia, East Java, Cambodia, Central Sumatra and Champa in the eleventh to thirteenth centuries (Stuart-Fox 1993).

Schoterman describes an illustrated manuscript, the *Aṣṭasāharsrikā Prajñāpāramitā*, from 1015 CE (2016, p. 115). The text contains many illustrations of Buddhist Divinities, mostly relating to India, but Sri Lanka, Java, Sumatra and the Malay Peninsula are also mentioned. There was little mention, however, of Nālandā. Similar Buddhist sanctuaries are mentioned in a 1071 CE manuscript, as is Sri Lanka, but this time only Java is mentioned in the list of essential sanctuaries (Jessup 2004, p. 115).

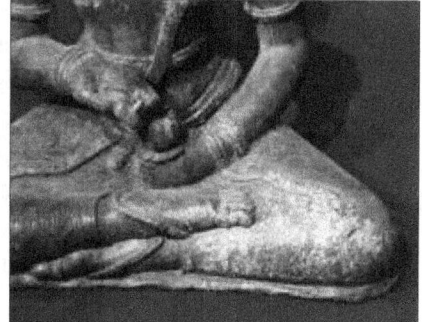

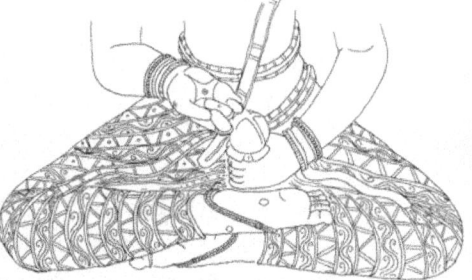

Figure 77 Vajradharma Lokeśvara, 9th–10th century. National Museum of Colombo. 61 cm, bronze. Inv. no. 14. Drawing of the textile pattern.

To place this material in context, it is useful to refer to the various compound textile patterns on the seated statues of Avalokiteśvara and the goddess Cundā/Mahāpratīsarā and on the statue of Vajradhara (fig. 77) in the Colombo National Museum, all three of which are dated to earlier. All three display a distinctly Indian textile pattern that is also seen in the later Tibet paintings and which closely resembles the textile pattern of the Green Tara at the CMA.[5] The *Aṣṭasāharsrikā Prajñāpāramitā* was produced three years after the departure of Atīśa for Sumatra. Atīśa was one of the most prominent saints of Tibet, who travelled from Tibet to Sumatra where he spent twelve years at the Buddhist site of Muara Jambi. This clearly shows that the Javanese developed their textile patterns at an earlier stage than the evidence given here of the later Indian material.

The techniques of ikat and block printing of textiles have been known from as early as the sixth century. Iwan Tirtha has suggested, however, that knowledge of ikat dates back to the Dongson period, to around the turn of the first millennium, as there are examples depicted in the mural cave paintings at Ajanta. The most notable of these is in Cave 1,[6] where the *Mahājanaka Jātaka* displays scenes of life at court and in the palaces (Christie 1998b, pp. 47 and 85). The central figure portrays a dancer, and also depicted are a number of musicians who are clearly wearing a striped cloth worn around the lower body. The pattern of "dashes" was probably replicating the ikat method. There appear, however, to also be other influences on the textile patterns of Central and early East Java—from the Indian painted resist and mordant dyed patterns seen in the Ajanta murals, and from Southern India in the style of the ornaments and the type of dress, especially in the uses of the *dhotī*. But despite the undisputed evidence suggested here, there is no doubt there was also a degree of interregional trade within Southeast Asia, as clearly reflected in some of the proposed textile patterns.

Fontein, Soekmono and Suleiman claim that whilst the art and architecture of Central Java was part of the mainstream of the intellectual life of the Buddhist world, the art and architecture of East Java was admittedly more self-centred, "as no new impulses from abroad stimulated a search for new forms and methods of expression" (1971, p. 45). The textile art of Central and early East Java was more predictable and perhaps formulaic, whereas the textile arts of East Java in the Kediri and especially the Singhasāri period were not predictable. Many of the statues were carved with unique textile patterns that were never seen either before or again in Java. In the case of the small gold Pārvatī though, we see early evidence of the kinds of patterns reflected in the *tapis* of Lampung of the nineteenth and twentieth centuries.

A comparative chart of line drawings is added at the end of the chapter to enable the reader to see in one place the variety of textile patterns depicted during this period.

Notes

1. http://jameelcentre.ashmolean.org/collection/6/1272/1274.
2. Despite the dating given by the British Museum, it is possible that these two gold statues were made in Sumatra, which would date them earlier, perhaps between the seventh and ninth centuries. The high matted hair, with the central tresses joining at the top, the long robe, overly large hands and feet, bulbous nose and very long hair curls hint at a rather more northeast and eastern Indian style, which can be termed "Śrivijayan style", reflected in local characteristics. Sumatra was of course known as "gold island", or *Suvarnadvipa*, with a ready supply of gold ore, which Java did not have.
3. The sculpture was taken by Colonel Colin Mackenzie, who travelled to Java in 1812, and was then donated to the Indian Museum in Calcutta. Mackenzie was Surveyor-General of India at the time, stationed in Calcutta. He went to Prambanan to survey and sketch the ruins. The Gaṇeśa, along with some other Brahmanical deities, were received by the Asiatic Society of Bengal as presents from its members. Unfortunately, no record was kept of their arrival in the museum or of who donated them.
4. The statue was bought at auction in Europe from a Chinese collector from Singapore with a good provenance, but the facial features and clean lines lead me to believe this is an early ninth-century bronze from Bangladesh or Odisha that just happened to be found in Java. This artefact highlights the early history of bronze icons that were traded from India to Java and vice versa. His open right palm is marked with a simple pattern that could be representing the *viśvajra*, similar to figure 54 of Mañjuśrī, which appears in the same form of Kumārabhūta.
5. Acri has argued "for treating Indonesia and India as an integral unit well into the ninth century" and has suggested that Borobudur Buddhism had an influence on India, although there is scant evidence of the inhabitants of Southeast Asia participating in the creation of the Tantras. He does indicate, however, that the contribution of insular Southeast Asia to Vajrayāna Buddhism in Tibet was acknowledged from the eleventh century. The transmission of Buddhist ideas from Java and Sumatra to the Himalayan region is beyond doubt. This is based on architectural and artistic similarities. As a consequence, I suggest the possibility that some of the textile patterns, such as the Green Tara and many other Tibetan examples, could easily have been inspired by Javanese designs.
6. The *Mahājanaka Jātaka* depicts a dancer with a full company of musicians. http://www.indian-heritage.org/painting/ajanta/dance4.html.

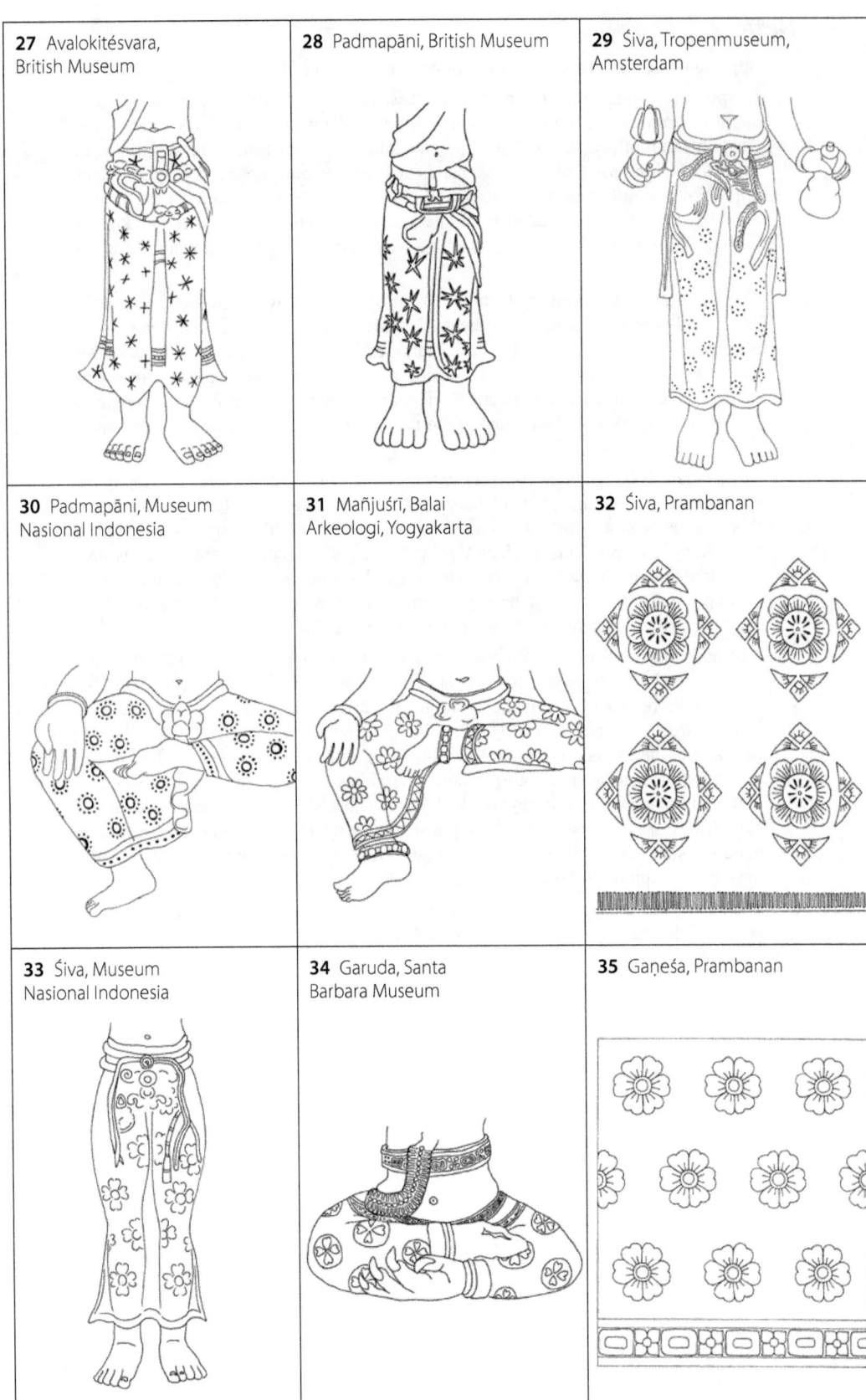

27 Avalokiteśvara, British Museum
28 Padmapāṇi, British Museum
29 Śiva, Tropenmuseum, Amsterdam
30 Padmapāṇi, Museum Nasional Indonesia
31 Mañjuśrī, Balai Arkeologi, Yogyakarta
32 Śiva, Prambanan
33 Śiva, Museum Nasional Indonesia
34 Garuda, Santa Barbara Museum
35 Gaṇeśa, Prambanan

Central and Early East Java – Comparative Chart of Line Drawings   **123**

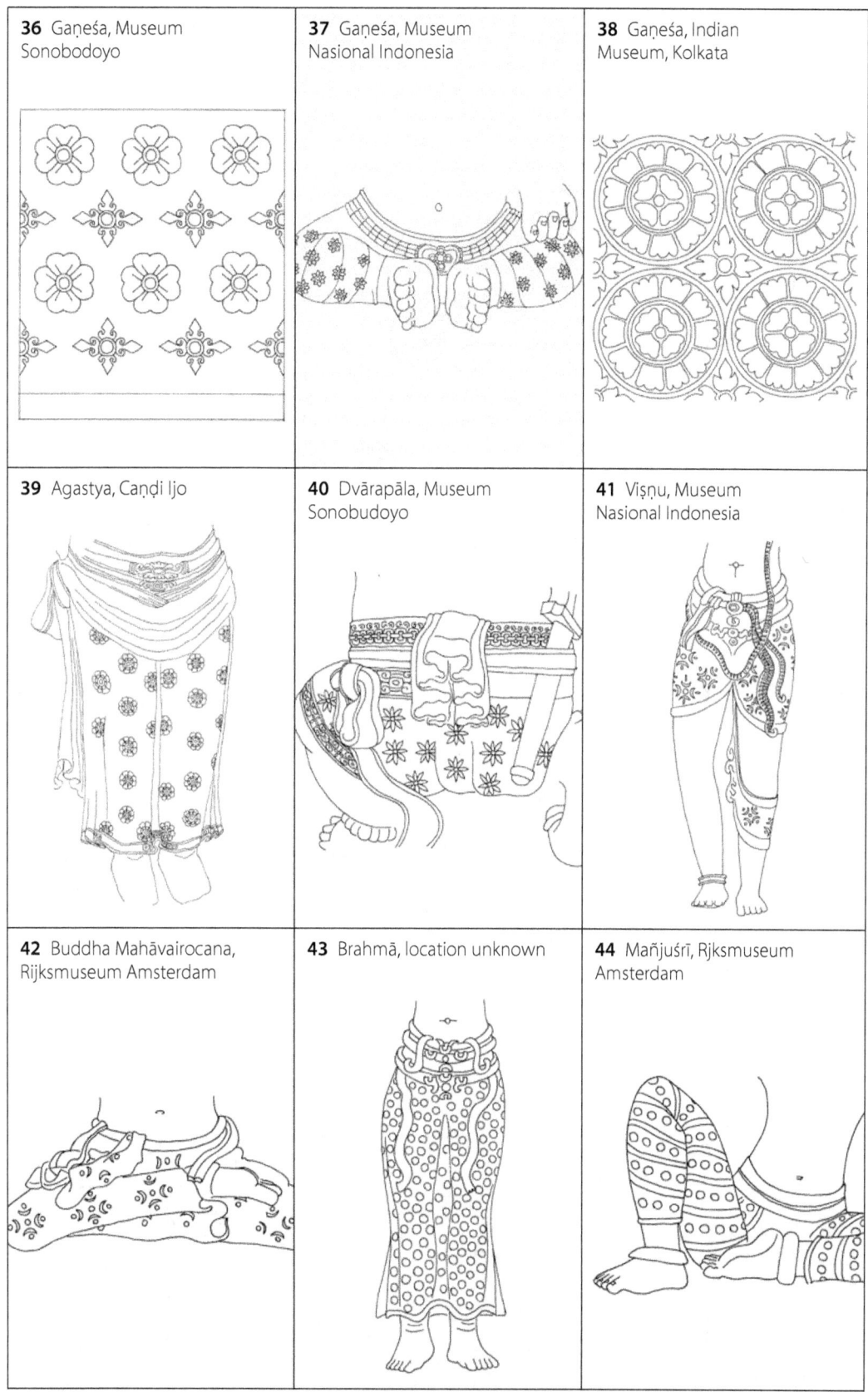

36 Gaṇeśa, Museum Sonobodoyo	**37** Gaṇeśa, Museum Nasional Indonesia	**38** Gaṇeśa, Indian Museum, Kolkata
39 Agastya, Caṇḍi Ijo	**40** Dvārapāla, Museum Sonobudoyo	**41** Viṣṇu, Museum Nasional Indonesia
42 Buddha Mahāvairocana, Rijksmuseum Amsterdam	**43** Brahmā, location unknown	**44** Mañjuśrī, Rijksmuseum Amsterdam

Central and Early East Java – Comparative Chart of Line Drawings

55 Śiva, Metropolitan Museum of Art	**56** Śiva, Museum Sonobodoyo	**57** Tara, Museum Nasional Indonesia
58 Avalokitéśvara, Franz Joseph, Naturhistorisches Museum	**59** Cundā, Museum Radya Pustaka, Solo	**60** Avalokitéśvara, BPCB, Yogjakarta
61 Royal Couple, Museum Nasional Indonesia	**61** Royal Couple, Museum Nasional Indonesia	**63** Viṣṇu, 's-Gravenzande Store, Leiden

64 Śiva, Museum Nasional Indonesia

65 Harihara, Museum Nasional Indonesia

66 Uma, Museum Nasional Indonesia

69 Buddhist maṇḍala, location unknown

69 Buddhist maṇḍala, location unknown

70 Gana, Museum Ranggorworsito

71 Pārvatī, Museum Nasional Indonesia

74 Arcā Leluhur, Site Museum Desa Bumiayu, Kecamatan, Sumatra

74 Arcā Leluhur, Site Museum Desa Bumiayu, Kecamatan, Sumatra

Central and Early East Java – Comparative Chart of Line Drawings 127

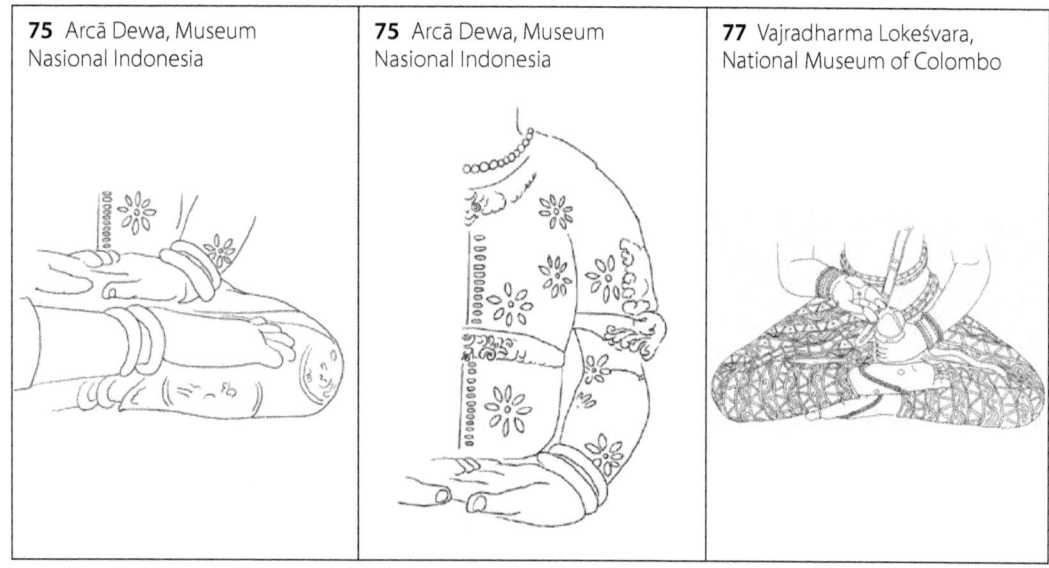

75 Arcā Dewa, Museum Nasional Indonesia

75 Arcā Dewa, Museum Nasional Indonesia

77 Vajradharma Lokeśvara, National Museum of Colombo

4. Kediri and Singhasāri
Stone Sculpture from the Eleventh to the Fourteenth Century

Many monolithic stone statues created during the Singhasāri period in the thirteenth century and some sculptures dated to the early fourteenth century were carved with a broad range of unique textile patterns. Almost all the statues were carved from a single piece of stone, either standing or seated against a backslab. This period in history gave rise to King Kṛtanāgara, the last of the Singhasāri kings. This extensive collection of statues was commissioned under his reign between 1269 and 1292 CE, the more significant part of which was placed at the Caṇḍi Singosari complex or at Caṇḍi Jago. This chapter illustrates all of the known sculptures that were carved with textile patterns. Where known, their places of origin are shown in map 4. These sculptures represent only a fraction, however, of all the sculptures made during this period—the remainder were generally of an inferior quality and exhibited no textile patterns.

There are little remains of importance from the Kediri period, from the mid-eleventh century to 1222 CE, except for the seated sculpture known as the Boro Gaṇeśa. This giant statue is arguably the sculpture that has been most frequently published in Southeast Asian textile and art history books. In my opinion, the Gaṇeśa does not fit into the Singosari style. This is evident from the position of the feet together and the rather stiff body. According to Edi Sedyawati, he fits more closely with the end

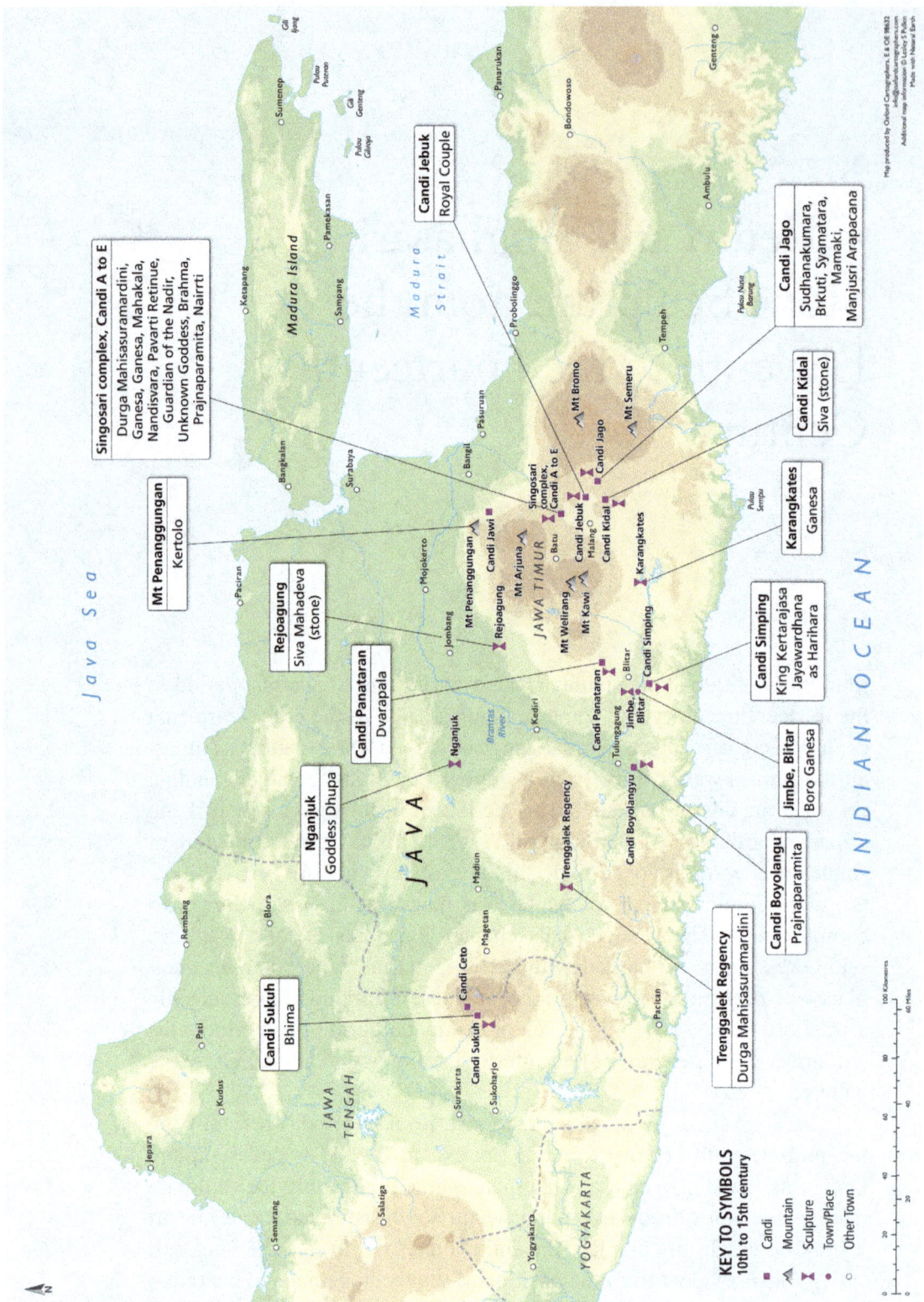

Map 4 Sculpture Locations in East Java, 10th to 15th century.

of the Kediri period, or, as she puts it, "the long empty interval between the last known Kediri inscription and the first Singhasāri inscription" (1994, p. 116). This therefore is a Kediri "style" statue with a Singhasāri date, and it is categorized as "Kediri" along with the Arcā Leluhur at the MNI. The rough andesite stone of the Boro Gaṇeśa results in a cruder form of carving; this establishes that he was made in a different region at a different time to the rest of the Singosari style sculptures. In contrast, the Arcā Leluhur is carved from a smooth and beautiful white andesite stone known as tuff, and is of a very different texture and quality.

The position of East Java within the interregional trade during this period might aid in our consideration of how some of the textile patterns in this chapter arrived there. The political system of east Java may have become more centralized, but the temples were no longer being funded by the state. This probably explains why there are no major temples of the scale of Borobudur or Prambanan in East Java. The changes in Chinese trade policy that enabled Chinese merchants to go abroad in the thirteenth century was another important factor.

> Singasari kings were silent epigraphically until 1264, when Kertanagara resumed the tradition of carving edicts on stone. In 1269 he issued the *Charter of Sawwardharma*, found on Mt Wilis near Penampihan, which exempted religious establishments from secular oversight. These religious establishments included many communities centered on *risi*. These communities gained autonomy from the ruler, but lost access to government funding. Thereafter Javanese temples became numerous but much smaller than their ancestors in central Java; architects adopted elaborate methods to make the temples appear taller than they are. (Miksic and Goh 2017, pp. 462–480)

The increased centralization—evident from the number of royal rituals and in the relationship of the royalty to their ancestors and the higher gods—was at the root of the spiritual prosperity of the Singhasāri dynasty. Much of the increase in financial wealth, however, was a result of the expansion of the trading networks and of the trade of Javanese rice and spices in return for foreign goods, which led to a financial boom. Chinese ceramics are widely distributed across archaeological sites, and literary and epigraphic evidence of the availability of "foreign" goods point to a monetized economy. This situation led the indigenous population to grow more rice to increase their wealth, with the result that Java became a centre of cross-cultural connections and international trade between Persia, China and the Indian world (Tarling 1992, pp. 225–26). From an analysis of the sculptures, these foreign influences appear to have made a considerable contribution to the visual culture of Central and East Java.

Extant textile examples from China and India from the thirteenth and fourteenth centuries are negligible. What do remain though of course are the stone sculptures, which have preserved the "patterns" from the past and which represent "hard and physical" evidence of what was in circulation at the time. What is not known though are the exact details about the textiles that were traded from India to Southeast Asia (Christie 1993a, pp. 17–18; Barnes 1997b, pp. 114–17; Devare 2009, p. 182). Let us assume then that it was Indian cotton that was in massive demand in Java and that it was imported over a long period, as recorded in the *Zhufanzhi*. The Chinese also seem to have needed cotton from India, such as white cotton, which was used for the uniforms of the Yuan soldiers who fought in the hot southern regions. This white cloth came to be known as *kanipha* in the Ming period, *bafta* in Thailand and *kain* in Malaysia (Devare 2009, p. 180). The Indian merchants traded this cotton cloth via Southeast Asian ports on their way to China. In the history of the Song dynasty, it is mentioned that arriving envoys—possibly from somewhere in Sumatra—brought with them, among other things, Indian textiles. This appears to be the first mention of Indian textiles exported to Southeast Asia (ibid., p. 180). Christie posed the theory that silk brocade cloth was probably traded both in and out of China and that some of the Javanese textiles identified by the Chinese as brocade were in actual fact probably embroidery work known as *songket* and weft ikat in silk (Christie 1998, p. 21). It is hard to substantiate what was being represented as there is no extant evidence apart from the stone patterns to indicate what techniques were used to make the cloth. But the statement by Wolters is partially incorrect as *songket* is in fact a type of brocade because the fabric is woven with a gold thread to create a supplementary weft pattern. The appearance of the resulting structure has a three-dimensional effect from the weave of the gold thread, and it appears carved as textile patterns on a number of the Singosari sculptures, which replicate a *songket* pattern, such as that of Nandīśvara, Durgā and the attendants of Amoghapāśa

Early Kediri and Singhasāri *Kawung* Patterns

The Boro Gaṇeśa (fig. 78) is seated on a cushion of skulls. It is carved from an andesite stone and the surface appears rough and uneven. The figure is seated on a large cushion of lotus flowers within a double circle, beneath which is an inscription in the vertical plane that reads "*hana, ghana hana bumi*". On the front half of the cushion are eight carved heads. On the reverse is a large *kāla*-head carved in deep relief. The statue is wearing a *sinjang* carved with a *kawung* pattern and held up with a woven sash, which is a relatively typical Singosari feature. The sash (fig. 79) is folded at the rear of the statue into a large loop. This is the first instance of this

Kediri and Singhasāri 133

Figure 78 Boro Gaṇeśa, 1239–40 CE (end of Kediri, beginning of Singhasāri period), Desa Boro/Bara, Jimbe, Blitar, East Java (in situ in a small, locked pavilion in Boro village). 1.70 m, andesite stone. Detail of the rear of the body. Drawing of the textile pattern.

Figure 79 Boro Gaṇeśa, details of the sash. Pullen photo. Drawing of the sash.

ubiquitous Javanese design carved in a simple arrangement. The sash, which noticeably drapes in two sections over the front of the legs at different lengths, is woven with a pattern reflecting a type of gold or silk thread. The edges are cut in a looped design, perhaps indicating a series of looped gimp or metal threads. The pattern on the sash indicates an overlapping triangular woven design, with the tassel decorated with a skull motif.

The sarong is folded over the sash, which is plainly evident as the *kawung* motif is visible at the rear of the body above the girdle. The patterns of the *sinjang* are very deeply incised. It is suggestive of a luxurious cloth—perhaps a design made with gold leaf, such as *prada*, or possibly a brocade or *songket*. We know from the earliest records that aristocrats in Southeast Asia owned and wore gold cloth, but no textiles from these periods remain. The carvings of luxury fashion that appear thickly brocaded, possibly with metallic threads, suggest these textiles were in vogue between the eighth and fifteenth centuries. We cannot say for sure, obviously, that this visual evidence represents metallic weaving. But we do know from the extant early Javanese inscriptions how prestige textiles have been valued by their weight in gold (Totton 2009, p. 33).

Guy suggests the Gaṇeśa is "wearing a prestigious imported Indian cloth" and that this design later became known as an important pattern in Java's batik repertoire (1998, p. 62). While this suggestion is certainly possible, the cloth is more likely to represent a brocaded textile with gold or silk threads; indeed, in Totton's opinion the fabric is "thickly brocaded, possibly with metallic threads" (2009, p. 33).

The statue of Śiva (fig. 80) at the Tropenmuseum is standing on a small lotus base that is damaged on one side. The andesite stone is relatively pale and smooth. The statue wears an abundant amount of jewellery, including the *upavīta* and a *kirītamukuta* or elaborate crown. His hair falls in long

Figure 80 Śiva, c.1260, Caṇḍi Kiḍal, Malang, East Java. Tropenmuseum, Amsterdam. Collection Nationaal Museum van Wereldculturen. Inv. no. TM-A-5950. 1.23 m, andesite stone.

Figure 81 Śiva, drawing of the *sinjang kawung* pattern and the sash.

locks over the shoulders. Silver adorns the neck, arms, waist and ankles. Wrapped around the waist is a long cloth belt. The *upavita* resembles a long, twisted strand of five strings of pearls draped over the knees with an intricate and sizeable jewelled clasp, which is a feature more typical of the Singosari style. The statue wears two cloths, indicated by a line just discernible below the knees. The plain *sinjang* falls to the ground, over which hangs a shorter fabric carved with a simplified *kawung* motif. Perhaps a regional artistic style was applied to the unusual dress of Śiva, specifically the double-patterned sash. The design has not been previously analysed. The unique pattern (fig. 81) has been deeply incised with a triangular motif and a vegetal pattern in the four quarters. The sash is tied in large knots; one end is just visible on the backslab and the other falls the length of the body. The pattern is visible over many delicate folds and, based on the complexity of the design, was probably made to represent a brocaded fabric. The *kawung* motif in this instance is closer to the Majapahit rendition of this pattern, as will be seen in the next chapter.

Caṇḍi Jago Statues

The next four sculptures originated from Caṇḍi Jago. The structure of the *caṇḍi* resembles a three-tiered "Temple Mountain" rather than a tall symmetrical structure, which is distinctly different from those of the other remaining Singhasāri *caṇḍi*. Each of the three terraces recede as one proceeds to the top, where the Central *cella* was based at the back of the temple.[1] The orientation is to the northwest, with two sets of double staircases leading to the top. Surrounding the three terraces are reliefs of stories all related to kingship.

The So-called *"Balah Kacang"* (Split Peanut) Pattern

The bodhisattva Amoghapāśa has four attendants: the male figure of Sudhanakumāra, the two female figures of Bṛkuṭi and Śyāmatārā, and the male figure of Hayagrīva. The last figure of Hayagrīva does not display any textile patterns, so it will not be included in this catalogue. These graceful and intricately carved figures are all slightly damaged. They highlight the early stage of the exact Singosari style statue that became evident from 1268 in the reign of King Kṛtanāgara.

Each statue is decorated with delicately carved ornaments, including a tall conical jewelled headdress with ribbons faintly incised on the backslab, extended earlobes inserted with round carved earplugs, a neckband, upper armbands, bracelets and anklets—some more substantial than others—and are finished with a border pattern indicating that the ribbon is representing a textile or fabric. Around the hips, holding the *sinjang*, is a highly decorated metal girdle with precisely carved plaques in the shape of peepul leaves. The *upavīta* is not visible on these statues; however, draped over both shoulders is a strand of three strings of pearls that hang to the waist, under which is a subtly carved *seléndang* laying across the upper body.

The *sinjang* on all three attendant statues of Sudhanakumāra, Bṛkuṭi and Śyāmatārā (fig. 82) fall the length of their bodies and have a delicate pleat at the front. The cloth in each case reveals the shape of the body beneath. The pattern of the cloth is made up of four elliptical petals, along the centre of which is a narrow oval (fig. 83). The ellipses are joined at the points to make a square, and this perhaps represents one of the combinations of the *kawung* pattern group. This pattern, however, is best described as *balah kacang*.[2]

Bart, an architect and weaving specialist, has described this pattern as a most complex one, and one that is very difficult to draw freehand. A sophisticated loom, such as an externally braced body-tensioned one with a reed, would therefore be needed to produce it (Buckley and Boudout 2015, p. 408), and not a simple externally braced backstrap loom, such as those used by most Austronesian speakers in Maritime Southeast Asia (ibid., p. 406). Bart states that this does not represent a *kawung* pattern, but is more likely the *balah kacang* pattern. Such a pattern is typical of those produced by the Minangkabau in West Sumatra, where the motifs are woven into ceremonial textiles made using the *songket* technique. The *balah kacang* type of pattern arrangement evokes a certain similarity with the style of patterns on these three sculptures. It is entirely possible the stone patterns were made to replicate an earlier version of this *songket*. Bart suggests that the design did not gain in popularity because it was too complicated to draw, and this is the reason it continued in Minangkabau *songket* weaving but not in Javanese batik patterns.

Figure 82 Details of the legs, Śyāmatārā, Bṛkuṭi and Sudhanakumāra, attendants of Amoghapāśa, 1268–1280 CE, Caṇḍi Jago, Tumpang, Malang, East Java. Museum Nasional Indonesia, acquired 1893. 1.14 m, andesite stone. Inv. nos. 247a, 247b and 112a. Pullen photos.

According to Bart, the patterns are carved with consummate skill, and they would have been complex and difficult to weave (2016, pp. 12–17). Based on the analysis by Bart, I suggest the textile patterns could well have been a response to some kind of luxurious cloth that was available at the time. As stated by Robin Maxwell, the exact nature of these textiles is unclear, but the sculptures from the Hindu-Buddhist temples clearly reflect the past and represent a legacy of the textile traditions at the time (Bautze-Picron 1993, p. 192).

Songket textiles are still woven today with patterns such as these. Many of them originate from the ancient village of Pitalah in Minangkabau, and have been made since at least the 1700s. Ann and John Summerfield describe the Minangkabau way of life as "centered

Figure 83 Drawings of the textile patterns on Śyāmatārā, Bṛkuṭi and Sudhanakumāra.

on a traditional belief system, *adat* (from the Arabic word *'adah*) which is translated as 'custom' or 'tradition'" (Summerfield and Summerfield 1999, p. 55). Garments in the Minangkabau tradition are made from *songket* textiles in accordance with *adat* specifications and worn during life-cycle ceremonies as emblems of *adat* (ibid., p. 171).

It is perhaps interesting to note that this type of geometric patterning is also depicted on the sash (fig. 124, p. 177) of the monumental, four-metre high, Mahākāla found in Sumatra (see map 2, p. 46), which is now housed at the NMI. This might indicate that these motifs were the beginning of the Minangkabau textile tradition. In the fourteenth century, the ruler of Hindu Jambi, the Majapahit prince Ādityavarman, conquered the Minangkabau heartland and founded the Minangkabau kingdom (ibid., p 45). A large statue was found in a remote village in the highlands (fig. 122, p. 175). The identity for the statue has been suggested by Bautze-Picron as possibly a deified Ādityavarman as Mahākāla. No inscription

Figure 84 Reproductions after Valentina I. Raspopova, "Textiles Represented in Sogdian Murals", in *Central Asian Textiles and Their Context in the Early Middle Ages*, Riggisberger Berichte 9, edited by Regula Schorta, Abegg-Stiftung, 2006, fig. 36.

exists however to prove it is Mahākāla (Bautze-Picron 2014, pp. 107–28). Previous scholars, such as Natasha Reichle, have suggested this is Bhairava (2007, p. 167). The statue remains in the MNI. Ādityavarman was known to be half Javanese and half Sumatran. It is entirely possible therefore to associate him with Minangkabau textiles, as we see on the pattern on his sash (fig. 124, p. 177).

The two textile examples represented in Sogdian murals shown in figure 84 date to the seventh or eighth century (Raspopova 2006, p. 64). The layout of the geometric patterning of these two show a remarkable similarity with the style of those on the statues from Jago. This similarity between the patterns attest to the longevity and perhaps to the popularity of this motif, and illustrates the continuity of designs that was a result of the interregional trade across the "single ocean".

Roundel Patterns

The seated statue of Māmakī shown in figure 85 is one of the *prajñās* or female counterparts of one of the four cosmic Buddhas associated with Amoghapāśa. In comparison to the previous group, the rough andesite stone of Māmakī does not lend itself to as detailed carvings of the ornaments or textile patterns. Since these statues are all from the same *caṇḍi*, this fact might indicate that this statue was made at a different time in a separate workshop that only had access to a lesser quality of stone.

Figure 85 Māmakī, female partner of Ratnasambhava, part of a set that represented the five Jinas and their female counterparts, 1268–80, Caṇḍi Jago, Tumpang, Malang, East Java. @Trustees of the British Museum. 48 cm, andesite stone. Inv. no. 1859, 1228.71. Gift of the Rev. Flint, executor of the will of Lady Raffles, 1859. Drawing of the textile pattern.

It is somewhat surprising that the textile patterns and the quality of the stone differ to such an extreme. The most delicate feature of the statue is the depiction of the sash ends, which are clearly shown flying upwards on the backslab. The now very faint pattern consists of concentric roundels with a double border consisting of a simple pattern of four scallop-shaped motifs around a central circle, with the interstices made up of four trefoil forms.

Mañjuśrī Arapacana, shown in figure 86, is seated on a lotus cushion. He carries a sword raised in his right hand over his head and holds the Prajñāpāramitā sutra in his left. He is accompanied by four attendants as replicas of the central figure. All the identifying features are of Arapacana. Mañjuśrī also originates from Caṇḍi Jago. In this case though, in comparison to that of Māmakī, the statue has been carved from a smooth, pale andesite stone. Other than some damage to the sutra in his left hand, the statue is in almost perfect condition. There are two visible inscriptions on the sculpture: one at the top of the sculpture on the front, and the other on the rear of the backslab. These inscriptions were first translated by Bosch (1921) into Dutch and then into English by U Kozok and Eric van Reijn:

> He Ādityavarman in the realm ruled by her majesty the supreme queen, from her lineage, having true intentions, endowed with excellent qualities, the highest ranking servant of the state, on Javanese soil, in the city of the Buddha temple, built an amazingly beautiful temple, to guide his parents and kin from the sublunary existence to the joys of nirvana. (Kozok and Reijn 2010, p. 139)

Kozok and Reign also suggested that, since the inscription (fig. 87) was written in Sanskrit, it is perhaps another indication of the patronage of Ādityavarman. The translation is somewhat ambiguous, however. Kṛtanāgara consecrated Caṇḍi Jago in 1280 to honour his father Visnuvardhana (Miksic and Goh 2017, p. 473). It is possible that Ādityavarman also built a separate shrine for Mañjuśrī Arapacana at the Jago site that now no longer exists. The original location of Mañjuśrī is unknown. The figures associated with the Amoghapāśa, however, have all been allocated positions on the upper levels of Caṇḍi Jago, so this information helps us to determine the original location for Mañjuśrī Arapacana as he is a man with an unusual manner of tying his hair.

Lunsingh Scheurleer hypothesises that "a Mañjuśrī statue is entitled to a separate shrine, and the statue seems to be rather small for this large building. If at Caṇḍi Jago, it must have been housed in a separate shrine in the compound" (2008, p. 296). Stamford Raffles suggested that Mañjuśrī would have been placed in a *cella* or niche on an elevated terrace about twelve feet tall (1817, vol. 2, p. 45) as the statue is set against a backslab, therefore a separate shrine or platform would seem to be appropriate.

Figure 86 Mañjuśrī Arapacana, dedicated in 1265 and inscribed in 1343 CE, Caṇḍi Jago. State Hermitage Museum, St Petersburg (in storage). Acquired in 1945 from Museum für Völkerkunde, Berlin. 1m, andesite stone. Inv. no. BD-610.

Various historical sources inform us that most of the highest honorary positions would have been filled by the king's relatives (Kozok and Reijn 2010, pp. 139–41). In 1343, Ādityavarman ordered the building of a "amazingly beautiful temple" to house the beautiful statue of Mañjuśrī according to the rules to foster *dharma* (the law and true faith in the Buddhist sense) (ibid., p. 143; Schnitger 1937, p. 9).

It is unknown, however, whether the statue was meant to be placed at Caṇḍi Jago or in its own pavilion, as there appear to be two completely different dedications written in different hands at different times. The sculpture is dedicated to commemorate the year Ādityavarman spent at court in East Java. This Sumatran prince who would later become King Ādityavarman (r. *c.*1347–79) returned to Sumatra and set up court in the Tanah Datar region of West Sumatra. He became the spiritual father of

Figure 87 Mañjuśrī Arapacana, inscriptions on the front and reverse of the backplate. Both inscriptions are dated 1343.

Figure 88 Mañjuśrī Arapacana, drawing of the textile pattern.

the Kingdom of Minangkabau. The statue was probably carved sometime after the consecration of Caṇḍi Jago in 1260, but before the dedication in the inscriptions of 1343. The statue should be dated, therefore, to a date not related to the temple at Jago but rather to his stylistic features, placing him closer to the earlier period of somewhere between 1260 and 1280 rather than the later date of the inscription. Based on stylistic similarities, the statue fits more closely with the attendants of Amoghapāśa, which are dated to between 1268 and 1280.

Mañjuśrī displays the most unusual textile pattern (fig. 88) on his carved *sinjang*, which perhaps suggests an earlier period in Asian history. The *sinjang* is held with a metal belt tied around the waist and can be seen behind the folded ankles. Here the *sinjang* finishes with delicate folds lying on the lotus cushion, with the fabric clinging to the legs. The pattern of roundels is in near-perfect condition and carved in deep relief, which might indicate a sophisticated woven brocade fabric.

Externally braced body tension looms, used by most Austronesian cultures, were known in Java at this time. Using such a loom, it would have been possible to weave a brocade type of fabric with the supplementary weft needed for this kind of pattern. The loom, or *pacadaran*, must have had a discontinuous warp that would have allowed for the use of a reed, or *suri*, required to produce a complex or brocade fabric (Christie 1993a, p. 14). Chris Buckley and Eric Boudout suggest that a reed was used on an ancestral loom with an elevated fixed frame (2015, p. 408). Christie has also commented that Sung Chinese reports from the eleventh century confirm that the Javanese were producing and weaving their own silk as well as importing threads from China. They were also making cloth that the Chinese classed as brocades and damask (Christie 1993b, pp. 188–89). The delicate and very unusual textile border pattern carved along the lower edge depicts pearl arches, candles and vegetal motifs. The body has been delicately modelled and carved with some unique features, including the design on the *sinjang* and its border, and the sophisticated pattern representing a series of roundels with triple outer bands. The pattern constitutes juxtaposing circles with motifs representing three different animals, both real and imagined. The animals appear to emerge from scrolling vegetation within each circle, which is reminiscent of Chinese cloud or rock patterns, and perhaps is also reminiscent of the carved roundels at Caṇḍi Lorong Jongorrang and at Caṇḍi Kidal (fig. 89).

The vegetal patterns take the form of part of the "recalcitrant spiral"—so named by F.D.K. Bosch. What we see in these roundels though is just the leaf part of the spiral vine—the complete spiral can be seen on some temple walls in Central Java. One roundel contains a clear and accurate depiction of an elephant. Elephants were known in Java, as they appear depicted in the relief panels at Caṇḍi Borobudur in many

Figure 89 Relief carving on the walls of Caṇḍi Kidal, commemorated to King Anuṣapati (r. 1227–48). The *caṇḍi* was completed in 1260 in time for the *śraddha* ceremony of King Anuṣapati, who was enshrined there as Śiva. Pullen photo.

fables that show the elephant as the future Buddha incarnated. None of the Central Javanese depictions, however, show the elephant in quite the same fashion as the roundel here does. The second roundel shows a dragon or griffin looking backwards and breathing fire, which curls into the roundel pattern.[3] The third roundel shows a mythical creature with wide open jaws and large teeth, and with his body emanating from the scrolling vegetation. This, I propose, could represent a mythical creature or the pseudo-*simurgh*—often referred to as a senmurv in current literature[4]—or possibly a representation of a *makara*.[5] It is most likely to be a local Javanese interpretation of such a mythical creature depicted on an imported textile. Within the interstices of each circle is a triangular outline carved with two different designs. These delicately carved patterns are placed around a central circle surrounded by petals to make a flower. The second pattern has a square centre surrounded by a square pattern. Overlaying the *sinjang* is a plain double sash (fig. 90), the ends of which are carved with a simple design of lines and circles and hang to the side of the body where they are tied in an overly large bow.

There are no known contemporary Indonesian textiles that replicate this pattern. The design perhaps came from China and drew on Indo-Persian roots, as suggested by the motifs. A textile bearing the pattern could have arrived with traders from China or with Arab traders from Persia. Another example from the mural paintings and relief architecture at Pagan (fig. 91) shows a direct influence of Pāla art. The temples at

Figure 90 Mañjuśrī Arapacana, detail of the sash tied on the right side of the body.

Figure 91 Relief architecture at Pagan. Pullen photo.

Pagan from the eleventh and twelfth centuries display Tantric features as a result of relations and marital links between the rulers of Pagan and those of Bengal. These features indicate how the influence of models from Bihar and Bengal had a direct bearing on the Burmese temple paintings.

Other than the examples presented here, there is no concrete evidence to attribute the textile pattern on Mañjuśrī to the Indo-Persia realm. It is possible though that textile samples or knowledge of these patterns could have ended up in Java. Heller describes the movement of such designs: "from Persia to China, medallions of single or confronting animals with a pearl roundel were among the most popular designs of the period. The creatures were frequently imaginary or hybrid birds or animals" (Heller 1998, p. 183). Marianne Yaldiz has suggested that influences were felt from Gandhara to Sogdiana and to Xinjiang in China (Yaldiz 2006, pp. 94–95, fig. 61). And even though we have no examples from Tibet, Heller has suggested that no matter the source of inspiration for the textile pattern on Mañjuśrī, it is evident that in addition to the mural paintings of textiles made in Tibetan monasteries between the tenth and twelfth centuries, the popularity in Tibet of Sasanian roundel motifs that enclose both animals and geometric forms remained long after their initial importation (Heller 1998, p. 175).

In contrast to Mañjuśrī, the grey andesite statue of Pārvatī (fig. 92) and her retinue remains in situ at Caṇḍi Singosari. She stands stiff and upright with two broken upper hands. The lower hands are held together, possibly holding the *padma*, or lotus bud, in *dhyānamudrā*—a gesture of meditation. The belt or girdle displays a *kāla*-head buckle, from which pearl chains fall on the *sinjang*. The *sinjang*, depicted in the Javanese style, falls the length of the body; it has a neat fold at the front, with the lower edge appearing to undulate, perhaps suggesting a large amount of fabric. The shape of her body is only just evident beneath the material.

Figure 92 Pārvatī Retinue, early 14th century, Caṇḍi Singosari, Caṇḍi B (now vanished) grounds, East Java. 2.15 m, andesite. Pullen photo.

The surface of the stone is clearly exfoliated, leaving the pattern visible only on the centre panel. Here we see the roundels with double borders, and the interstices pattern is clearly visible, but it is only partially evident on the left side. Close examination of this intricate pattern suggests a motif of juxtaposing circles with double outer rings (fig. 10a, p. 37) that appear to contain zoomorphic figures (fig. 93). A small duck is distinguishable. A part also remains of what appears to be a four-legged animal, possibly a deer. Bautze-Picron has described a mural painting "in the Lokahteikpan (monument 1580) which can be ascribed to the early twelfth century, [where] Māyā wears a skirt with roundels alternatively adorned with flowers and *haṃsa*". She notes how such a motif appears again as an ornament pattern on a bodhisattva from Bengal, and which also occurs in a simplified form in a later Nandamanya-hpaya mural at Pagan (2014, p. 6). A goose or *haṃsa* motif is apparent carved on the cave pillars at Ajanta Cave 23. Along the lower edge of the *sinjang* appears a border carved with horizontal bands in a "teardrop" pattern. The plain double sashes are draped over the thighs, with the ends arranged in neat folds at the side of the body and tied in an overly large bow. The neck is decorated with a metal band. It should be mentioned that the sculptor has depicted the fall of the cloth, which has been arranged with consummate skill.

The textile examples presented here range in date from the sixth to the eleventh century. Following a careful and extensive study of textiles and paintings from India, Central Asia, Burma and China, it can be suggested that there are a number of examples that fit closely to the pattern on Pārvatī. These examples undoubtedly indicate that the sculptor of this unique pattern did not use a Javanese textile, but rather those from Central Asia or China.⁶ The delineation of a fowl within a roundel pattern, either woven in silk or block printed on cotton, appears on many different textiles and wall artwork, as textiles have for millennia been part of a tradition of gift giving and tribute and have been carried by traders to foreign lands.⁷ Even though

Figure 93 Pārvatī. Drawing of the textile pattern.

the duck with a feathered head as depicted in the roundel on Pārvatī is not apparent on any known Sasanian or Chinese examples, the concept of a duck or the goose (*haṃsa*) and other animals in roundels is clearly evident from India to Central Asia. The most obvious comparisons can be made with the mural paintings at Ajanta and the Taq-i Bustan rock carvings (figs. 94a–d). The next group of examples from India also depict geese (*haṃsa*) as a pattern on Indian cottons in the Newberry Collection, where a certain similarity to the duck or *haṃsa* motif can be seen in a number of examples of garments depicted in Jain Kalpasutra manuscripts (figs. 95a–b).

The *kāla*-head clasp, the depiction of the sash and the pattern of animal roundels on the *sinjang* all signal a closer similarity to the Singosari style classification. The textile pattern is closer to the variety of designs found in the Singosari period, as the core Majapahit sculptures all appear with a variation of the *kawung* motif. On this basis this sculpture will be classified as belonging to the Transition style. The remains of the lotus plant appear on each side of the accompanying acolytes, who stand in *añjalimudrā*. The two acolytes are adorned in a similar style to the central figure, but without the *kāla*-head belt. There appear to be faint markings of a similar textile pattern, but because of the extreme wear on the stone this is only apparent on first-hand inspection, and it is not detailed enough to replicate with a drawing.

Figure 94 Central Asia and India, 6th–7th century, examples of a fowl in wall paintings, textiles and carved in stone. **94a** Palace scene (detail), wall painting 5th–6th century, Ajanta cave 1. Reproduced from Madanjeet Singh, *India: Paintings from the Ajanta Caves* (New York 1954), pl. IV. **94b** Detail, relief of elephant rider, boar hunting relief, Taq-I Bustan. Reproduction after Karel Otavský, "Zur kunsthistorischen Einordnung der Stoffe", in *Entlang der Seidenstrasse. Frühmittelalterliche Kunst zwischen Persien und China in der Abegg-Stiftung*, Riggisberger Berichte 6, hrsg. von Karel Otavský, Abegg-Stiftung, 1998, fig. 66. **94c** Silk fabric with embroidered ducks, Abegg-Stiftung, Ch-3132 Riggisberg. Inv. no. 4902. © Abegg-Stiftung, CH-3132 Riggisberg, 2015 (photo: Christoph von Viràg). **94d** Textile sample (reconstruction), boar hunting relief, elephant rider, from Taq-I Bustan. © Abegg-Stiftung, CH-3132 Riggisberg, 2015 (drawing: Vendulka Otavská after Fukai Shinji and Horiuchi Kiyoharu, "Taq-i-Bustan. Vol. I Plates", The Tokyo University Iraq-Iran Archaeological Expedition Report 10, Tokyo 1969, pl. LI and LXV resp. XXXIX).

Figure 95 **95a** Textile fragment with *haṃsa*, or geese, and quatrefoils c.1400. Inv. no. EA 1990.807. ©Ashmolean Museum. **95b** Detail from the Kalpasutra Manuscript, Mahavira Distributes Wealth: Folio from a Kalpasutra Manuscript,1461. The Met Museum of Art, New York. Rogers Fund 1918, 11.1x 25.7cm. Inv. no. 18.104.7.

Complex "Brocade" and Skull Motifs

The *Tantu Panggelaran*, a late East Javanese text from the sixteenth century, mentions a group of gods in a Śaiva temple. Evidence taken from existing Śaivite temples built throughout the Classical Period include sculptures such as the next group of four sculptures. The four all originate from Caṇḍi A or the Tower Temple at Caṇḍi Singosari, and they all now reside in the RV.

Figure 96 Durgā Mahiṣāsuramardinī, c.1292, Caṇḍi Singosari, Tower temple, Caṇḍi A, Malang, East Java. Volkenkunde, Leiden. Collection Nationaal Museum van Wereldculturen. Inv. no. RV-1403-1622. 1.57 m, andesite stone.

The smooth pale grey statue of Durgā Mahiṣāsuramardinī (fig. 96) is one of a kind. The goddess stands with her legs wide apart and her knees slightly bent astride the buffalo demon Mahiśa. Her stance could be described as "dramatic and defiant". The statue is decorated with elaborately carved ornaments, including a conical headdress *kirītamukuta*. The top two levels of this are inset with a motif of a sizeable skull with teeth that appears to bite into the crescent moon. Her body possesses a fleshy naturalism, with a soft swelling belly—a new phenomenon in Javanese sculpture. There is some damage to the upper arms, nose and

Figure 97 Drawing of the upper body and of the jacket textile pattern; Persimmon motif in *songket*. Textile Museum, Kuala Lumpur. Pullen photo.

lower right leg. Most of the backslab is missing. The andesite stone shows many inclusions and is worn in places.

Durgā is adorned with a double necklet, large and heavy ear ornaments, large upper armbands and bracelets, and snake ornaments encircle her ankles. Her hair falls in long braided curls. The *upavīta* is carved in the image of a thick snake that appears on the multiple belts on her belly, where the head and tail come together. Her upper body is dressed with a decorated jacket that is carved with a clear pattern of stylized lotus flower motifs or rosettes. The model consists of rounded and pointed petals, with a triangular vegetal design filling the interstices between the circles. The border at the top and bottom of the jacket has a pattern representing a series of small motifs that appear as a cross-section of the *kapāla*. The persimmon theme taken from a present-day Malay *songket* (fig. 97) shows a similarity to the structure of the jacket pattern, perhaps highlighting the longevity of this type of weave and patterning. The *kapāla* or skull in Sanskrit represented the skull cup or human head used as a ritual implement. The term "brainpan" describes the object held in the hand of the Gaṇeśa during the Singhasāri period, which has been described as a "demonic feature" (Pott 1962, p. 131). The *kapāla* pattern on the border of the jacket is a motif that also appears as part of a relief pattern on the upper walls of Caṇḍi Kidal *c.*1260[8] (fig. 98).

Figure 98 Detail of relief architecture on Caṇḍi Kidal. Pullen photo.

Wrapped around the lower half of the body is an elaborately decorated *sinjang* consisting of two cloths, with the lower *sinjang* overlaid by a shorter fabric. The shape of the body beneath is clearly revealed. The *sinjang* is carved with a lotus-flower theme set within a geometric scheme known as *rantai*, which is another idea that is reflected in present-day Malay *songket* textile patterns (Pullen 2013, p. 12). The alternant motif recalls a stylized head shape carved upside down. The addition of the inverted head motif is not random but appears this way all over the cloth. It is not possible to account for why the heads are placed this way other than to please Durgā herself (fig. 99). The shorter fabric is carved with a similar pattern as on the jacket. Both are decorated with a border incorporating the *kapāla* form interspersed with four small squares within vertical bands. The lower body garment is held up with a plain cloth belt, the ends of which drape on to the thighs with elaborately carved tassels that are suggestive of gold work decoration. The costume is completed with two sashes (fig. 100) draped over her legs carved with a *bunga bintang* or star motif, a pattern that continues today in Malay *songket* designs. The sash ends are tied at each side in a large bow.

The precision with which the textiles have been carved mean that the designs are unlikely to have been an invention of the sculptor's imagination and are more likely to have replicated a cloth that existed at the time. The delineation of stars and rosettes set within chains is reflected in *songket* textiles (fig. 101a and 101b) originating from Palembang in Sumatra. There are also remarkable parallels with a number of the *batik kraton* at the Danar Hadi and Galerie Batik Kuno in Surakarta. These similarities indicate the longevity and continued popularity of such patterns in Java, Sumatra and the Malay Peninsula.

Kediri and Singhasāri   **155**

Figure 99 Durgā, detail of the lower leg, showing the upper cloth and the *sinjang*. Drawing of the textile pattern on the *sinjang*.

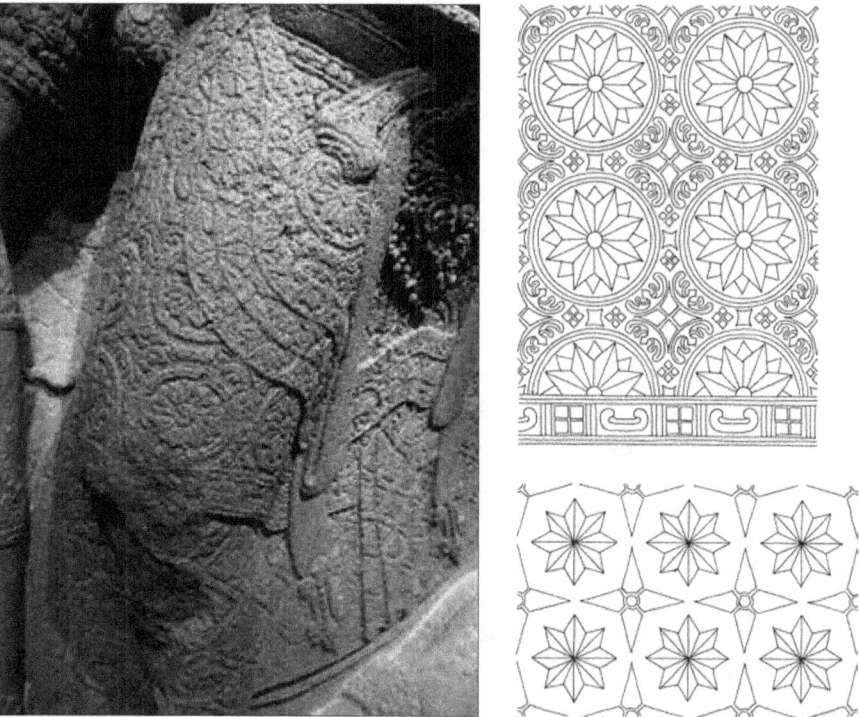

Figure 100 Durgā, detail of the short cloth and over sash. Pullen photo. Drawing of the textile patterns.

Figure 101 **101a** Detail of a *kain songket limar*, Palembang, South Sumatra, 200 years old. Private collection. **101b** Detail of a *seléndang songket limar*, Palembang, South Sumatra, 20th century. Private collection

The carving of Nandīśvara (fig. 102) is of a similar quality to that of Durgā and of the following statue of Mahākāla. Nandīśvara is the principle form of Śiva as the benign door guardian (Blom 1939, p. 51). He is standing to attention as would a guardian, in an upright position with his feet together. His ornaments are few but are carved in great detail. There is a broad, jewelled band around his head, with the ribbons carved on to the backslab, which is a feature typical of east Javanese sculptures of this period. The earrings, neckband and upper arm bands suggest gold jewellery work. A broad, plain *seléndang* is clearly draped over the upper body and marked with a single line through the middle, with the end depicted over the left breast. The carving of the garments on this statue can undoubtedly be attributed to a similar hand to those of the other sculptures in this group.

Nandīśvara wears a sleeveless jacket and a *sinjang*. The jacket is delineated with a central line and is adorned with the pattern of an eight-petal "daisy" flower set within horizontal and vertical *rantai* or chains. The stylistic grammar of this pattern is reflected in a popular motif illustrated in Malay *songket* textiles known as *bunga kemunting Cina* (Chinese rose myrtle). The term *bunga teluk berantai*—in chained bays—also describes the overall *bunga* or flower within the pattern. This striking pattern has been in existence since the early twentieth century. An example of such a *songket*[9] textile (fig. 103) exhibits a pattern that clearly reflects the design on the sculpture, suggesting that this statue is the earliest evidence of this kind of textile construction in East Java. The mangosteen and its imitation textile pattern can also be attributed as a likely influence behind the six- to eight-petal rosette flower. The pattern has a small rhomboid-shaped centre around which are arranged eight solid circles representing the corolla of the mangosteen fruit (*Garcinia mangostana*) (Selvanayagam 1990, pp. 77, 189–90).

Kediri and Singhasāri 157

Figure 102 Nandīśvara, c.1292, Caṇḍi Singosari, Tower temple, Caṇḍi A, Malang, East Java. Volkenkunde, Leiden. Collection Nationaal Museum van Wereldculturen. Inv. no. RV-1403-1624. 1.7 m, andesite stone. Detail of the upper body. Drawing of the torso jacket.

Figure 103 Detail of the jacket textile pattern. Detail of a *kain songket*, Palembang, c.1920. Pullen collection.

The *sinjang* (fig. 104) on the lower body falls stiffly to the ankles. It has a pleated central panel. The form of the body is not revealed beneath, which suggests a more substantial material. The *kawung* pattern[10] appears with two different designs that radiate in vertical bands. In this version, the emphasis is on the star-shaped central pattern rather than the plain vesica. A plain sash is draped over the *sinjang* in two sections. It falls naturally over the lower legs and is gathered up and tied at the side in a large bow and in front of the body into a huge knot.[11] This sculpture proves a valuable contribution as a template for textile patterns that are depicted in *songket* textiles today. Examples of this rosette flower pattern are also represented in a fragment of lampas silk dated to the thirteenth century, as seen in the David Collection, Copenhagen.

The carving in figure 105 depicts Mahākāla as Śiva's fierce door guardian in his second principle form, known as the Destroyer (Blom 1939, p. 51). His distinguishing features are his flaring hair, goatee beard, bulging eyes and large belly. He holds a sword and a club. His open stance is marginally more aggressive than that of his partner Nandīśvara. He is also dressed in a sleeveless jacket (fig. 106) that joins at the front and he wears a short hip wrapper. The pattern on the jacket is carved in deep relief in horizontal bands set within a rope design with alternating circles of scrolling leaves, or the leaves from a recalcitrant spiral motif (Hoop 1949, p. 272), along with a lotus with eight-pointed petals. This style of the lotus is a naturalistic or conventionalized disk form, which

Figure 104 Nandīśvara, depiction of the lower limbs, indicating the sash tied with a large knot. Drawing of the textile pattern.

is a popular motif in many areas of Mahāyāna Buddhism, and is a pattern that is very similar in construction to that on Mahākāla. The design also recalls Tibetan stylistic norms, as with the carved textile patterns on a clay statue of Buddha Amoghasiddhi from Kyangbu in Tibet dated to the eleventh century[12] (Fischer 1997, p. 140; Maxwell 2003, p. 128, fig. 78). Despite the earlier date, Mahākāla highlights the continuity of these textile patterns.

This sculpture and the others in the destroyed temple indicate the artistic achievements and the assimilation of foreign influences that eventually led to a cohesive Tibetan style. Another such Tibetan example from 1328 is an Esoteric Buddhist *maṇḍala* woven in silk tapestry, or *kesi* (Clunas 1997, p. 122, fig. 60). The background motif on the *maṇḍala* visibly depicts a series of meandering vines and lotus flowers[13] that is remarkably similar to the pattern on the jacket of Mahākāla.

Figure 105 Mahākāla, c.1292, Caṇḍi Singosari, Tower Temple, Caṇḍi A, Malang, East Java. Volkenkunde, Leiden. Collection Nationaal Museum van Wereldculturen. Inv. no. RV-1403-1623. 1.7m, andesite stone.

Mahākāla is also dressed in a short hip wrapper (fig. 107) tied with a long cloth belt. The long cloth is folded over and tucked in at the front of the body to the right. The sash is then tied off in a large bow at the rear of the figure, shown on the backslab of the body. Here the sash (fig. 108) appears carved with the loose end looping over the front on both sides, falling to the edge of the short *kain*. The *kain* falls to the knees with a small pleat at the front and is carved with a *kawung* pattern with differing central motifs and three different border patterns. One interpretation of the border pattern is that it represents a simplified *banji* (fig. 109). The *banji* motif is derived from the swastika, a theme associated with many different countries. In India it is the symbol of Viṣṇu and Śiva, while in China it is closely associated with Buddhism. The *banji* pattern used in Indonesia is probably the oldest known pattern from the Chinese word ban, meaning ten, and *ji*, meaning thousand, and

160 Patterned Splendour

Figure 106 Mahākāla, detail of the upper body jacket. Drawing of the textile pattern. Pullen photo.

was believed by the Chinese to come directly from heaven. The motif could easily have been imported from India during this period. In Java today, the *banji* motif is seen as an old and very traditional batik motif (Warming and Garwoski 1981, p. 172). The swastika pattern (fig. 153, p. 205) is also apparent on the *kain* border of Harihara Ardhanari, now in the State Hermitage Museum (SHM).

The border pattern on the sash of Mahākāla is decorated with horizontal lines depicted on the folded ends at the rear of the body. The long cloth belt pattern shows a stylized flower in a repeated square motif. The pattern on the *kain* exhibits two bold designs: the focus on the circle of the four vesicae motifs, and the points touching to make up the circle. The artist has carved the pattern on the sash across the hips and has taken into account the fact that the design on the cloth is

Figure 107 Mahākāla, detail of the sash around the waist. Pullen photo. Drawing of the textile pattern.

folded and can only be seen in parts. The textile, known as *gěringsing* (fig. 110), is woven here with a pattern called *gěringsing pepare*. The *gěringsing* textile appears very similar to the pattern of the cloth replicated on Mahākāla (fig. 109). Indeed, this figure could be depicted with an early version of a *gěringsing* hip cloth.[14]

The carvings in deep relief on a pale, smooth andesite stone allows for precise interpretation of textile patterns and ornaments. It is entirely possible therefore that the sculptors were replicating textiles that were in existence at the time, as is evident from the diversification of the patterns. The study of these textiles has contributed to our knowledge of textiles that were either in production at the time, such as the *songket* patterns, or that were brought in as valued textiles and interpreted and replicated on the statues.

The first known inscription issued by King Kṛtanāgara, known as the *Sarwadharma* charter, and dated to 31 October 1269, is seen as a proclamation of his programme at the beginning of his reign, in which he intended to continue the policies his father had established. As a token of the temple priests' loyalty, it was written that they would not be liable for fines for using and wearing certain ornaments and cloths. The *Sarwadharma* charter ends with a homage to Śiva alone, and it seems to be of purely Śaivite origin (Sidomulyo 2010, p. 23). The dating of this charter to one year after Kṛtanāgara came to the throne appears to signal a shift in the stylistic interpretation of the types and styles of the

Figure 108 Mahākāla, detail of the lower limbs showing the *kain*. Pullen photo. Drawing of the textile pattern.

sculptures produced and hints at his predilection for Buddhism, which is taken from the inscription of *Dharmāśraya* (Padang Arcā) (ibid., p. 23). The change is evident in the shift we see in the increase in textiles types and in the elaborate patterns carved on the statues.

Blom has suggested that the three figures of Durgā, Nandīśvara and Mahākāla were the "present *kotangs* of the *kraton padjurits* of Jogjakarta and Surakarta". This term probably represents the prototype of the present-day guards of the *kraton*. The actual meaning, however, of the term *kotang* is of a brassier—the term used for a service jacket. Jákl and Hoogervorst use the term *kalambi/klambi* describing it as "the neutral word for a 'shirt, jacket'" (Jákl and Hoogervorst 2017, p. 215). These terms are interchangeable, but as we have no extant examples of these jackets, we do have the statues as representations. The statues are best described therefore as protective guardians, for, if the ashes of Kṛtanāgara were interred at the Tower Temple, then they would have been suitably guarded

Figure 109 Detail of the right leg showing the looped sash. Pullen photo. Drawing of the textile pattern.

by these images of the gods in "military jackets" as part of the entourage of the king (Blom 1939, p. 132). This does not explain though why each "guardian" wore a different dress depicted with different patterns, when guards are generally dressed the same.[15]

A question that arises with respect to the textile patterns is, do they represent tantric iconography? The patterns on both Śaivite and Buddhist sculptures originating from Caṇḍi Singosari would indeed appear to offer sufficient evidence of a Javanese version of tantric practice. Lunsingh Scheurleer suggests that a skull is a tantric attribute, with the images

Figure 110 *Gĕringsing pepare*, double ikat textile from Tenganan, Karangasem, Bali, 20th century. Hand-spun cotton, natural dyes. Private collection.

of Gaṇeśa seated on heads being an indication of the cremation ground (Lunsingh Scheurleer 1998, pp. 4–5). These unusual tantric or esoteric depictions on some of the textile patterns could well have been a result of the unusually devout religious affiliations of Kṛtanāgara. During the latter half of the king's life, he adopted the name Śiva-Buddha, as seen in the *Nāg.* (43:5) (Robson and Prapanca 1995, p. 56; Casparis 1983, p. 16). The term is best described in the *Sutasoma*. But, as Hunter suggests, in "terms of religious praxis we are not looking at a merger of religious establishments or a complete synthesis of religious doctrines, that has often been put forward as a characteristic of East Javanese religion" (2007, p. 33).

This merger of religious establishments was evident in the period. The description of Kṛtanāgara as Śiva-Buddha[16] and the idea of a syncretic fusion of religions in the Singhasāri period is apparent in the image of Kṛtanāgara undertaking initiations as Akṣobhya and as Bhairava. To illustrate this further, the work of Kate O'Brien on the *Sutasoma* explains the unique concept of kingship that emerges from the text; for example, the Buddhist ideal that substantiates the divine nature of a king as the incarnation of Buddha. These have far-reaching implications for our understanding of Kṛtanāgara's kingship (O'Brien and Mpu 2008, p. 3).

Another inscription, the Mūla-Mulurung charter,[17] refers to rituals connected to the traditions of royalty. The early rulers of Tumapĕl (the capital of Singhasāri) carried on the traditions of their predecessors at Kediri. Hadi Sidomulyo describes "irrefutable evidence for a major shift in the religious orientation of the royal line of East Java sometime after 1255" (Sidomulyo 2010, p. 22). Revolutionary changes were introduced following the accession of Kṛtanāgara in 1254, although what these might have been and when they were implemented are unknown. It is quite likely however that the changes were influenced by the threat posed by Kublai Khan, and they should probably be linked in part to this threat (ibid., p. 22). The charter is important for the new light it sheds on the history of the Singhasāri period.

Efforts by Kṛtanāgara to ensure an enduring legacy have left an indelible footprint (Hunter 2007, pp. 52–53)—one that is above all characterized by the wide variety of sculptures and their diverse array of textile patterns. If the ashes of Kṛtanāgara were indeed interred at the Tower Temple, they have never been found. The Singosari temple was erected as a memorial to the dead rather than as a funerary monument:

> Ruins of seven or eight stone temples stood around a palace square or *alun-alun* in the nineteenth century, but only one survives today, and it is unfinished. The remaining temple on the site is now called Caṇḍi Singosari. It resembles Kidal in its general plan and cross-section, but is larger. The superstructure was never finished. It is possible that it was under construction when Kṛtanāgara was assassinated.... An inscription of 1351 reports that a shrine was built to commemorate the *risi* who were slaughtered along with Kṛtanāgara. (Miksic and Goh 2017, pp. 462–80)

The sudden death of the king appeared to result in a swift end to the production of statues. The royal atelier perhaps continued to produce sculptures in a similar style, however, such as the remainder of the sculptures at Caṇḍi Singosari that did not originate from the Tower Temple. In some cases we have no confirmation of the exact dating for some of the statues in this chapter, with only the type and style of the textile patterns on the sculptures to place them in a certain period.

The two seated Gaṇeśa that I will discuss next also originated from Caṇḍi Singosari. The first of these, which now stands in the RV (fig. 111), is the fourth statue to originate from Caṇḍi A or the Tower Temple. Figures of Gaṇeśa appeared in many forms during the Hindu-Buddhist periods of Java, but, stylistically and by size, they appear to have reached their peak during the Singhasāri period. Sedyawati suggests there seems to be a wider variety of "art" styles associated with the religion in the Singhasāri period; however, there is generally a single predominating formulation of traits—that of Gaṇeśa with skulls (1994, pp. 255–56). In this example, Gaṇeśa is seated with his right leg raised and his left leg placed flat on the base. His two lower arms carry the *kapāla* or skull cup. The statue appears on a large cushion of realistically carved skulls. The sun and moon appear within his headdress, at the top of the backslab. A full-page very realistic drawing of Gaṇeśa is in the *Raffles History of Java*, volume II, on the inside front cover.

The Gaṇeśa wears extravagant jewellery, including the *upavīta*, a patterned upper-body garment and trousers or *lañciṅan* covered by a

Figure 111 Gaṇeśa, c.1292, Caṇḍi Singosari, Tower Temple, Caṇḍi A, Malang, East Java. Volkenkunde, Leiden. Collection Nationaal Museum van Wereldculturen 1.54 m, andesite stone. Inv. no. RV 1403-1681.

second short cloth finishing at the knees. The *lañcinan* perhaps denotes "soldier's trousers" or a form of warrior's lower garment, an element of battle dress (Jákl 2016, p. 189), as befits the status of Gaṇeśa in his context at Caṇḍi Singosari. A plain *seléndang* is hidden across the upper body, with the flap appearing on the left shoulder just visible beneath the skull ear ornament. The carving of the pattern is identical to that on the same garment on the previous statues of Mahākāla and Nandīśvara. The *udharabhanda*, or stomach band, consists of hinged metal plaques with a pattern of adjoining peepul leaf (*ficus religiosa*) ornaments, the design of which is reflected in the remainder of the adornments. The garments are arranged in three parts. The sleeveless jacket covers the upper body and finishes at the *udharabhanda*. Its pattern is carved on a horizontal axis and depicts a large square design with a flower with four pointed petals surrounded by a circular repeat pattern set within a square motif. The border is ornamented with a pattern of lappets or downwards lotus petals[18] (fig. 112).

The stylistic grammar of the decoration would suggest an embroidered or a brocade fabric such as a *songket*.

On closer inspection the lower garment can be seen to be depicted as a form of trousers (fig. 113), proven by the fact there are no folds of the cloth apparent on the lotus cushion. This cloth is carved with a design of skulls set on a diagonal axis, with a forward-facing head alternating with a pattern of "one-eyed *kāla*-head[s]" (Lunsingh Scheurleer 1998, p. 192).

Figure 112 Gaṇeśa, drawing of the jacket textile.

Figure 113 Gaṇeśa, detail of the trouser pattern on the right leg garment. Pullen photo. Drawing of the textile pattern.

168 Patterned Splendour

Figure 114 Gaṇeśa, detail of the skull motif on the upper of the left leg garment. Drawing of the textile pattern.

Figure 115 Gaṇeśa, c.1292, Caṇḍi Singosari, Caṇḍi D, then moved to the *alun-alun*, Malang, East Java. National Museum, Bangkok. 1.70m, andesite stone. Inv. no. SR1V1J01.

Kediri and Singhasāri   169

A short cloth (fig. 114) is on the upper thighs and carved with a design of confronting stylized *kāla* heads. It is finished with a border pattern of a *kapāla* motif set between double lines. The extensive sash is tied at each side and drapes over the ankles on the left side falling over the skull base.

The next statue of Gaṇeśa (fig. 115) remains at the Bangkok Museum. It could be considered a matching partner of the previous figure of Gaṇeśa, although no evidence has surfaced of its possible location, and the figure

Figure 116 Gaṇeśa, detail of the jacket. Pullen photo. Drawing of the textile pattern.

Figure 117 Gaṇeśa, details of the trouser on the right leg. Pullen photo. Drawing of the textile pattern.

170 Patterned Splendour

Figure 118 Gaṇeśa, detail of the left thigh. Pullen photo. Drawing of the textile pattern.

Figure 119 One-eyed *kāla*, part of a stone relief or lintel. Trowulan Museum, Trowulan, East Java. Pullen photo.

 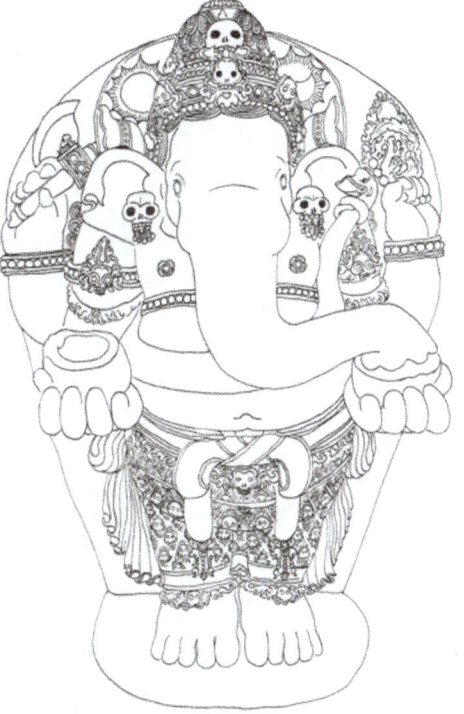

Figure 120 Karangkates Gaṇeśa, Desa Sumber Pucung, near Karangkates, East Java (in situ on a concrete platform in the open air) *c.*1300. 2.7m, andesite stone. Pullen photo. Drawing of the sculpture.

Figure 121 Karangkates Gaṇeśa, detail of the lower right leg. Pullen photo. Drawing of the textile pattern.

does differ in a number of ways. His posture and attributes are the same as the RV Gaṇeśa but his apparel is depicted with different patterns. The sleeveless jacket (fig. 116) is defined by a repeated decoration of a large square design on the horizontal axis, which encompasses a four-petal flower surrounded by a scrolling circular motif set within a square grid. Again, as with the previous statue, this was probably intended to represent a brocaded or embroidered fabric. The trousers (fig. 117) exhibit a decoration carved with skulls placed on the diagonal axis. The forward-facing skull motif alternates with a pattern of a "one-eyed *kāla* head". The depiction of the skull is identified by the long upward-thrusting tusks, and the one-eyed *kāla* head by the protruding teeth. The border pattern consists of four-petal flowers interspersed with four leaves, around which are placed on each quadrant a *kapāla*-shaped motif. The short upper cloth is carved with only a one-eyed *kāla* head engraved in two different ways, with each head set within a double border creating squares on the diagonal. The border (fig. 118) comprises a *kapāla* motif interspersed with an eight-petal rosette, over which the sash appears on the thighs and finishes in a large knot, with the ends draped to the ankles.

The textile patterns on both Gaṇeśa depict esoteric iconography in the form of skulls and one-eyed *kāla* heads. Lunsingh Scheurleer has described these four sculptures that originated from Caṇḍi Singosari as part of a tantric circle. Despite some of them appearing with demonic characteristics, it has been suggested that this demonic iconography would have had other meanings in association with the many ancient aspects of the Indonesian people, such as headhunting, ancestors, fertility and the concept of regeneration (Juni 1998, pp. 15–16). It is my opinion, though, that the overt depiction of skulls and *kāla*-head patterns are an iconographic representation of the heightened tantric activity initiated by King Kṛtanāgara.

Evidence of a number of carvings of one-eyed *kāla* heads (fig. 119) would suggest that the stone in the Trowulan Museum is testament to an evolution of this style. Lunsingh Scheurleer suggests that in East Java there was a "demonization" of the skull and *kāla* motif (1998, p. 192). The *kāla*-head motif appeared by the thirteenth century to have evolved to be represented eventually as a one-eyed *kāla* head, as seen at Trowulan. Willem Sutterheim, Bernet Kempers and Lunsingh Scheurleer have all discussed the evolution of the *kāla*-head motif (Stutterheim 1929, fig. 11; Bernet Kempers 1959, figs. 315–16; Lunsingh Scheurleer 1998, p. 192). Unfortunately, we have no context or answers as to how these large, one-eyed *kāla* of stone were used or placed, and there is no clear answer as to how or why this style developed. Bernet Kempers discusses the variables of the *kāla*-head features, asking how the fangs and the horns extended and why only one eye remained. Solar connections are perhaps plausible, resulting in the development of the cyclops-type one-eyed *kāla*, where possibly the single eye represents the sight of the sun. Indeed, with the development of the Singosari sculptures, we see a flowering of this unusual rendition of the *kāla* head in the textile patterns on the statues.

The monumental stone statue known as Karangkates Gaṇeśa (fig. 120) stands against a backslab carved with the sun and moon. Gaṇeśa is placed on a lotus base set within a platform of a row of nine large skulls. The statue and the base are made from two different types of stone. Considering that the figure remains outside without any cover, it appears in near perfect condition.

Gaṇeśa is richly arrayed with rather simple yet beautifully executed and carved ornaments. As with all the Singosari Gaṇeśa, the snake *upavīta* is apparent around his waist as a belt. It has a foliate design and a small skull for the buckle—a feature unique to this Gaṇeśa. His *sinjang* falls to the ankles, low cut under his copious belly. The outline of his legs are clearly visible. The pattern on his *sinjang* is carved in a very different fashion to those of the previous Gaṇeśa, and it seems finely incised in low relief with a design of skulls set in a diagonal axis. The traditional skull motif (fig. 121) of Śiva is depicted with a crescent moon; in this case, however, the moon now resembles fangs (Lunsingh Scheurleer 1998, p. 192) that curl up each side of the skull—a pattern known as *candrakapāla*. The double sash lies over the lower part of the legs, where considerable attention is paid to the sizeable and elaborate bow. The bow tied at the side of the body finishes with a particular flourish, with the two ends falling to the ankles. The carving of the pattern is in shallow relief compared to that of the previous Gaṇeśa, and it appears to be considerably worn. I propose that this thinly incised skull pattern set within a triangle differs only slightly to that on the *sinjang*; it is not well-defined enough though to be able to create a drawing. The *candrakapāla*[19] patterning of the *sinjang* is very similar in design and carving to the next sculpture of a monumental Mahākāla (fig. 122), which is now in the MNI. The key difference, however, lies in the carving of the skull motif.[20]

As Lunsingh Scheurleer has suggested, the term *candrakapāla* was perhaps known in the Central Javanese period. But, as the term does not appear in the Old Javanese dictionary translated by Petrus Zoetmulder in 1972, there is little evidence of such knowledge (Lunsingh Scheurleer 2013, p. 25). The *kāla*-head motif used over doorways is an entirely separate motif from the skull-on-crescent-moon depicted on images of Śiva and Gaṇeśa, differing in both form and function. By the East Java period, however, they had more or less come together with other motifs and were being used in a completely different way. In East Java the skull motifs have gained teeth and bite into the crescent moon below, and the moon has become so elongated that it has become tusks. No images of Śiva were produced in this period, but this iconic image now adorns other gods in East Java; for example, the Durgā from Caṇḍi Singosari and a number of the Gaṇeśa. This motif also takes on a different form, depicted as a one-eyed *kāla* head carved into the textile patterns of the two Gaṇeśa (figs. 111 and 115) from Caṇḍi Singosari (ibid., pp. 22–25).

The drawing that accompanies this statue reveals an otherwise invisible pattern that indicates the importance of the *candrakapāla* motif in

Figure 122 Mahākāla, attributed to Ādityavarman, 14th century, Padang Roco, Sungai Langsat, West Sumatra. Museum Nasional Indonesia. 4.14 m, sandstone. Inv. No. 6470. Pullen photo.

Figure 123
Mahākāla, detail of the right side *kain*. Pullen photo. Drawing of the textile pattern.

East Java in this period. Two further examples can be seen on two stone inscriptions, or *prasasti*, dated from the earlier Kediri period of 1120 CE. They were both commissioned by King Bameswara.[21]

Among the highlights in the MNI is the monumental figure of Mahākāla shown in figure 122. It is carved of a smooth, pale andesite stone. The figure does not originate from Java but from Sumatra. This statue has been included to highlight a certain similarity with other sculptures in the two textile patterns on his *kain* and sash. This is the only sculpture from Sumatra that portrays any form of tantric iconography, which can be seen in the motifs on his short *kain*.

A brief historical background for this sculpture will support the connections with the Singhasāri ruler Visnuvardhana (r. 1248–68). Before his death, Visnuvardhana had appointed his son Krtanāgara as heir, and by the end of his life in 1268 he had transferred all his powers to his son. He abdicated and became a hermit (Krom 1926, p. 463). His son Krtanāgara then laid the foundations for the following Majapahit period (Tarling 1992, p. 215). By the year 1275, both Palembang and Malayu Jambi[22] in Sumatra had become the target of Krtanāgara's expansionist policies. He launched what was known as the *Pamelayu* expedition to Jambi, where his Javanese soldiers claimed suzerainty of South Sumatra (Munoz 2006, p. 261; Kulke 1991, p. 18; Schnitger 1937, p. 8; Hall 1981, p. 72; Bade 2002, p. 34). The figure of Mahākāla is thought to represent the first king of the Minangkabau, Ādityawarman, who was likely the patron of this sculpture. It is believed that whilst he was a youth at the Majapahit court he became acquainted with the Bhairava sect. In 1370 CE, after he had moved to Sumatra, he was initiated as a Bhairava (Schnitger 1937, p. 8). At a discussion at SOAS, University of London in September 2018, Bautze-Picron suggested that this is in fact a statue of Mahākāla, as indicated by the bulbous hairstyle, the garland of skulls and the fact the statue carries the *kapāla* and dagger.

The extraordinary sculpture stands at a height of 4.4 metres. Half of the backslab is missing, the face and hands are damaged, and the small lotus cushion and the ascetic are broken. There is wear on the lower legs, thought to have been made by the statue being used as a knife sharpener when it lay horizontal in the field. The statue is decorated with a profusion of carved ornaments—a large necklet, ear ornaments, upper armbands, bracelets and ankle bracelets—all representing serpents. Toe rings are also visible. The figure is decorated with a very detailed *seléndang*, depicted by fine lines across the breast and beneath the right arm. There is a remarkable similarity in the styling of this figure with that of the attendants of Amoghapāśa, also in the NMI. The short *kain* is portrayed falling to the mid thighs. It appears pulled up in the centre in the style of a South Indian *dhotī*. The pattern on the *kain* is made up of a series of diamond shapes carved on the vertical axis.

Figure 124 Mahākāla, detail of the left side sash. Pullen photo. Drawing of the textile pattern.

The carving of the designs is delineated in a very similar style to that of the previous Gaṇeśa. The pattern in each diamond (fig. 123) represents a skull motif resting on a sickle moon known as *candrakapāla*. Depicted around the central theme is a vegetal motif carved to create a rough outline for each diamond. Around the lower edge of the *kain* is a clearly delineated border pattern of three rows of circles, with a larger one in the centre (which appears to be unfinished). The detailed patterning of the sash (fig. 124) is distinctly different from that of the *kain*. Both are carved within a triangle on the vertical axis. One of the small triangles is filled with four trefoil motifs, around which are placed four scallop-shaped patterns. The alternating triangular pattern consists of the theme of an elongated flower and trefoil. The carving of the *kain* and sash have been skilfully executed and the sculptor clearly understood how cloth falls in folds, as the pattern is often half obscured.

In 2001, Bart designed a *songket* textile pattern based on the sash design of the Mahākāla[23] (fig. 125). This reproduced design suggests that this type of weaving was entirely possible in the fourteenth century, and it highlights the longevity of weaving using the *songket* technique by the ancestors of the present-day Minangkabau in West Sumatra. The origins of *songket* were unknown prior to the fifteenth century. The technique of weaving with gold threads originated from the Indo-Persian world. This knowledge arrived through the old trading ports of Palembang and the commerce in cloth and gold threads. With details gained from the *Zhufanzhi*, however, we know that the Chinese were also trading silks and brocades from at least the twelfth or thirteenth century and probably earlier.

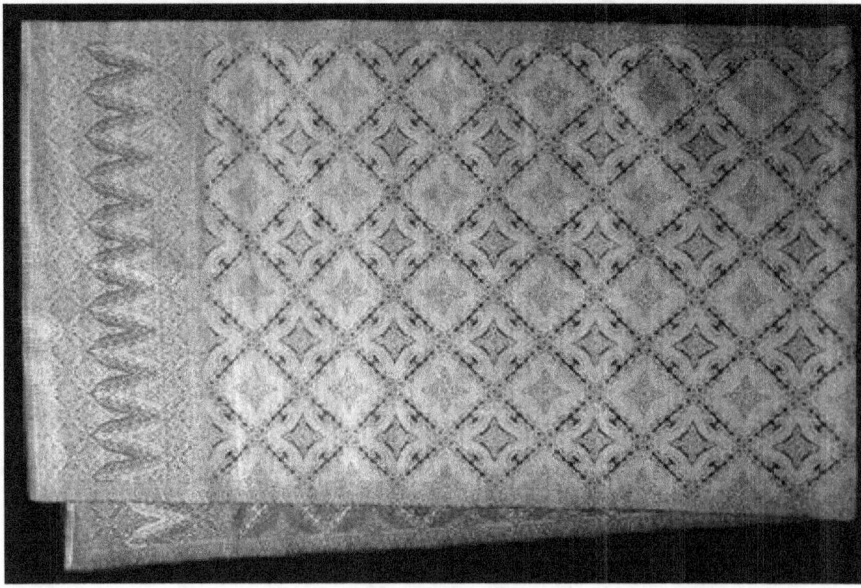

Figure 125 *Kain songket seléndang*, 2001 by PT Studio Songket Palantaloom. 194 x 55 cm. Private collection.

Embroidery and Lotus Motifs

Undoubtedly, the seated statue of the goddess Prajñāpāramitā[24] shown in figure 126 is the finest in Indonesia, and it is regarded as one of the country's national treasures. She remains in a secure room in the NMI. The statue is carved from a pale, almost white, andesite stone with an incredibly smooth surface. She originated from the now lost Caṇḍi E in the Singosari complex and is the lone Buddhist sculpture from the Singosari group. Of all the East Javanese sculptures, her execution is the most perfect, and she has only slight damage to her fingers. The fineness of the carving was possible because of the smoothness of the white stone. The figure is seated in the lotus position *padmāsana* on a lotus cushion placed on top of a square pedestal. The pedestal is carved with a frieze of small rosettes, probably representing lotus flowers, a typical Buddhist motif. The pattern has also been termed a "heart medallion", referring to the pattern used to decorate a Tibetan book cover dated to the mid-ninth century and which probably corresponds to Buddhist symbolism. This consequently led to a blending of Buddhist design vocabulary with those of secular or regal designs. As this rosette motif is also depicted on an eleventh-century Tibetan lion throne, it lends support to the idea that the motif could transgress on to different media and to religious and royal affiliations (Heller 1998, p. 115–16). The lotus stem, with the book on top, curls around the left upper arm. This, along with her hands in *dharmachakramudrā*, are identifiable features of Prajñāpāramitā. The base of the lotus growing from its roots is just visible at the left side of the sculpture. The statue is decorated with a profusion of extravagantly carved ornaments designed for a queen, such as a double necklet, upper arm bands and bracelets, large ankle bracelets, and rings on her fingers and toes. A notable feature is the evidence of pearls, which appear

Figure 126 Prajñāpāramitā, c.1280, Caṇḍi Singosari, Caṇḍi E, also known as Caṇḍi Wayang or Putri (now vanished), Malang, East Java. Museum Nasional Indonesia. Acquired in 1923. 1.26 m, andesite stone. Inv. no. 1403-1387. Photo by Gunawan Kartapranata, licensed under the Creative Commons Attribution-Share Alike 3.0 Unported licence: https://creativecommons.org/licenses/by-sa/3.0/deed.en.

on the lower and top edges of the broad upper arm bands. The *upavīta* (fig. 127) is carved as a three-strand pearl chain (*ratnopavīta*) and is joined with a clasp resembling gold work that is depicted at her left breast. The long chain of this falls on to the folds of her *sinjang*.

The *seléndang* is draped across the upper body. It is portrayed by faint lines embossed with rosettes suggestive of metal flowers or perhaps jewels. The flap is depicted on her left shoulder. Around her waist are portrayed a number of belts decorated with floral metal plaques that fall over the lower legs with a detailed tassel. The depiction of the *seléndang* clearly reflects Pāla styles; however, in this case, unlike with the Pāla Sena School of sculpture (Huntington and Huntington 1993, ch. 18), the carving of the sash is more realistically portrayed. The many folds of the cloth have been carved with a well-defined pattern of large roundels. The following description of where the roundels meet is purely suggestive and interpretative of the pattern. The interstice between the circles represent a star shape consisting of vegetal designs. Each of the circles differ slightly, as the petals around the circle on the right knee vary in number from ten to eleven and on the left knee there are thirteen. The pattern of the roundels is particularly interesting, as the study of textile patterns in Java and Sumatra over the last two hundred years has not revealed any

Figure 127 Prajñāpāramitā, detail of the lower legs depicting the twisted pearl *ratnopavīta* and the flower-decorated waist sash and *sinjang*. Pullen photo.

Figure 128 Prajñāpāramitā, detail of the right side of the body depicting the *sinjang* and the sash. Pullen photo. Drawing of the textile pattern.

designs that come even close to this one.²⁵ My reading of the contiguous roundels (fig. 128) is that they represent four quadrants around a central circle. Each quadrant contains two misshapen paisley motifs—a pattern that is difficult to describe but which evokes so many possibilities. The most exuberant aspect of her dress is the double sashes (fig. 129). This distinctive decorative item has been carved with such flourish, with a large double bow on either side of the body and with the loose ends draped over the lotus cushion to the pedestal. Two different and distinct patterns are drawn on the sash reflecting a repeated vegetal design. This pattern perhaps represents a brocade fabric to give the material body.

There has been little discussion in previous literature of the likely inspiration behind the textile patterns on Prajñāpāramitā. I suggest therefore some ideas here. The Tang rosette silk flower known as *karahana*, or Chinese flower, was a typical pattern at the end of the seventh and in the early eighth century. The pattern is also evident from Panjikent (figs. 130a–b), the ancient city of Sogdiana. In the first quarter of the eighth century, according to Valentina Raspopova, the design was mostly used on saddle cloths, and also for samples for a cushion on a royal throne (2006, p. 68).

Figure 129 Prajñāpāramitā, drawings of the two sashes worn across the thighs.

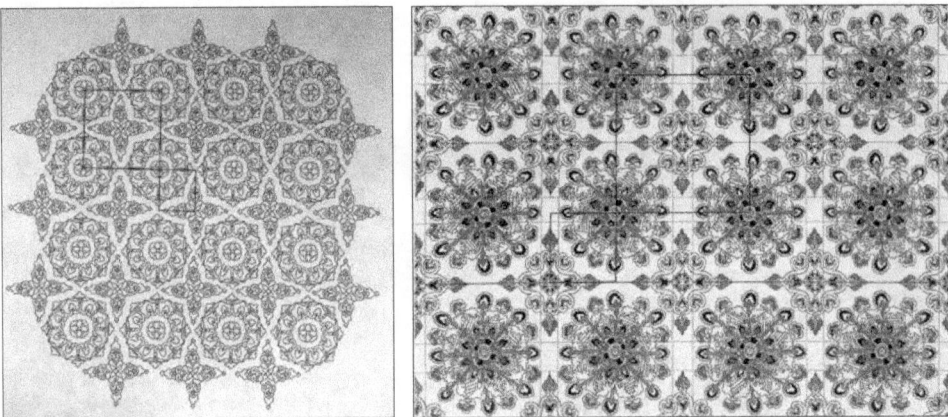

Figure 130 **130a** Rosette motif from a depiction of a saddlecloth. **130b** Rosette motif from a cushion, early eighth century, Panjikent Room 28, Sogdiana. Reproductions after Valentina I. Raspopova, "Textiles Represented in Sogdian Murals", in *Central Asian Textiles and Their Context in the Early Middle Ages*, Riggisberger Berichte 9, edited by Regula Schorta, Abegg-Stiftung, 2006, figs. 39 and 40.

Designs such as these could have provided indirect inspiration for the patterns on the Prajñāpāramitā statue. The concept, though, of vegetal motifs making a circle infilled with a star-shape have appeared on many textiles, yet there are nevertheless some remarkable parallels here. On the other hand, this pattern could also be representing a *gĕringsing* double ikat textile, where the "star" pattern between each roundel is often so prominent, just as depicted on the Mahākāla in figure 108, where the *gĕringsing* is worn as a protective cloth. We have, however, no contemporary extant examples.

From the intricacy of the design, it is of course possible that Prajñāpāramitā was carved in the earlier period of Kṛtanāgara's reign. Jan Fontein and Reichle have both dated this goddess to circa 1300. As Kṛtanāgara died in 1292, it could be argued that Prajñāpāramitā was made during the early phase of construction of the Caṇḍi Singosari complex. Looking at the way she has been carved and at her textile patterns, we can see that they represent a complete departure from any other sculpture found at the site. Perhaps this assertion of her geographical separation and differences in style from the remainder of the Singhasāri statues can help in dating her to an earlier period rather than to the time of the construction of the Tower Temple. A suggested date of circa 1280 fits more closely with the style of the carving on the Caṇḍi Jago statues. This image of the goddess Prajñāpāramitā is thought to be the posthumous image of Queen Rājapatnī, the consort of King Kĕrtarājasa. However, as Fontein has stated, we have no way of proving this (Fontein 1990, p. 160; Reichle 2007, p. 53).

The seated stone figure of Prajñāpāramitā shown in figure 131 has been considerably damaged and is missing its arms and head. In comparison

Figure 131
Prajñāpāramitā, mid-13th century, Caṇḍi Gumpung, Muara Jambi, Jambi Sumatra. Muarajambi site Museum, Jambi. 80 cm, sandstone. Pullen photo.

to the previous statue, Prajñāpāramitā has been carved seated in the lotus position with her garments covering the lotus cushion. She has also been carved from a pale white andesite stone. This statue remains in situ in Sumatra at the Buddhist site of Muara Jambi (map 2, p. 46), housed in a small site museum and pushed up against a corner. The damaged hands would have been in *dharmachakramudrā*. A small amount of the lotus stem curls around her left upper arm, and a small lotus plant is visible at the rear of the sculpture. Her hair falls in long curls down her back. She has also been attributed to the Singhasāri period as she appears stylistically similar. These similarities perhaps suggest close political, religious and artistic connections between the two regions of Jambi and East Java (Pullen 2020, pp. 38–45). This stylistic comparison is based on the ornaments of the figure and on her general physiognomy. The way her garments fold over her crossed legs suggest the two sculptures could have been made by the same hand in the same place. The patterning of her textile differs considerably, however, and does not show any parallel with the rest of the carving. It has been suggested that Kṛtanāgara despatched either the statue or the artisans, who then produced a similar sculpture

Figure 132 Prajñāpāramitā, detail of the *sinjang* on the lower legs. Pullen photo.

for the kingdom in Jambi. This cannot be proved one way or the other as there is no inscription or text to say a statue of Prajñāpāramitā was sent by Kṛtanāgara to the ruler in Jambi. To be able to make proposals regarding aspects of style, place of origin and workmanship, the intended purpose of the sculptures, and the general trends of production it is necessary to test the volcanic andesite stone in both Java and Sumatra. As this is not possible, I propose that these two statues were made separately and are not connected in any way.

The arrangement and decoration of the garments have been executed with precision. The statue wears the *upavīta* over both shoulders, finishing on the cushion in front of the body. The carving represents a five-strand twisted pearl chain *ratnopavīta* joined with a clasp depicted at the left breast of the statue, probably representing gold work. Spacer ornaments appear every ten to fifteen centimetres along the chain. The faint marking of a *seléndang* is portrayed falling between the chest and beneath the right arm. The *seléndang* is clearly visible across the back of the body, finished with a pleated end over the left shoulder.

The dress of Prajñāpāramitā is arranged with the *sinjang* finishing at the ankles (fig. 132) and lying over the cushion base in a multitude of delicately carved folds. The pattern on the *sinjang* appears unfinished—this is apparent on the lower folds, where a series of small rosettes is carved but there is no other design. The pattern on the *sinjang* (fig. 133) is completed with a small border that shows a stylized triangular-shaped motif.

Figure 133 Prajñāpāramitā, detail of the border pattern at the ankle on the right leg. Pullen photo.

This motif is often known as a "tree of life", bamboo shoot or by the Malay terms *pucuk rebung* or *tumpal*. This motif was traditionally woven into *kain limar*—Malay silks in weft ikat—but in this case the pattern can also be described as a cockspur, or *lawi ayam* (McIntosh 2012, pp. 202–13). It is tempting to state that this sculpture represents the first evidence for the development of a particular "Malay" textile design. The design can also be clearly seen woven on a nineteenth-century *kain limar cual* (fig. 134) from Muntok, Bangka Island, and in weft ikat *hol* from Pattani, Thailand. It is also apparent along the borders of a number of textiles in the Tilleke and Gibbins Collection. In the thirteenth and fourteenth centuries, new regional powers further reduced the options for the local Malay rulers in Sumatra. Siamese military activities of the Sukhothai followed by those of the Ayutthaya kingdoms in the mainland spread down as far as the Straits of Malacca (Tarling 1992, p. 175). The incursions of the Siamese and the influence of the Chinese under the Song could certainly have had an impact on the textile patterns of this statue. The Siamese royalty gave Cambodian silks to members of their court and to less powerful rulers of their kingdoms as gifts of allegiance. Similar patterns are depicted in the kinds of Indian trade cottons that were commissioned for consumption in Siam. Evidence of the extant textiles at this time date back to the time of

186 Patterned Splendour

Figure 134 Detail of the end panel of a *Kain limar cual*, Muntok Banka Island. Private collection.

Figure 135
Prajñāpāramitā, detail of the right side showing the *sinjang* and sashes falling over the lotus cushion. Pullen photo. Drawing of the textile pattern on the *sinjang*.

the Prajñāpāramitā and possibly attest to the roots and longevity of this particular motif.[26]

The garments consist of the *sinjang* and two sashes. The pattern on the *sinjang* appears to be unfinished or to have been poorly executed in comparison to the intricate details on the sashes. The design has been carved in relief consisting of large concentric circles. The interstices are filled with a triangular motif made up of four trefoil patterns. The decoration within the circles is unique to this particular sculpture; it consists of a four-petal lotus flower set with a double roundel that contains a simple pattern of the outer petals of the lotus flower. The sashes are draped over the thighs in two sections. They are depicted tied off in a large soft bow at each side of the body. The two ends are shown on either side, completely covering the lower cushion (fig. 135). There appear to be two different and distinct patterns: one of a realistically carved lotus flower within a scrolling vine motif, and one of a stylized lotus flower within a scrolling vine pattern.

The patterns on the two sashes (fig. 136) denote an embroidery technique that has been executed with crisp detail, making it easy to interpret the intricate design. Embroidery has always been very popular in China, and has been used to create the intricate details needed for Buddhist textiles (Lin 2006, p. 62). An eleventh-century Liao period embroidery roundel also exhibits the same aesthetic qualities as on the sashes on Prajñāpāramitā, as does an example of a Song *kesi* flower border (Kuhn 2012, p. 290).

Ernst Gombrich wrote that if "style" is used descriptively for alternative ways of doing things, the term "fashion" can be reserved for the

Figure 136 Prajñāpāramitā, drawing of the two sashes worn across the thighs.

fluctuating preferences that carry social prestige (1998, p. 151). Fashion or style could also account for the differences between these two sculptures, where local fashion and regional trends or influences might have played a part. It is my opinion that influences from international sources played a crucial part in informing the style of these two Prajñāpāramitā (Pullen 2020, pp. 45–50). The original placing of the statue of the Muara Jambi Prajñāpāramitā at Caṇḍi Gumpung in the Muara Jambi complex remains an enigma. Further research is needed on this statue and on the other archaeological remains at Muara Jambi.

Ceplok Patterns – *Kawung* motif

The *ceplok* pattern group was by far the leading group during the Singhasāri and the following Majapahit period. The statue of Prajñāpāramitā shown in figure 137 is the third of four acknowledged statues of the goddess. The fourth is damaged and remains at the Caṇḍi Singosari site, and does not show any visible textile pattern—the pattern has likely been entirely worn away. I propose a high proportion of the existing damaged Singosari statues were also decorated with textile designs.

The large stone seated statue of Prajñāpāramitā originates from Caṇḍi Boyolangyu. The statue remains in situ under a small bamboo pavilion on the remains of a brick base at the now ruined *caṇḍi*. Boyolangyu is located a hundred kilometres southwest of Caṇḍi Singosari in the Tulungagung District of Kediri, a wealthy rice-growing area. The statue is seated in a lotus position against a severely damaged backslab. The surface is worn and she is missing her head and forearms. Along with the remains of Caṇḍi Boyolangyu there are also many Buddhist stupas in the Kediri region and an eleventh-century meditation cave known as Gua Selomangleng.

The broken hands would have been in *dharmachakramudrā*. The small remains of the lotus stem that appear growing from its roots at the side of the sculpture and curling around her upper left arm are the only remaining distinguishable feature of Prajñāpāramitā. She appears unmistakably to be dressed in royal attire, with the *ratnopavīta* as a large five-strand pearl chain joined with an ornate clasp that sits on the lower folds of her *sinjang* and another metal clasp at her left breast. The band clearly represents a plain and very wide *seléndang* depicted by faint lines across the upper torso, finishing on her left shoulder with a large flap in the typical Singosari style. She wears many belts of both metal and fabric. The ends are draped over the lower legs, but the detail is very faint due to the erosion on the surface. The depiction of the pattern on the *sinjang* is also considerably worn, with very little detail still visible to the naked eye. On close inspection there was enough pattern for us to be able to create a reconstruction of the design in this drawing. What we see is a repeated pattern of four vesicae that form a square when viewed from the inside and a circle when viewed from the outside. Within each of the four vesicae is a small five-petal flower and two elongated petals.

Figure 137 Prajñāpāramitā, c.1362, Caṇḍi Gayatri/Boyolangu, Tulungagung District, East Java, in situ. 1.05 m, andesite stone. Pullen photo.

The pattern within the circles represent four sections in which there is a scallop-shaped motif. This motif is part of the *ceplok* group of designs. Her *sinjang* is just visible at her ankle (fig. 138). The pattern is not carved in deep relief, as was the case with the previous two sculptures, but appears to have been incised in fine lines. Overlaying the sarong is a narrow sash tied in a large bow at the side of the body, the two ends of which fall the length of the legs. There appear to be remnants of a vegetal pattern on the sash, drawn in fine lines, which is different from the design on the *sinjang*. This pattern appears to consist of a series of finely executed squares with a four-petal flower overlaying the crossed demarcation of the centre pattern.

In terms of the style categorization for this sculpture, the Transition style would be appropriate, notwithstanding the late date of 1362, which puts her well into the Majapahit period. The style of the carving, the ornaments and the unusual textile pattern places her closer to a Singosari sculpture. The textile patterns are defining features. The design undeniably fits more

Figure 138 Prajñāpāramitā, detail of the faded pattern on the *sinjang* lower right leg. Pullen photo. Drawing of the textile pattern.

closely with the attendants of Amoghapāśa in the NMI, placing the *ceplok* patterns of the following Majapahit sculptures in the fourteenth centuries.

A close study of this version of the *kawung* pattern reveals certain Chinese stylistic qualities, as evident in two textile samples that date to the Liao period in China (907–1125) (Langewis and Wagner 1964, p. 164), which demonstrate a remarkable similarity with the style of roundels of the next statue of an unidentified goddess in the depiction of the "star" motif and in the general aesthetic of both Javanese and Chinese patterns. Despite the earlier Liao dating, these textiles reflect the type of complex brocade weave structure that could have been the inspiration behind the pattern on this deity. Regula Schorta has suggested that Liao art displays influences from the arts of the Tang and Central Asia, which they held constant contact with. Central Asian art was highly eclectic, as for centuries Central Asia remained a hub of influences from every part of Eurasia (Schorta 2007, p. 14). Such similarities, however, do not appear in the designs of present-day Javanese or Malay textile traditions. This pattern, then, could well have been of a local weave, perhaps representing a valued imported Chinese silk textile. In her original condition, the dress and ornamentation on this damaged sculpture would have been of the highest quality.

The next four sculptures originate from Caṇḍi Singosari. Two of them remain within the grounds of the Tower Temple at Caṇḍi Singosari and two are located in museums.

Details of the statue of an unidentified goddess (fig. 139) were published in 1939 by Jessy Blom, and prior to that by J. Knebel in 1909 when he completed excavations with the renowned scholar J.L.A Brandes; however, no known photographs were taken of the sculpture. I published details along with photographs of the statue in 2019 (Pullen 2019, pp. 20–21). I visited the site three times for field work in 2009, 2014 and 2016. In the intervening period the delicate textile pattern had almost entirely disappeared. What was visible in 2009 was a

Figure 139 Unidentified Goddess, *c.*1300, Caṇḍi Singosari, Caṇḍi B (now vanished), Tower Temple, grounds in situ, Malang, East Java. 1.37 m, andesite stone. Pullen photo.

192 Patterned Splendour

Figure 140 Unidentified Goddess, lower right leg detail. Pullen photo, 2009. Drawing of textile pattern.

small area of the pattern on the front of the right leg, where enough detail was still discernible to be able to make line drawings of the repeat design. By 2014, even this small area of pattern had all but disappeared (ibid., p. 22).

The four-armed goddess is missing her head and the back two arms. She is seated in the lotus position against a severely damaged backslab (fig. 140). Her lower hands are possibly holding a lotus or a censer. The surface of the stone is badly exfoliated, leaving only hints of the jewellery, including the *upavīta*, neckband, armbands and anklet. The *sinjang* is much worn and has a barely discernible pattern that was probably carved in deep relief. The design is of concentric interlocking circles decorated with a four-pointed star and a small rosette flower, and it is a pattern that is unique to this sculpture. Her sash is clearly visible carved across her hips and on to the backslab at either side of the body, tied in a large bow—a feature typical of the Singosari style.

Figure 141 Dikpāla, guardian of the nadir, carried by the *vāhana*, a tortoise, c.1300, Caṇḍi Singosari, Caṇḍi B (now vanished) Tower Temple grounds, in situ, Malang East Java. Andesite stone. Brandes photo from 1904; Pullen photo from 2014.

The lowers limbs of a Dikpāla (fig. 141) also remain on the grounds at Caṇḍi Singosari. He is one of the Aṣṭa-Dikpāla—the eight regents or guardians of the sky quarters or directions—originating from Caṇḍi Singosari. The 1909 photographs taken by J.L.A. Brandes clearly show how the textile pattern on the *sinjang* was quite evident over both legs. Enough of the design still remained visible in my 2014 photo, but by 2016 the pattern had virtually disappeared (Pullen 2019, pp. 23–24). On account of this deterioration, I have presented here two photos—the current one and the Brandes photo—which were used to reproduce the pattern template for this Dikpāla.

The Dikpāla is seated in lotus position with the left hand placed on the left knee, palm upwards and decorated with a flat rosette. The limbs appear on a lotus cushion carried by the *vāhana*, a tortoise, with only the neck and feet visible. The tortoise is also decorated with a neck ornament, which probably was replicating the decoration on the Dikpāla. The feet of the *vāhana* clearly distinguish him as a tortoise, along with his shell that sits over his body. The worn surface of the remaining section of the goddess hints at her jewellery, which includes her belt, an anklet and a toe ring. The tortoise appears to be inserted or "carrying" the deity between the lotus cushion and his own base. The surface of the limbs has been severely eroded by the elements, with the ornaments and *sinjang* barely visible, and the head of the tortoise is missing. The *upavīta* is just discernible falling over the waistline as a string of three pearls. The *sinjang* lies in neat

Figure 142 Dikpāla, drawing of the textile pattern.

folds on the front of the cushion. On the right knee, the faint outline of a pattern can be interpreted as a *kawung* motif (fig. 142). In this instance, the four vesicae constitutes a circle around a four-pointed flower (ibid, p. 24).

Examples of contemporary batik, some dated to the early nineteenth century, exhibit similarities to this style of patterning and attest to the longevity of this *kawung* motif. The carved pattern could however also represent a woven brocade cloth. This type of pattern is closer in style to the *kawung* designs on the Majapahit sculptures of the fourteenth century than to similar patterns of the thirteenth century. The stylistic grammar of the statue, however, is clearly in the Singosari style.

Large Daisy Flower Pattern

Nairṛti, the statue in figure 143, is known as the guardian of the southwest. Here he is seated in the lotus position and is borne by his *vāhana*, known as a *bhūta*—only the head and arms of which are visible. The statue was found in the ruins of Caṇḍi B in the Singhasāri complex during the excavation of 1901 and was subsequently removed. It currently remains in a locked cabinet in the Vihara Buddhayana in Jakarta. Raffles writes that the period in which the statues in the Chinese Vihara were collected is unknown "and the subjects in general are not so well executed" (1817, vol II, p. 55). Access to the statue is restricted. It was only after much persuasion that permission was granted for the case to be opened so I could have a closer look at the sculpture, without which I would not have been able to photograph the patterns.

The right hand holds a flaming sword; the left lies on his knee with the palm upwards and is carved with a flat rosette, as was the case with the previous statue. The *bhūta* is portrayed with flaring long hair, bulging eyes, and fangs at the corners of its mouth; likewise, bulging eyes also appear on the Nairṛti statue, and small tusks protrude from the side of the mouth. In the past, thick varnish and gold paint had been applied to the surface. The gold has now mostly disappeared. Despite the adverse surface conditions, however, the statue remains in a near-perfect state. Deciphering the textile pattern has been difficult though on account of the excessive surface applications. The barely visible patterning on the *sinjang* covers the lower part of the body (fig. 144). The pattern is still just discernible on the front of the right leg. The design appears to represent a large daisy with rounded petals, interspersed with a square in a circle. The sash carved on the backslab is depicted with the typical Singosari feature of a large knot. The anklets and bracelets are visible, but the remainder of the body decorations unfortunately have been obliterated somewhat by the varnish and gold paint (Pullen 2019, pp. 24–25).

Kediri and Singhasāri 195

Figure 143 Dikpāla, Nairṛti, carried by his *vāhana*, an anthropomorphic being or *bhūta*, guardian of the SW, *c*.1300, Caṇḍi Singosari, Caṇḍi B (now vanished), Vihara Buddhayana. 85 cm, andesite stone. Inv. no. 154b/3631. Pullen photo.

Figure 144 Dikpāla, Nairṛti, detail of the lower legs. Pullen photo. Drawing of the *sinjang* textile pattern.

The textile pattern is almost identical in construction to that on the next sculpture, a statue of Brahmā (fig. 145), which also originates from the Caṇḍi Singosari complex. The fact that both these statues appear with an almost identical pattern is highly unusual, which suggests they originated from the same workshop. The artist has drawn the two patterns the same, as it is impossible to see enough of the pattern on Nairṛti to be able to make a more precise interpretation.

The statue of Brahmā as an ascetic is large at 1.7 metres tall and is an exceedingly rare figure in East Java. He remains on view at the RV and adds to the group of previous sculptures from the Tower Temple that have also been retained in the RV. The backslab is badly damaged, but the statue is generally in good condition apart from the lower legs and the surface of the stone, which has severely exfoliated. The Brahmā has been carved from a grey granular stone that differs in colour from the other Singosari statues. The rock appears to be of the same quality as the sculptures from Caṇḍi A in the Singosari complex, only lighter in colour. This would indicate these sculptures were all made at a similar period with an equivalent type of andesite rock. Anatomically, this is an exceptional figure, where the sculptor has clearly defined the sheer volume of the torso. This statue has four heads and stands in a stiff upright position with the two upper hands holding the attributes against the backslab. The lower hands together hold the lotus bud in *dhyānamudrā*, a gesture of meditation. The leaves of the lotus plant appear carved on the left side of the statue, while on the right side only the stalks are visible curling over the head of his *haṃsa vāhana* or mount.

Brahmā appears carved with a broad *seléndang* that drapes across the upper body and with the end falling over the left breast. The band is impressed with a line across the centre, as is the case with the sculptures from the Tower Temple. In this instance though the pattern is rather too worn to be able to decipher any further details. The five-strand pearl *ratnopavīta* is draped over the *seléndang* and finishes at the knees with a sizeable elaborate clasp decorated with peepul leaf ornaments. The style of the *ratnopavīta* fits more closely with the Majapahit style, as do the position of the lower two arms; however, the form and pattern of the *sinjang* match more closely with the Singosari style; therefore, the statue is placed into the Transition style. The *sinjang* falls the length of the body and has a small well-defined pleat at the front. The carved textile pattern in shallow relief is worn on most of the *sinjang*, as the surface of the stone has exfoliated on the right side, but it is discernible on the left side. The pattern represents three different motifs. There is an eight-petal daisy flower with eight rounded petals—perhaps a version of the Chinese design I described earlier. Juxtaposing this is a pattern constituting a square within a circle filled with four trefoil scallops and

Kediri and Singhasāri 197

Figure 145 Brahmā, late 13th century, Caṇḍi Singosari, Caṇḍi D, Malang, East Java. Volkenkunde, Leiden. Collection Nationaal Museum van Wereldculturen. 1.74 m, andesite stone. Inv. no RV 1403-1582.

carved around a small inner circle. The diamond-shaped pattern that fills the interstices is made up of a four-leafed vegetal design, the same as in figure 144. A plain sash is draped over the *sinjang*. The long patterned ends of the sash (fig. 146) hang stiffly to the side; they bear the same design as the *sinjang*. The sash is tied in a large bow held with a jewelled band in a way very similar to that on the figure of the Pārvatī retinue. The long belt draped on the thighs is suggestive of heavy fabric or leather and is decorated with circular plaques that are probably representing gold.

Figure 146 Brahmā, detail of the left side of the *sinjang*. Pullen photo.

There are some parallels to be explored between the design on the textile on Brahmā (fig. 147) with older textile patterns such as the design on the jacket on the harp player on the seventh-century Sasanian rock reliefs at Taq-i-Bustan (Iran) (fig. 12, p. 39). The relief panel of the Sasanian rock reliefs that depict the boar hunt includes a harp-player in the right-hand boat whose costume is carved with a textile pattern. The pattern is best described as a series of four rosettes and diagonal crosses (Otavsky 1998, p. 130, Abb 60). The reliefs show royal fashion and textile designs depicted in the utmost detail (Canepa 2014, p. 5). There appears a certain similarity in the geometrical layout and design of the floral

Figure 147 Textile sample (reconstruction), boar hunting relief, elephant rider, from Taq-I-Bustan © Abegg-Stiftung, CH-3132 Riggisberg, 2015 (drawing: Vendulka Otavská after Fukai Shinji and Horiuchi Kiyoharu, "Taq-i-Bustan. Vol. I Plates", The Tokyo University Iraq-Iran Archaeological Expedition Report 10, Tokyo 1969, pl. LI and LXV resp. XXXIX).

rosettes seen in figure 11 (p. 39). This type of rosette pattern is also visible on a king's robe illustrated on a wall painting at Pagan (fig. 148), where large rosettes are painted on the garment worn by the king. And there is undoubtedly a certain similarity in the wall paintings of the tenth to the eleventh century in the Patothamya and Nanpaya (Mahler 1958, p. 37). Bautze-Picron describes mural paintings of the Kubyauk-gyi at Myinkaba of 1113 CE where the "lay people are dressed with garments richly adorned with numerous different patterns", highlighting the many possibilities across Asia of patterns with concentric circles (2014, p. 2).

The Patothamya temple, dated between the tenth and eleventh centuries, is typical of the first phase of Pagan building. The characteristics of the Mon people were evident at this phase of construction, and the textiles were strong in design, although they were treated as flat patterns. The ceiling paintings, however, depict numerous Chinese patterns influenced from the Tang period. For example, the lotus blossom, which was reduced to an abstract pattern, often reflected a strong resonance of Sassanian and Chinese ideas, which appeared over the centuries to be interchangeable. After Pagan became the capital, ideas also became exchangeable with the outside world, particularly with India and Ceylon and other neighbouring countries in the wake of the increase in trade relations and diplomatic exchange (Mahler 1958, pp. 37–38;

Figure 148 Fresco painting of a king, Gubyauk gyi, Pagan, Myanmar, 11th–12th century. Pullen photo.

Bautze-Picron 2014, p. 1)—ideas that we see transposed on to statues such as the thirteenth-century figures of Nairṛti and Brahmā.

Finbarr Flood has suggested that if the royal figures at Pagan and in Ladakh in the eleventh century are wearing robes from another land, it is likely that these items would have been gifted and would be regarded as objects of identity. The suggestion can also be made that the gifting of robes was observed as a way of gaining the loyalty of the recipient king or regent (Flood 2009, p. 84). In this case, however, the Javanese elite did not wear robes; they wore a *kain* or *sinjang*, which was uncut and worn wrapped around the body. One can only imagine nobles sweating in Chinese robes at Javanese and Sumatran courts. The gifting of textiles was common practice between the Chinese elite and local envoys. In the tenth century, a hundred pieces of various textiles amongst gilded objects and other products were gifted. In return, the foreign envoys to China were gifted with gold, silk, horses and military implements (Bielenstein 2005, pp. 65–66). In the *T'oung Pao*, there are constant mentions of local people wearing a long skirt wrapped around their loins or a cotton sarong; there is never any mention of a jacket or upper body garment of any sort (Rockhill 1915).

The patterned textiles that appear on a number of the sculptures of Persian, Indian or Chinese origin were quite possibly brought into the region and treasured as gifts or as statements of political power.

The statue of Brahmā appears to fit into the Transition style for the following reasons. First, the concept of a Hindu deity not depicted as a monarch, as was the case with the statue of Pārvatī as a queen; second, the juxtaposition of the Singosari portrayal of garments and the style of textile patterns, along with his hairstyle; third, the rigid upright stance and *mudrā*; and lastly, the overly long, five-strand *ratnopavīta*. All of these point to a later Majapahit style. This leaves the statue in neither one style or the other; hence, the Transition style is the closest fit.

Brocade Patterns

The last group includes two sculptures that both fall into the Transition style. Their textile patterns do not bear any particular relation to each other, and each statue is a different colour and was carved from a different type of andesite stone. Despite the *sinjang* on Durgā Mahiṣāsuramardinī (fig. 149) displaying a pattern in the *ceplok* group, she does not fit into the previous *ceplok* pattern group because of the late dating and the distinct Transition style of the body

This particular stone statue of Durgā Mahiṣāsuramardinī is of a similar size to, but represents a complete departure in style and quality to, the previous Durgā from the Tower Temple. The figure also stands astride the buffalo demon. This statue, however, presents a gentle sway of the right hip and none of the aggressive stance of the previous Durgā. The face is damaged and the statue appears considerably worn, with the carving of the textile patterns in shallow relief in comparison to the previous Durgā where the design is in deep relief. The difference in quality of the andesite stone is a

Figure 149 Durgā Mahiṣāsuramardinī, early 14th century, found in Trenggalek Regency, East Java. Museum Mpu Tantular, Surabaya, East Java. Approx. 1.5 m, andesite stone. Inv. no unknown. Pullen photo.

Figure 150 Durgā Mahiṣāsuramardinī, detail of the lower right side showing Durgā holding the buffalo tail and a detail of the textile pattern. Pullen photo. Drawing of the textile pattern.

testament to the different workshops involved in the production of statues during this period. This Durgā statue remains in a small regional museum, the Mpu Tantular Museum in Surabaya, East Java.

The statue of Durgā is decorated with ornaments that include a small tiered crown, a neckband, armbands, bracelets, anklets, the *udharabhanda* and many belts. The *ratnopavīta* of four strings of pearls finishes over the upper thighs. The *sinjang* is arranged in neat folds at either side with a textile design (fig. 150). The pattern is part of the *ceplok* pattern group, seen here as a *kawung* design. When viewed on the vertical plane, the design constitutes four vesicae emphasizing the joined points to make a square, with each filled with a simple four-leaf trefoil placed around a small circle. The sash is draped over the thighs almost at the knees and is tied in a large knot with the ends falling the length of the body and flaring outwards. The construction of the pattern does not continue in the Malay tradition of *songket* weaving; however, it does show parallels with twentieth-century *batik kraton* patterns from Java.

The *tribhaṅga* pose, where the body bends in three directions, is a common feature of Indian sculpture, and the pose is represented here in Durgā Mahiṣāsuramardinī. The pose is in sharp contrast to many of the sculptures from the same period, which either remain stiffly upright or bend in *contrapposto*. In light of this, the statue probably dates to the beginning of the fourteenth century, which fits more closely with the

Transition classification. The earlier dating suggested is based on various factors: first, her smaller size compared to the Majapahit sculptures; and second, there are few remaining statues of Durgā from the mid to late fourteenth centuries. Her textile pattern, however, fits more closely with the prevalence during the Majapahit of the *kawung* motif. She is therefore neither Singosari nor Majapahit.

The last figure in stone covered in this chapter is of Harihara Ardhanari (fig. 151)—believed to represent the deified figure of King Kṛtanāgara. The statue remains an enigma. Its place of origin is unknown, although it was thought to be in the vicinity of Malang at a place called Sagala. Here,

 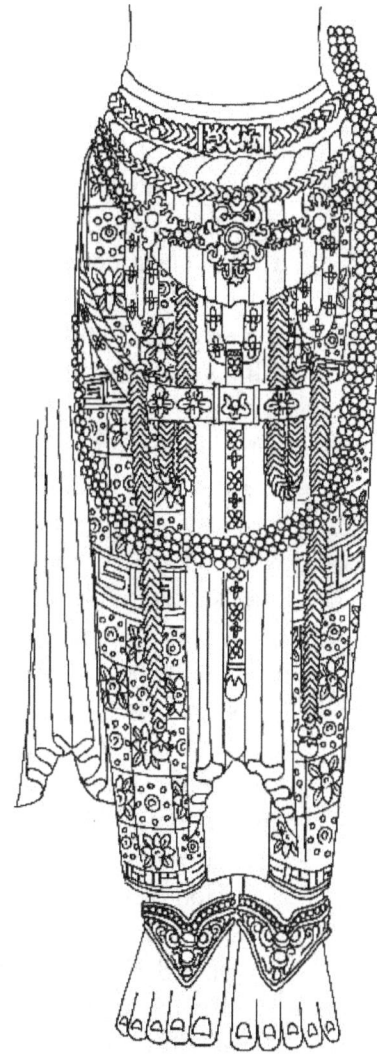

Figure 151 Harihara Ardhanari, deification image of a god, possibly King Kṛtanāgara, early 14th century, Majapahit. State Hermitage Museum, St Petersburg. Acquired in 1945 from Museum für Völkerkunde, Berlin. 1.45 m, andesite stone. Inv. no. BD-543. Drawing of the lower body.

Kṛtanāgara was placed as a Jina in a subsidiary *caṇḍi* to Singosari, as the figure of Ardhanari, Vairocana and Locana in a single statue (*Nāg.* 43:5). The sculpture was acquired by Germany from Dutch sources in 1861, along with Mañjuśrī Arapacana (Stutterheim 1932, p. 47). The figures were subsequently acquired by the Russians sometime around 1945 and 1946 and taken to Leningrad (today's St Petersburg) and subsequently placed in the SHM, where they now reside in the museum's storage. Along with the Mañjuśrī Arapacana, the statues were positioned in an exhibition at the SHM in the spring of 2016. A book cataloguing all the Southeast Asian sculptures in the Hermitage collection was published in Russian by Olga Deshpande (2016, pp. 389, fig. 337).

The statue appears to be in relatively good condition, although the upper right side of the backslab was repaired by the SHM and the lower right arm is missing. The andesite stone is grey and very smooth, which enabled the fineness of the carving, particularly of the ornaments and the multitude of belts. The ornaments include the chain, which ties at the waist and falls to the lower legs with a detailed tassel. The *ratnopavīta*, as a three-strand pearl chain, drapes to the upper thighs and is held with a large clasp depicted beside the left breast. A stylized ornament of a *makara*—a sea-creature from Indian mythology described as a half-terrestrial and half-aquatic animal—appears at either side of the head, falling on to the shoulders. This ornament is exceptionally unusual and is unique to Singosari/Transition period sculptures. The long cloth sash is tied at the side of the body with a knot, with one end on the backslab and the other falling along the body. The *sinjang* is carved to denote three layers (fig. 152), which is unusual, and it visibly signifies a textile wrapped around the body. At the right side, the fabric appears folded over the left at the lower edge, with a pleat in the fabric, which is typical of a Javanese sarong. The two shorter *kain* fall over the *sinjang*. At the front of the body, the structure seems to be tucked over one of the belts at the waist. The pattern on all three textiles give the impression of a grid-like ornamentation, rather than being on the diagonal, as is the style in most other cases. It is carved in a straightforward fashion and the pattern appears unfinished (fig. 153). The lower *sinjang* is carved with a border of small squares, whilst the borders of the upper two *kain* are carved with a version of the *banji* or swastika pattern, a motif that was also popular in Thai, Lao and Balinese textiles. The *banji* motif is often described as being derived from China; however, it could also be interpreted as a "meander or cloud border" used to indicate the edge of a garment (Hoop 1949, pp. 56 and 64), regarded by the Chinese as "the motif of ten thousand". The *banji* pattern is regularly used today as a border pattern on batik textiles, and the Balinese use this motif as a border pattern on a batik cloth decorated with *prada*, or gold-leaf glue work. The *banji* motif

Figure 152 Harihara Ardhanari, detail of the lower right side of the body. Pullen photo.

may well have been imported during the Hindu-Buddhist period from India or, as has been suggested, from China.

If we compare the pattern on this *kain* to that on the Durgā in the RV from the Tower Temple, the carving can be considered to be relatively simplistic. One suggestion is that it was carved to replicate a brocaded fabric. Another suggestion is that it could represent a cloth with a block printed pattern applied with gold leaf, such as *prada*. An example of a twentieth-century *batik prada* that is set with small flowers within squares is the *kain kelangan*, which has a *batik banji* motif (Cutsem-Vanderstraete 2012, p. 295). Another is the border pattern on a silk *lokcan kemben* shown in figure 154 (Hauser-Schäublin, Nabholz-Kartaschoff and Ramseyer 1991, p. 126, fig. 9.8). These examples highlight the continuity and longevity of this auspicious design up to the present day. There are undoubtedly some aesthetic parallels between the examples mentioned here with the thirteenth-century stone textile pattern.

Figure 153 Harihara Ardhanari, drawing of the textile pattern.

To give a clear definition of the pattern on the statue of Kṛtanāgara is challenging. The two examples though highlight the variety of textiles that could have been in use at the time. Details about the figure have only been published once in a 1932 article by Stutterheim. He summarizes his analysis of Kṛtanāgara by saying:

> Thus, appears the portrait statue of the Javanese king, who believed himself to be like the Kublai Khan ... at the same time he was a man who devoted his entire attention to the secret teachings of the Tantrayana attaining the highest reaches thereof of any Javanese prince. (Stutterheim 1932, p. 50)

Further support for this claim by Stutterheim is provided by the evidence of a considerable amount of tantric iconography depicted on a number of the statues from Caṇḍi Singosari. A brief account of the statue will be beneficial here, as this is the last figure in the Singosari and Transition style.

The *Nāg.* (43:5–6) describes Kṛtanāgara in the place he was enshrined as Śiva-Buddha with a Jina figure and as a figure who is also Ardhanareśvarī and Vairocana-Locanā[27] in the one statue (Stutterheim 1932, p 48; Robson and Prapanca 1995, p. 56). It is likely this refers to the statue of a youthful Kṛtanāgara now held in the State Hermitage Museum (fig. 151). Stutterheim continues to discuss the possibility of this statue being created in the likeness of Kṛtanāgara, considering that the burial places and associated figures of all the previous Singhasāri kings are already known. In Sutterheim's opinion, this figure is without a doubt the commemorative statue of King Kṛtanāgara. The statue's fine features certainly give him a royal air. Sutterheim also surmises that the figure would surely have been placed with Mañjuśrī Arapacana. But as we have no record from which temple the statue originated, it can only be supposition. What is clear though is that the textile patterns and the way they have been carved differ considerably. There is a phrase in the *Nāg.* that reads "*atyanta ring sobhita*". A literal translation of this is, "bright, beautiful, extraordinary",

Figure 154 Detail of a *batik lokcan kemben*, silk, early 20th century. Private collection.

and it refers to the idea that few ancient Javanese sculptures have been modelled so correctly—down to the jewellery—and with such precision as this one (Stutterheim 1932, p. 49).

Placing the statue within the Transition period has been judged on the basis of his attributes and his stance as the deified figure of a king. The detailed descriptions and drawings of the textile patterns of this statue are, however, an essential addition to the Deshpande catalogue and to the earlier Stutterheim article. I also maintain that this statue is a portrait of the Javanese king in the form of a god. Stutterheim has suggested that Kṛtanāgara believed himself to be like Kublai Khan. Both these figures wanted to be perceived as incarnations of Mañjuśrī.

There are also some Singosari features depicted on this statue; notably, the *makara*-type ornament on the shoulders. The most important such feature though is the depiction of the three layers of the *kain* and the unique textile pattern, which is not at all in keeping with the later Majapahit styles of a purely *kawung* aesthetic.

Summary

A typology of textile patterns has been presented in this chapter in the form of eight groups. I hope this has significantly contributed to the knowledge and understanding of the history of textile production in East Java during this period. There are an extraordinary variety among the statues and many individual characteristics, but there are also many similarities that allow them to be grouped. I have noted how each statue displays a unique and entirely personal textile pattern, and yet the designs can often be seen to have been carved with the same hand, and they show a similarity in the style and type of models.

In discussing the accomplishments of the Singosari craftsmen, Sedyawati has suggested that their achievements and the sophistication of their carvings led them to attain a certain degree of authority. She recalls Bernet Kempers, who stated that the pinnacle of beauty was reached during the Singhasāri period, as new influences were felt from India, particularly from Bengal.[28] It is also possible to suggest, however, that these fresh influences were imported as a result of the increase in prosperity and control of the Singhasāri. The wealth and prosperity enabled the leaders to participate in the international culture and trade that arrived from Bengal (Sedyawati 1994, p. 256n6). If this was the case, then perhaps, as Andrea Acri has stated, the Newar artists were situated at Caṇḍi Jago. This suggestion could explain how the unusual textile pattern of roundels on the Mañjuśrī Arapacana reached Java.

The most dominant feature that unifies the sculptures of the Singosari style is the "movement or expression" depicted in the form of the body, and the "plastic volume" created by the sculptor to indicate a certain realism in the anatomy of the human form. Other features include the smoothness of the andesite stone and the large size of the figures, which are seldom carved in the round, with the artists having chosen instead to carve the deity against a stone backslab. The only statue we know that is not in this category is the Prajñāpāramitā from Muara Jambi. It also has some distinguishing features. First, consider the delineation of the *seléndang* across the upper body. This feature has certainly been taken from the art of the Pāla period—it is evident on the late Pāla sculptures in the National Museum, New Delhi. Secondly, note the flourish with which the cloth sash has been carved across the hips and has been depicted as tied in large, soft bows that "sway" to the side of the body. To place the textile patterns in a historical timeline along with the sculptures though is problematic; however, the apparent similarity in the andesite stone of the Singosari statues clearly links them together.

The broad variety of patterns depicted in this chapter suggest a high quality of craftsmanship and apparent evidence of international textile designs that appear in some instances to have influenced a number of the designs carved on the sculptures. The comparative textile examples given for these groups have been based on a certain similarity in design, pattern layout and general aesthetic. These patterns, which are often of an international nature, exhibit some explicit similarities to the Javanese sculptures they have been compared with. Having said this, it has been essential to keep certain groups of statues together if they originated from the same *caṇḍi*, for example. The groups of complex "brocade" and skull motifs depict skull and *kāla*-head imagery, but they also display brocade patterns and *kawung* themes. The largest group of patterns are in the *ceplokan* category, with designs known as *kawung*. On some sculptures, more than one textile is evident, but the *kawung* motif appears to be in the majority. The carving of rosettes, for example, as we saw on the Central Javanese statues, are carved here much larger in size and have taken on a sophisticated form, with the inclusion of an additional pattern with a circular motif around a vegetal design.

Transition Style

The two sculptures of Nairṛti and Brahmā are both supposed to have originated from the Caṇḍi Singosari complex; however, one statue is in the Transition style whilst the other is in the Singosari style. And yet they both feature virtually the same textile pattern. The interpretation of this pattern was relatively simple in the case of Brahmā, as the remains of the design were evident. But in the case of Nairṛti the design has all but been obliterated by the addition of varnish and gilding. After careful analysis, Ms Huang proposed that the layout of the textile design was very similar.

Two Prajñāpāramitā, from Java and Sumatra, have been suggested by previous scholars to have been made in Java. The Muara Jambi statue, however, originated in Sumatra, and is carved with a pattern exhibiting some similarities with Chinese textiles. It also exhibits parallels with Buddhist iconography in the large stylized lotus patterns. The MNI statue, on the other hand, originated from Java. And even with her Buddhist iconography, her textile pattern shows far more significant similarities with Balinese textile patterns, or perhaps similarities to past textiles from Indo-Persia.

The three statues depicting patterns of consecutive roundels all differ: from the andesite stone used, to the style and types of designs, which bear no relationship to each other. The animal roundels on Mañjuśrī Arapacana portray motifs that appear to reflect patterns from the past; some from relief designs in Central Javanese *caṇḍis* and some from Indo-Persian designs. The sophistication of this design is the most elaborate and complex of the entire group in this chapter. In the case of the statue of Pārvatī, which also depicts animals in roundels, the patterns are reflected in earlier Indian textile paintings, on wall paintings in Pagan, and in Central Asian roundel designs.

Bart has described how the patterns on the three sculptures in the second group of "*balah kacang*" models consist of a complex series of designs that would have been challenging to weave. To create such a repeat pattern so accurately with such fine detail, and making each textile outline on each statue a little different, would have taken a very skilled hand. The extraordinary similarity of the layout of the patterns on the three sculptures in comparison to existing Minangkabau textiles from West Sumatra is uncanny. It is quite possible that they were the templates for some of the motifs seen on Minangkabau textiles today.

Some of the textile patterns perhaps represent a *songket* or brocaded textile, or perhaps reflect *prada*, a gilded pattern. This assumption is based on the examples of contemporary Malay, Javanese and Balinese textile patterns that are reflected in the sculptures. This is particularly evident in the sculptures with *kawung* patterns. Evidence from the *kidung* and *kakawin* poems—as discussed in chapter 2, inform us of the use of these types of textiles during this period of history. It is entirely possible therefore that a number of the textiles on the sculptures could be representing woven or gilded gold cloth; particularly considering the royal nature of the patron and the apparent importance given to the statues. Gold is after all the material of choice for kings: the verses, "adorned with canopies of red *lobheng lĕwih grinsing*" (painted with gold) and "the carriage of the king, adorned with gold and glowing jewels" are taken from the *Nāg.* (18:4–5). Another example relates to a journey by the king into the countryside, where he met Śaivite and Buddhist priests who gave him gifts of food. The king repaid them "with gold, clothing and titles" (*Nāg.* 34:3) (Robson and Prapanca 1995, pp. 38 and 48).

Taking all of these ideas into consideration, perhaps the court of King Kṛtanāgara mastered the rules of religious statuary with luxury textiles. The creation of the figures in this chapter include statues belonging to the Hindu triad—the grouping that often appears in many Central and East Javanese *caṇḍi*. None of the statues in the previous *caṇḍi* though have been carved with textile patterns or are as grand or imposing as these sculptures.

The three sculptures (figs. 137, 149 and 151) given the term Transition cannot be defined by their textile patterns alone, as there is no one pattern or thread of a design that connects them. Lunsingh Scheurleer has discussed the issue of where to place some sculptures that did not automatically fit into the Singosari style. She stated:

> A sculpture belongs to the Singosari style when a connection can be established between it and a member of the Singhasāri dynasty, or the dynasty as a whole. Provenance from the Singosari site is not sufficient. Because styles develop, objects in the Singosari style may have been produced before or after the Singhasāri period. (Lunsingh Scheurleer 2008, p. 290)

Lunsingh Scheurleer presents many possibilities in her informative article, which covers some of the sculptures included in this publication. She has clearly delineated the Singosari style figures, and on the whole I agree with her analysis and the conclusions she has drawn. She was, however, working on the premise of only having two stylistic groups in East Java to fit into the two dynastic periods of Singhasāri and Majapahit, wherein lies the problem. While recognizing that the physical style of these six figures is similar, the stylistic grammars of their textile patterns differ considerably. Clearly, the critical distinctive stylistic traits of the Transition style are of a rigid upright stance and a *mudrā* with hands together; the depiction of a small representation of the lotus plant, which appears not as is the previous group but is beginning to show the rigid traits of the Majapahit style; and an exuberance of elaborate ornaments, particularly the depiction of a three- to five-strand overly long *ratnopavīta*. The textile patterns, however, do not display any elements that could group them together.

As a result of this analysis, two stylistic classifications have been created: Singosari and Transition. As a reminder to the reader, the term *Singhasāri* is in reference to the historical period and the term *Singosari* refers to the style and to the *caṇḍi* of the Singhasāri period. The Singosari style is a well-known description and it has been quoted here from Lunsingh Scheurleer. *Transition*, however, is a term that has been created here for a group of six sculptures that do not "stylistically" fit into the previous group, nor into the Majapahit style, which will be treated in the next chapter. The research carried out by Blom on the sculptures of the Singhasāri period does not refer to the textile patterns as a means of style recognition. She does, however, reference the ornamentation and the *mudrā*, as discussed in chapter 1, but not as a means of style recognition. Nandana Chutiwong's paper on Caṇḍi Singosari describes many sculptures from the Singosari site that "show clear stylistic features of the Majapahit period of the fourteenth centuries". She raises the issues of Pārvatī, which I have placed in Transition style. Stutterheim mentions the lotus plant and its particular depiction in the Singhasāri period versus the Majapahit period, with the lotus growing without a vessel for the Singosari and from a jar in the Majapahit.

As a result of these anomalies, the textile patterns themselves could not be placed into a template as there are too many variations. Furthermore, each of the textile patterns are unique and have remained as visual templates from the thirteenth century until today. The critical distinctive stylistic traits of an upright stance, the *mudrā* of the lower two hands, a smaller depiction of the lotus plant, and an abundant amount of elaborate ornaments, particularly the representation of a three- to five-strand overly long *ratnopavīta*, enables them to be placed in the Transition style classification.

The textile examples can be used as evidence to suggest what might have been in circulation in East Java in the thirteenth century. Let us assume that we know what patterns they were since some of the examples that remain today demonstrate strong, often uncanny, similarities with a number of the stone textile patterns. The evidence from Chinese sources of traded textiles has also been highly significant, particularly from the *Zhufanzhi* and the *Historical Notes on Indonesia and Malaya* (Hirth and Rockhill 1965; Groeneveldt 1960). The stone patterns and the evidence from the *Zhufanzhi* support the theory that some of these textiles must have been in circulation in East Java at this time, even if some comparisons are not ultimately persuasive. The evidence of skull designs themselves cannot be seen solely as an iconographic sign of tantric activity at Caṇḍi Singosari. It is quite clear, however, that King Kṛtanāgara was a follower of esoteric rites and held "the Gaṇcakra" or tantric feasts (*Nāg.* 43:3) (Robson and Prapanca 1995, pp. 55–56). The suggestion therefore that the skull and *kāla*-head textile patterns on this group of sculptures is unique and is perhaps suggestive of more than tantric practices reflects a deep connection the ancient Javanese had to their ancestors and the past. All the details recounted in the *Nāg.* provide further clues as to the types of textiles used in the thirteenth century, and so these sculptures are not our only evidence.

In order to emphasize the significance of these sculptures, it is perhaps important to remember that numerous statues were lost at sea when they were removed from Java by the Europeans. Others were stolen, damaged, destroyed or used as building blocks for houses in the years following the decline of the Hindu-Buddhist period. The most critical loss has been to the elements and through on-site human destruction. The sculptures that remained outside on the grounds of Caṇḍi Singosari have, for example, all but lost their textile patterns and jewellery designs (Pullen 2019). The data gained from these fast-disappearing patterns create a typology for the future as a reference for the remnants of the hidden patterns of the past. Someday these figures will have completely disintegrated, and there would have been no tangible record of the extraordinary detail carved on them.

To summarize, I have referred to the often complex and dense textile patterns depicted on the sculptures from the thirteenth and fourteenth centuries, which contrast unmistakably with the Indian renderings in the drapery and the small flowers, circles and lines of the sculptures in chapter 3. The differences are astonishing. With the use of the line drawings, the variations can be discerned at a glance. It is apparent from the analysis of the textile patterns on the sculptures in this chapter that the Javanese absorbed, assimilated and imitated in order to create distinct stylistic characteristics, and it is through these that the statues and the textiles can be identified as Javanese. The focus here has been to determine how the textile patterns can be realistically placed chronologically. Earlier studies of these sculptures have not tried to place the textile patterns into a time frame. When new statues have been discovered, suggestions for dating—such as those made by R. Soekmono in 1969—have been made based only on the sculptures themselves. At the village of Gurah, in a Kediri site, three deities and one Nāndi were found that all had similarities to the Prajñāpāramitā at the NMI. Soekmono described them as undeniably Singhasāri. Some features were apparent, but the most evident was the "ornamental girdle" and the loop of the cloth on the hips, perhaps indicating the bow of the sash. The deities were identified as Surya and Chandra (Soekmono 1969, pp. 14–17). There is no mention in Soekmono's article of any textile patterns on the sculptures. They are now housed at the NMI, with no identification plate to accompany them. I advocate that these statues could be in the Singosari style despite there being no textile patterns to go by. The most telling feature is the depiction of tiny beaded chains that hang from the *udharabhanda*, the chest band, and from the upper arm bands. Another is a faint marking of the *seléndang* across the body. Other than these features, the carving of the statues lacks a certain sophistication in execution that would place them clearly within the Singosari style.

A comparative chart of line drawings is appended at the end of this chapter to enable the reader to see at a glance the various textile patterns depicted during this period

Endnotes

1. Hadi Sidomulyo has spent many years studying the architecture of East Javanese temples and Mount Pěnanggungan. In conversation he stated that all mountain temples are made up of three terraces with a platform at the top—part of the concept of four and nine (nine peaks at Pěnanggungan).

2. The pattern called *balah kacang* is primarily known today in the Minangkabau highlands. It is entirely possible that Ādityavarman brought the motif from these three Buddhist deities with him to his Malayu kingdom in Sumatra. He subsequently moved from Dharmasarya to Pagaruyung following interference from the Javanese, and the patterns must have moved with him. This pattern and the motif on the sash of the Bhairava are both known today in the repertoire of the Minangkabau *songket*. Bernhard Bart is a weaver in Minangkabau who has completed research on the geometry of the *kawung* and *balah kacang* motifs. He has created modern *songket* to exactly replicate this pattern. The basic difference between the two textiles is that the *kawung* consists of five circles whilst the *balah kacang* consists of eight.

3. Textiles featuring images of dragons, griffins and phoenix within roundels have been known in the Yuan period between 1279 and 1368, which was contiguous with the carving of the Mañjuśrī in Java,

4. This composite creature has been much discussed by Matteo Compareti: "the winged dog with a peacock tail commonly identified with *simurgh* of Iranian mythology should be identified most probably as a manifestation of the very important concept of 'glory' or 'charisma' that was called in Persian texts *farr*" (Compareti 2020, p. 115). Compareti's research has concluded that this creature is of Central Asian rather than Persian origin, as has been suggested in previous literature. He also proposes that this composite creature was not popular amongst the Buddhists of Central Asia (2020, p. 116), and it is not what we are seeing here in this drawing. My interpretation of the drawing is that it shows an animal with a doglike head, an open mouth displaying a forked tongue and a row of pointed teeth. The forelegs and paws are canine or feline, with sharp claws. The forepart of the animal comes to an abrupt halt and the back half of the creature is a bird. Wings come from the shoulders, and long slender feathers rise above the head. A rich tail of double plumes curves out behind it. The lion-griffin and the serpent-dragon appear similar in many ways to the pseudo-*simurgh*. The feathered, realistic birdlike termination of the body of the pseudo-*simurgh*, however, is not to be found in any of the animal chimera known from the heart of the ancient Near East, Iraq or Iran. The wings of the pseudo-*simurgh* are composed of fine feathers on the lower section, and longer waving tendrils form the outer part, which usually turn forward towards the neck rather than back towards the tail. Of course the representation of a pseudo-*simurgh* in this textile pattern is a proposal, on which Compareti does not agree; he suggests this figure is typically Indian, specifically from Gupta art, where similar motifs are seen at the Ajanta caves (in conversation, 23 September 2020).

5. The *makara* is a mythical creature. Its Sanskrit name means "water monster" or "sea dragon". The Rijksmuseum in Amsterdam describes it as follows: "The *makara* is a

mythical creature associated with water. In Central Java, they often stood guard at temple entrances. This example has the muzzle of a dragon, the trunk of an elephant and the horns of a ram. Seated on the tongue of its wide-open mouth is a lion."

6. In conversation at SOAS in January 2016, Anna Contadini described how Sassanian designs of the fifth and sixth centuries moved west to Tibet and then to the Arab world and Java via Indian and Arab traders. In the early trade of Indian textiles from the fifth century, according to one Chinese document, an Indonesian diplomatic mission carried textiles from India and Gandhara to China. This indicates that textiles from northeast India could have been available in Indonesia at this time. It is therefore evident that Indian textiles would have been available in Java from at least the eighth century as the statues provide corroboration of this. In conversation at the Abegg Stiftung, Dr Regula Shorta suggested that the patterns are "stylised"—the artist's depiction of a real cloth to make it more elaborate or suitable for the local taste. This suggestion is entirely possible, but these clear similarities tell us that textiles or ideas such as the examples given here must have been a template of some sort; otherwise, why would there only be one sculpture with this particular pattern.

7. The idea that woven silk textiles made in India were subsequently traded to Tibet and Central Asia, with the textiles often then used as a form of gift-giving, was discussed by Rosemary Crill in a conference on Assam at the British Museum on 8 July 2016. Rosemary's paper was titled "Trans Himalayan Textiles: Indian woven Silks in Tibet".

8. In 1260 CE, Caṇḍi Kidal was built as a *śrāddha* temple—a ceremony in honour of a dead ancestor—for King Anuṣapati during the early reign of Kṛtanāgara. The *caṇḍi* has a panel of *kapāla* cup relief that encircles the entire building. This would indicate that in this first stage of Kṛtanāgara's reign he was already leaning towards the extremes of Esoteric practices. The term "*kapāla* motif" will be used for the motif that runs around the upper levels of Caṇḍi Kidal. The same shape is clearly evident on a number of the textile borders on the Singosari sculptures. The pattern's appearance on the walls of Kidal is the first instance of it occurring until it appears in the textile patterns on the Singosari sculptures.

9. This *songket* was inherited from a distant relative whose ancestors had lived in Palembang, South Sumatra around the 1900s.

10. The *kawung* pattern could also have been inspired by the Chinese coins the Ssu Shu. A textile in the Singapore National Museum has a batik described as "*batik tulis ceplok*" inspired by Chinese coins from the 1960s. It is unlikely, however, that in the thirteenth century this pattern would have been inspired by Chinese coins—it is far more likely to have been developed from nature.

11. This has often been described as a pouch. But in studying the way a sarong is tied today—particularly in Myanmar—the knot can obviously be seen to be a part of the fabric of the sash, and not a pouch.

12. The resolution of the photograph in the original publication is too poor to include here. This statue and the entire body of sculptures no longer exist.

13. The resolution of the image is insufficient to show here.

14. In Bali, three sections of the pattern would be sewn together and used to form a single overgarment (*saput* or *kampuh*). Joined red *gĕringsing* cloths are worn by both men and women at important rituals in Tenganan village today.

15. As is evident from my personal observations at the Kraton in Surakarta today.

16. The term is used when a king is unified with a god—in this case Śiva—or with a bodhisattva or Dhyani Buddha. *Bhaṭāra* in Old Javanese means "divine ancestor". It is an honorific term.

17. The charter refers to the establishment of five monuments in the years preceding

1255, all of which are listed among the twenty-seven royal shrines in the *Nāgarakṛtāgama*. Sedyawati talks of the three Kṛtanāgara inscriptions, one of which is the *Mūla-Mulurung*, in which it states the highest rank of officials were in direct line to the king's commands.

18. This is a typical Chinese stylistic attribute on Yuan blue-and-white ceramics, used around the foot and upper edges of a vase, often called "upward lotus petals". Jingdezhen China Ceramics Museum, 2016.

19. Hadi Sidomulyo has proposed that the *candrakapāla* motif was also known in the early twelfth century in Kediri and was used as the emblem of some of the kings. An example is on the top of a large *prasasti batu*, or inscription, in the Airlangga Museum in Kediri. Another is on the site of Caṇḍi Plumbungan, dated to the early thirteenth century (Trawas, in conversation, May 2016). The carving of the c*andrakapāla* symbol, however, appears quite different on the *prasasti* to the rendition on the textile patterns.

20. Karangkates has a skull pattern with round eyes, long curving teeth and double fangs curving to the widest part of the head, whereas the pattern on the Mahākāla in the MNI is depicted with almond-shaped eyes, short teeth and single fangs curving to the top of his head.

21. The emblem of the Kediri kings is known as Argha *candrakapāla*—literally meaning "half-moon head". This information was gained from the Airlangga Museum. To explain the use of this emblem and its subsequent interpretation of the textile of the Gaṇeśa is a subject beyond the scope of this book. What it does show however is the apparent longevity of this motif over nearly two hundred years, which would in my opinion indicate the underlying tantric religion of the kings of East Java. The use of this symbol reaches its height with Kṛtanāgara and the statues of Gaṇeśa.

22. Śrivijaya, or *Sānfóqí*, no longer existed after 1030 CE. Wolters was of the opinion that by 1080 the name was believed to refer to Malayu Jambi and not Palembang. References to *Sānfóqí* in the tenth and early eleventh centuries could relate to Palembang or Jambi (Miksic and Goh 2017, p. 396).

23. In 1996, Bernhard Bart, a Swiss architect who was learning Indonesian in Padang, made a sketch of an intricate old Minangkabau *songket* that was on display at the Padang Museum. When he tried to find a similar weaving in the markets of Pandai Sikek and Payakumbuh, he found only poor-quality textiles with simplified patterns. Intrigued, Bart began to research Minangkabau *songket*, eventually photographing around fifteen hundred pieces, including many in museums in Indonesia and Europe. Along the way he became convinced that he had to do something to keep the tradition alive. His studio, PT Studio Songket Palantaloom, has turned its attention to reproducing textile motifs found on stone statues in the Museum Nasional Indonesia, including the lotus flower motif on the statue of the Hindu deity Durgā from Candi Singosari, East Java and the *balah kacang* (split peanut) motif on the statue of Śyāmatārā from Candi Jago, East Java. The *balah kacang* motif, which is found almost exclusively on Minangkabau *songket* textiles, has important symbolic meaning for the Minangkabau. It is not at all clear how this motif found its way from several thirteenth century Javanese statues to Minangkabau weavers in West Sumatra. http://www.nowjakarta.co.id/reviving-minangkabau-songket.

24. There are in fact two known statues in Sumatra: one at Muara Jambi and another from Pugungraharjo, Lampung. The second is of a poor-quality stone, but it does provide evidence of Prajñāpāramitā statue production in Sumatra. There are three in Java: the two mentioned here and another headless statue in the grounds of Caṇḍi Singosari.

25. The website www.digitalheritage2013.org describes this pattern as a *jilamprang* motif. In modern Indonesia it is regarded as a traditional batik pattern.

26. The town of Muntok on Bangka Island was part of the Regency of Palembang where most of the *kain limar* were woven for the Palembang courts. Knowledge gained from personal communication with weavers in Palembang during a 2016 research trip.

27. The interment of Kṛtanāgara as the Buddha Vairocana ties in well with the image of his father as Amoghapāśa, whose central position he occupied in Jago's *maṇḍala*. The Javanese concept of ideal kingship notes the importance of the right queen and of the king's obligation to pursue that quest since the queen is the person who embodies the fertility and good fortune of the kingdom. Based on this, Kṛtanāgara was deified with his queen and as Vairocana and he became the most important of all the Javanese kings in this deified image. This has not, however, had any effect on his textile patterns, on which there are no signs of esoteric imagery.

28. North Eastern Indian or Newar elements have long been noted in the statuary and decorative aspects of East Javanese Buddhist art. There was believed to be a diaspora of Newar artisans in the realm of the Sino-Tibetans who became evident at the court of the Yuan emperor Kublai Khan. This coincided at a time when the reign of Kublai and that of Kṛtanāgara were parallel. It has been suggested, based on some inscriptions at Caṇḍi Jago associated with Kṛtanāgara, that there were links with Newar and Northeast India.

Kediri and Singhasāri – Comparative Chart of Line Drawings

Kediri and Singhasāri – Comparative Chart of Line Drawings

108 Mahākāla, Volkenkunde Leiden	109 Mahākāla, Volkenkunde Leiden	112 Gaṇeśa, Volkenkunde Leiden
113 Gaṇeśa, Volkenkunde Leiden	114 Gaṇeśa, Volkenkunde Leiden	116 Gaṇeśa, National Museum, Bangkok
117 Gaṇeśa, National Museum, Bangkok	118 Gaṇeśa, National Museum, Bangkok	121 Karangkates Gaṇeśa, Desa Sumber Pucung

123 Mahākāla, Museum Nasional Indonesia

124 Mahākāla, Museum Nasional Indonesia

128 Prajñāpāramitā, Museum Nasional Indonesia

129 Prajñāpāramitā, Museum Nasional Indonesia

129 Prajñāpāramitā, Museum Nasional Indonesia

135 Prajñāpāramitā, Muara Jambi Site Museum

136 Prajñāpāramitā, Muara Jambi Site Museum

136 Prajñāpāramitā, Muara Jambi Site Museum

138 Prajñāpāramitā, Caṇḍi Gayatri/Boyolangu

Kediri and Singhasāri – Comparative Chart of Line Drawings

140 Unidentified Goddess, Caṇḍi Singosari

142 Dikpāla, Caṇḍi Singosari

144 Dikpāla, Vihara Buddhayana, Jakarta

150 Durgā Mahiṣāsuramardinī, Museum Mpu Tantular, Surabaya

153 Harihara Ardhanari, The State Hermitage Museum, St Petersburg

5. Majapahit
Stone Sculpture from the Fourteenth to the Fifteenth Century

A group of eight sculptures dated to the Majapahit period represent deified figures of kings and queens dressed in royal attire, which is evident from their high crowns, their substantial garments and the heavy ornaments on their ankles. The detailed pattern of the *sinjang kawung* repeating itself in slightly different variations on each sculpture indicates the reverence with which the Majapahit rulers held this particular motif. As Klokke has suggested, the presence of four arms is an unmistakably divine feature, with the attributes indicating the specific qualities of the various gods represented. The highest god is one who combines the visual characteristics of two deities to express the oneness of these gods, such as Ardhanarīśvara, the supreme concept of one god, joined as one in both male and female. They stand in a stiff, upright stance—a distinctive feature. Their eyes are downcast in deep meditation, combined with the limited *mudrā* of the lower two hands. Their deification led them to attain the highest spiritual knowledge (Klokke 1994, pp. 190–91). H.G. Quaritch Wales has suggested that at the foundation of the Majapahit there was a resurgence of pre-Indianized culture, which appeared to have little reference to the Indian legacy of the past. This was evident in the culture of non-Indian gods and ancestors, who appeared to reign supreme (Wales 1977, pp. 89–90).

The statues in this chapter, unlike with the previous sections, will be ordered chronologically where possible during the mid-fourteenth and early fifteenth centuries, as the textile patterns all fall within two group. The first will include the *ceplok* patterns, and the second will consist of the different models in Java and in Sumatra.

The practice of deifying the ancestors was known at the beginning of the thirteenth century during the Kediri period and continued throughout the Singhasāri and Majapahit periods. The assumption that the images bear facial features of a certain king or queen is in contrast to ancient Indian and Southeast Asia sculptures whose features are generally without any specific character and appear to follow the convention or the style of the period. However, in East Java the sculptors did not deviate from this practice, as it would be necessary to have more than one statue bearing exactly the same features to be able to consider a statue as a portrait of a person. Klokke suggests that the Majapahit statues were symbols of royalty and symbols of divinity. These symbols were incorporated into the iconography of the statues, and hence should not be referred to as portrait or mortuary statues (Klokke 1994, pp. 182–84). In Klokke's opinon, these statues are not portrait statues, as has been suggested by past scholars, but "images of kings and queens who were deified after death. Their deification implies attainment of the highest knowledge which entails release of the material world and unification with god". This suggests they are neither gods and goddesses or kings and queens, for they are both (ibid., p. 191).

The epic poem the *Kakawin Sumanasāntaka* talks of the deification of royal ancestors and discusses the cultural and social environment of the court. It tells us that when a queen dies prematurely she is transported to Indra's heaven where she becomes a "royal ancestor" (Hardjonagoro 1979, pp. 603–11). If her husband the king dies first, the queen commits suicide, and both king and queen are cremated at the same time. The poem recounts how "they are deified as ancestors in the form of a god and goddess united, Ardhanarīsvara, and enshrined in a temple where their influence becomes ritually available to their ancestors" (ibid., p. 611).

The author of the poem Mpu Monaguṇa recounts that royal power was considered incarnate in the person of the queen, who was identified with Lakshmi the female, stating that the power of the god was embodied in the consort. The power of the king, therefore, was incorporated in his queen. As a consequence, royal couples are imagined to be Ardhanarīsvara—the union of Śiva and his consort. There appear to be some deviations from the previous Indian norms of sculpture production, as seen in the significant number of East Javanese sculptures created in the appearance of portrait statues of deceased kings and queens. It was assumed that this move away from the more "Indian features" meant that figures were now being made to represent deified kings rather than gods. It is clearly apparent that the statues had been given crowns and not the matted hair, or *jaṭā*, a characteristic of ascetic gods such as Śiva (Klokke 1994, p. 180). This is a feature of all the statues in this chapter.

This group represents just a fraction of the sculptures created during the fourteenth and early fifteenth centuries that appear with a carved textile pattern and that are clearly representative of the Majapahit style. Whether a sculpture has been carved with a textile pattern or not does not appear to alter the amount of jewellery adorning the statues, especially in comparison to the earlier figures of the Central Java period. The four- to five-strand pearl *ratnopavīta* and the overly long chain belts carved in deep relief are a distinct feature of the Majapahit style. It is perhaps interesting to note that many of the small and medium Majapahit sculptures in the museums of Java and Europe are without any textile patterns.

So, do the faces of the statues represent those of gods or those of deified monarchs? By this point, there were diverse Majapahit styles that differed entirely from the previous Transition and Singosari forms. The type of statue had changed entirely from the previous association with Northeast India to dominant affinities with a Javanese Buddhism. This was clearly reflected in the forms of esoteric practices seen during the reign of Kṛtanāgara. By the fifteenth century, Islam was well established on the north coast of Java, but at the same time there appeared to be a strong resurgence of classical Hinduism. Some inscriptions have been found that exhibit a high standard of Sanskrit scholarship. J.G. de Casparis suggests that the Javanese were in contact with the Vijayanagar kingdom in the Deccan in India. And despite the lack of "direct cultural relations" between these two kingdoms, it would appear that the flowering of the use of Sanskrit in East Java would connect these two great empires during the fourteenth and fifteenth centuries (Casparis 1983, pp. 17–18).

There is unmistakably a remarkable difference in the East Javanese style of statues, as evident from the textile patterns and the carving of the facial features. It is apparent in the jawline, which often appears too heavy, and in the lips and nose, which are too fleshy to be the refined features of a god, in comparison to the deities from the Singhasāri period. There are two clear stylistic differences between the statues in this group. Some figures are significant at 2 metres in height, whilst a further four statues are all on average 1.6 metres. The faces of this second, smaller group differ considerably; the ornaments appear even more prominently from the body; and the *sinjang kawung* pattern has simplified. In fact, if it was not for the breasts of Pārvatī, there are no distinguishing features to identify a statue as male or female from either their dress style or textile patterns. The conclusion therefore is that rather than portraits, the sculptures are indeed deified figures carved to follow the preferred aesthetics of the period: "they represent figures who bear royal or divine features and are absorbed in meditation" (Klokke 1994, p. 188).

Convincing evidence rests with the stone patterns on the Majapahit statues. Despite a lack of any archaeological reports or particular textual references to these textile patterns, the statues support the theory that textiles with designs of *kawung* were popular during the fourteenth century. In addition, the garment known as a *sinjang kawung* has been a particularly longstanding one.

Ceplok Patterns

Two massive stone statues of *dvārapāla* (fig. 155) remain in situ at the entrance to the Main Temple at Caṇḍi Panataran. Panataran functions as a state temple consecrated to Śiva (Kinney 2003, p. 180). There is evidence of a skull and crescent moon in the hair of the guardians. They are accompanied on either side by a small female attendant. The *dvārapāla* and the attendants stand upon a skull base. Both statues exhibit some damage; one more so than the other. The sheer authority and strength they exude as guardian figures though is still apparent. Despite the rough grey andesite, which is marked by many inclusions, the statues have been carved with some exceptional details.

Figure 155 *Dvārapāla*, guardian figure, 1347, Majapahit, Main Temple, Caṇḍi Panataran, Blitar, East Java. 1.55m, andesite stone. Pullen photo.

Wrapped around the torso is the *sarpopavīta*, defined as a sizeable realistic snake, with the damaged head rearing over the left shoulder. The statues are adorned with several belts and sashes. The girdle consists of metal plaques and pearls or gold beads that hang in loops. It is closed with a large detailed *kāla*-head buckle. The chain belt with looped pearls is apparent on a number of the Singhasāri and Majapahit sculptures. The *sinjang* is held with a fabric sash, the ends of which fall to the ankles with an overly large and detailed tassel representing a gold ornament with jewels (fig. 156).

The female attendants on the outside of the central figure are dressed identically, with a similar *sinjang kawung*. The attendants do not wear the *sarpopavīta*, but instead a four-strand pearl chain. Both statues are carved with a small cloth overlaying the *sinjang*. The *kawung* pattern is visible on both textiles, each with a different border (fig. 157). Across the upper thigh, one above the other, are two broad sashes. These appear to be tied at the rear with an overly large knot. The ends of these sashes fall the full length of the sculpture.

The colossal statue of Harihara deified as a king shown in figure 158 remains in the NMI. It is carved from a much smoother andesite stone

Figure 156 *Dvārapāla*, detail of the lower legs showing the long sashes and patterned *sinjang*. Pullen photo.

228 Patterned Splendour

Figure 157 *Dvārapāla*, close up of the sash border pattern on the lower left leg. Pullen photo. Drawing of the *sinjang* and the sash.

to that of the *dvārapāla*. This type of sculpture of Harihara is not unusual in East Java. This particular statue was believed to represent King Kertarājasa Jayawardhana, the first king of Majapahit. It was found in the ruins of Caṇḍi Sumberjati, also known as Caṇḍi Simping. The structure is thought to be the commemorative *caṇḍi* of the first Majapahit king, the son-in-law of King Kṛtanāgara (*Nāg.* 70:1–2). It has also been suggested that the figure of Queen Tribhuwana as Pārvatī was the companion of this statue (Kinney 2003, p. 219). Although Kinney bases this deduction on their similar sizes, the comparable jewellery and on details of the clothing, they do also exhibit certain differences and the two figures should not be described as a pair. Arguably, the lack of a textile pattern on Queen Tribhuwana could be because she is unfinished. The indented design on the areola behind her head remains the defining difference between the two statues.

The Harihara is decorated with a profusion of elaborately and meticulously modelled ornaments. The tall, heavy-looking crown has a diadem tied with ribbons carved on the backslab. The earlobes are enlarged and adorned with heavy earrings recalling goldwork. He wears clearly defined multiple necklets and bracelets. The anklets, unfortunately, are damaged. The *seléndang* is carved in the typical East Javanese style. The long *ratnopavīta*, a string of four strands of pearls, is draped across the upper thighs. The chain is interspaced with two elaborate clasps: one on the chest and the second on the upper leg. Around the waist

Figure 158 Harihara, King Kertarājasa Jayawardhana, early 14th century, Majapahit, Caṇḍi Simping or Sumberjati, south of Blitar, Malang, East Java. Museum Nasional Indonesia. 2m, andesite stone. Inv. no. 256a/103a.

Figure 159 Harihara, drawing of the textile pattern on *sinjang* and sashes.

Figure 160 Pārvatī as a queen, late 14th or early 15th century, Majapahit. Museum Nasional Indonesia. Andesite stone. Inv. no. 113a. Pullen photo.

hang both metal and jewelled belts held with an ornate belt clasp. The ends of the chain belt fall to the ankles with a detailed tassel. The chain is made to depict gold plaques linked together. Both consorts appear identically dressed to the central figure.

The *sinjang kawung* folds at the waist, where the pattern is visible above the belts. Draped over the upper thighs are two broad sashes, which are tied with a large knot and with the ends arranged in neat folds. The pattern carved on the sash is identical to that on the *sinjang*. The drawing (fig. 159) shows interlocking circles with double borders. The motif in the centre of each circle consists of a vegetal pattern finished with a plain edge.

The smaller stone statue of Pārvatī as a deified queen (fig. 160) appears considerably rougher in quality compared to the previous two figures. The origin of the statue is unknown. Depicted at the side of the body are two broad sashes tied with a large knot. The two ends fall almost to the ankles. The pattern is so precisely carved that the fabric appears folded. The figure is adorned with a profusion of carved ornaments (fig. 161) consisting of metal and jewelled belts. Most notable are the detailed clasps and gold plaques. Two ties fall to the ankles with a detailed tassel. The male consorts attending the queen appear somewhat worn. Their dress is similar to that of the central figure. The garment on the leading figure consists of the *sinjang kawung* comprising large juxtaposing circles with a double border. The centre of each circle is made up of four semi-circles—a geometric pattern based around a small central circle.

In a rear corner of the MNI remains a unique carving representing a royal or divine couple (fig. 162), where the female appears seated on the left knee of the male. The couple are placed against a partially broken but decorated backslab on a decorated lotus base. The arms and legs of both figures are damaged. At the upper right side only is a small *kāla* head (fig. 163), a Sanskrit term that means time or death. The *kāla* was initially a lion's face in a stylized demonic form, who assumed a demonic character. The face appears with long fangs and the tip of his tongue is folded back into the mouth. The head is surrounded by swirling vegetation—a feature unique to this statue.

The pair are dressed as a royal couple, with elaborate jewellery, including the *upavīta*. A considerably damaged patterned *sinjang* covers the lower part of the body to the ankles. The smooth stone surface is of an exceptional quality andesite. Given that the characteristics of the faces of the royal couple are highly personal, this statue would appear to be a "portrait" representing a royal couple united with the gods upon death. The rendering of both sculptures has been well conceived and meticulously carved with a profusion of elaborate ornaments, all of which remain visible. The earlobes are enlarged with heavy earrings recalling gold work. The meticulous detail on both the male and female is apparent in the many necklets—which differ between the two statues—and in the double upper arm and triple bracelets. The *ratnopavīta* is carved as a five-strand string of pearls draped on the lower legs. Along each strand are embellishments of different types of ornaments. Some metal belts are tied around the waist. A chain belt also links and falls the length of the body, between the legs and on to the lotus base with an overly large tassel. Both figures are carved with a *sinjang kawung* noticeable at the ankles. Despite the statue's considerable surface damage and missing limbs, the textile pattern is visible on the legs of the female and the right side of the male's sash (fig. 164). The photograph shows the

Figure 161 Pārvatī, detail of the *sinjang* and chain belts on the lower left leg. Pullen photo. Drawing of the textile pattern on *sinjang* and sashes.

Figure 162 Divine or royal couple, late 14th or early 15th century, Majapahit, from Jebuk, Tulungagung, East Java. Museum Nasional Indonesia. 1.67m, andesite stone. Inv. no. 5542. Pullen photo.

delicacy with which the male has his hand around the sash bow of the female. The designs consist of a series of carved double circles that overlap each other. The rings are made up of *vesicae*. In the centre of the circles are four teardrop motifs around a central circle. This straightforward yet sophisticated rendering of the *kawung* pattern is reflected in some modern batik textiles. The design in the modern batik in figure 165 echoes the layout of the *kawung* motif on the *sinjang* and the sash, which demonstrates the continuity and longevity of this pattern. As suggested earlier, in the fourteenth century textiles would probably have been decorated with gold or woven with gold thread. Both sculptures are no doubt wearing a sash, as a considerable knot is discernible at each side. Around the neck of the knot is a detailed beaded ornament, which is a feature that is seen on many Singosari sculptures. One end of this falls on to the lotus base and the other is depicted on the backslab. The meticulous detail with which this sculpture has been executed is outstanding, particularly in the crafting of the dress and the ornaments on both figures, as the jewellery follows the curves of the body and gives proof to the artist's considerable talent.

The idea of a god and goddess seated together is by no means unique to Java, as this grouping is well known in similar gatherings of divine couples in the art of the Pāla produced between the tenth and twelfth centuries. There are examples in the SHM, the Assam Museum and in the Metropolitan Museum of Art, to name just a few. In the South Asian convention, Pārvatī would look at her partner, or forward as in the Assam sculpture, whereas the Javanese female is looking away. This highlights another reason to suggest this is a royal couple, despite the halo, and not a figure of Śiva and Pārvatī. As there are no textile patterns and only simple ornamentations on the Pāla figures, I suggest this undoubtedly indicates the noble status of the Javanese couple.

Figure 163 Divine or royal couple, detail of the *kāla*-head on the upper right side of the backslab. Pullen photo.

234 Patterned Splendour

The one-metre high statue of Pārvatī (fig. 166) as a queen is believed to represent a member of the royalty. There is a similar statue in the Metropolitan Museum of Art (possibly a replica). This statue is flanked by her children Gaṇeśa and Kārttikeya, or Skanda. The group stands upon Nandi, Śiva's vehicle. Pārvatī wears a *sinjang kawung* with a pattern of overlapping circles made up of four vesicae. The centre of each circle constitutes a four-leafed vegetal motif. Draped over the thighs and knees are two plain sashes carved in deep relief and tied with a large

Figure 164 Divine or royal couple, detail of the left hand of the male holding the sash bow of the female. Pullen photo.

Figure 165 Detail of a batik wall hanging by Dudung, 2016, Pekalongan, Java. Cotton. Private collection. Drawing of the textile pattern.

Figure 166 Pārvatī as a queen, late 14th or early 15th century, Majapahit. Museum Nasional Indonesia. 1.06 m, andesite stone. Inv. no. 126. Pullen photo.

236 Patterned Splendour

Figure 167 Pārvatī, detail of the *sinjang* and sash on the lower left side. Pullen photo. Drawing of the textile pattern.

knot (fig. 167), with one end flying upwards and the other falling to the side of the body. Contemporary batik textile examples (fig. 168) demonstrate how the *kawung* pattern on this statue has been replicated on a modern textile, demonstrating once again the longevity of this popular and auspicious pattern. Fastidious detail in the carving is apparent with the multiple necklets, dual upper armbands and triple bracelets. The long *ratnopavīta* as a string of four strands of pearls drapes to the upper legs, with a simple clasp between the breasts. Draped around the waist are several metal belts inset with jewels and looping pearl chains, joined with an overly large buckle. Another long belt is tied at the waist and falls to below the knees, finished with a large metal tassel. The two accompanying figures appear decorated with jewellery.

Figure 168 Detail of a *batik sakti tulis*, Bīma Sakti, Imogiri, Java, 2010. Cotton. Private collection.

As a point of reference, jewellery with looping pearl chains of this type are also visible in some Tibetan paintings. For example, the figure of Vajravārāhī from Western Xia, Khara-Khoto of the late twelfth to the thirteenth century at the State Hermitage Museum is decorated with a pearl-chain belt and pearl-chain upper armbands. This feature is also typical in some earlier Singosari sculptures, such as Prajñāpāramitā in the NMI and the headless Prajñāpāramitā at Caṇḍi Singosari also carved with a pearl upper armband.

Śiva Mahadeva (fig 169) is the last sculpture in the Majapahit group. The rough andesite stone and again the appearance of the ubiquitous *kawung* textile pattern on this late fourteenth or early fifteenth century statue indicates the continuity of this pattern layout throughout this long period.

Figure 169 Śiva Mahadeva as a king, late 14th or early 15th century, Majapahit, Rejoagung, Pare, East Java. Museum Nasional Indonesia. Approx. 1.5 m, andesite stone. Inv. no. 5620. Pullen photo.

238   Patterned Splendour

Figure 170 Śiva Mahadeva, detail of the lower legs showing the *sinjang* and long chain belt. Pullen photo. Drawing of the textile pattern.

Draped over the thighs and knees are patterned sashes with the *kawung* design. The cloth is tied at the side with a large knot, and the two patterned ends realistically but stiffly fall the length of the body. The rendering of this statue does not have the intricate, realistic detailing of the previous Majapahit sculptures. The *sinjang kawung* is once again carved in a schematic fashion (fig. 170), with a series of vesicae joining at the points to create a circle. Within the ring is a leaf design. This pattern appears, however, to be carved with a little more detail than the previous sculpture. The *ratnopavīta* chain is draped between the breasts, falling to the upper thighs, and is finished with an excessively large clasp. Fastened around the waist are metal and jewelled belts held with a detailed jewelled buckle. The long chain belt represents a series of reticulated metal plaques. It finishes at the ankles with a tassel representation in metalwork or perhaps a gemstone.

Miscellaneous Patterns

Bhīma and Kertolo are both part of the Panji stories. The two statues presented here are examples of statues at the culmination and the very sudden collapse of the Majapahit. With the collapse, the production of deified statues ceased, the types of textile patterns changed and there was no further evidence of the *kawung* design.

Panji stories became very popular, with the figures of Bhīma and Kertolo also appearing in relief carvings and as *wayang kulit* figures. But by this stage, the type of patterned garments reflected on the statues was very different from the styles worn by the previous deified statues of kings and queens.

Bhīma is seen as the mighty protector and mediator, and represents one of the principal characters in *wayang kulit* shadow theatre drama (Duijker 2010, p. 37). The statue of Kertolo is approximately the same size and uses the same quality of stone as that of Bhīma. They both appear in the same stylistic category and possess similar morphological characteristics.

Bhīma (fig. 171) wears a loincloth that ties around the waist and falls as a narrow band between the legs. The loincloth on Kertolo (fig. 172) in contrast opens to one side to reveal the swelling of the genitals. The arms of both statues are overly long and reach to their knees. Their legs are bare. Both figures have open eyes, a handle-bar moustache and a pointed nose. They both also have snake-style ornaments wound around their necks and wrists. In their ears are heavy ornaments, or *sumping*. The hairstyle, or *gĕlung*, on both statues is alike.

Bhīma's loincloth is carved with a *polèng*, or chequered (fig. 173) layout. This is usually presented in black and white, and sometimes with a red border. The pattern is carved in deep relief, suggesting a heavy or folded woven cotton textile standing proud of the body. The cloth is gathered at the front and rear, and reaches to the ankles. He wears the fabric as a remembrance of his initiation. Kertolo wears a simple loincloth tight around his waist. The only decoration on it is a border pattern along the lower edge. The design (fig. 174) is of small circles and a peepul leaf shape, which was probably woven into a cotton textile or embossed in gold. The *polèng* is a *kain bebali* (fig. 175) that is used for sacred stones, trees, shrines and divine symbols and worn by human beings. Cloths made up of alternating "black or grey and white checks, are held to be antitheses—antitheses, however which mutually condition each other and without which the whole world would be inconceivable" (Hauser-Schäublin, Nabholz-Kartaschoff and Ramseyer 1991, pp. 89–92).

Figure 171 Bhīma, 15th century, possibly Caṇḍi Sukuh, Mt Lawu, Central Java. Museum Nasional Indonesia. 68 cm, andesite stone. Inv. no. unknown. Pullen photo.

Figure 172 Kertolo, one of the acolytes of Prince Panji, 15th century, Mt Pĕnanggungan, East Java. Museum Nasional Indonesia. Inv. no. 310d. Pullen photo.

For the Balinese, it is this principle of dualism that makes up the whole. *Polèng* textiles are used today in Bali for numerous occasions and remain one of the most visible forms of textile identification in Indonesia.

Two further relief figures highlight the continuing uses of textile patterns on stone carvings in both Sumatra and Java (fig. 176). The figures are of dancers with demonic faces, carved in yellow andesite. They originate from stone casements at either side of the stairs of Biaro Pulo at Padang Lawas in West Sumatra, shown in map 2 (p. 46). F.M. Schnitger has suggested that the site was probably Mahāyāna Buddhist judging from the various remains found in the vicinity (1937, p. 29). Both figures (figs. 177a and 177b) wear a loincloth. The dancing monk is depicted with a demonic face, with skulls at the ears and a hip wrapper that ties at the back (unseen). The fabric represented would have been quite firm, as the double U-shape at the top indicates a brocade of some sort.

Figure 173
Bhīma, detail of the lower limbs highlighting the textile pattern on the loincloth. Pullen photo. Drawing of the textile pattern.

The motif on the *kain* is one of circles juxtaposed with each other and the pattern of a trefoil or perhaps a simple type of *vajra*. The dancing figure with a bull's head appears to be wearing a *kain* in the style of a South Indian *dhotī*. The view appears to be from the back of the figure, as his head is twisted around in an energetic dancing pose. The double U-shape perhaps represents a heavy cloth with a dual band at the top and the motif of a scrolling pattern set within vertical lines.

These patterns are unique to this set of sculptures and they appear nowhere else in Sumatra or Java. These figures are depicted in an animated attitude and could be dancers at tantric ceremonies of the kind that can be seen today in monasteries in Tibet, Bhutan or Mongolia (fig. 178),

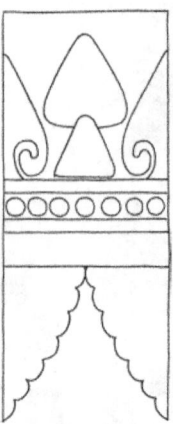

Figure 174 Kertolo, detail of the lower limbs highlighting the patterned end to the loincloth. Pullen photo. Drawing of the textile pattern.

Figure 175 *Polèng, Kain Bebali*, detail, 21st century. 147 x 117 cm, cotton. Threads of Life, Ubud, private collection. Pullen photo.

for which the dancers wear similar masks. This practice is more likely, however, to have travelled in the opposite direction, with the Buddhist monk Atīśa. *Sānfóqí*, or Śrivijaya, was part of an active international Buddhist network. Atīśa moved there from India and stayed there for twelve to thirteen years before returning to Tibet. A Nepalese manuscript written circa 1015 CE contains drawings of well-known Buddhist images. The drawings are thought to be of Lokanatha, as found in the vicinity of Bukit Seguntang with only the remains of the lotus pedestal and a fragment of the topknot (Krom 1931, p. 248; Schnitger 1937, p. 3; Miksic and Goh 2017, p. 396). The bull, who appears as the servant of Yama, represents the god of death (Haulleville 2000, p. 50).

Figure 176 Bas relief of dancers, 13th–14th century, Biaro Pulo, Padang Lawas, West Sumatra. Museum Nasional Indonesia. 55 x 33 cm, sandstone. Inv. no. 6121. Pullen photo.

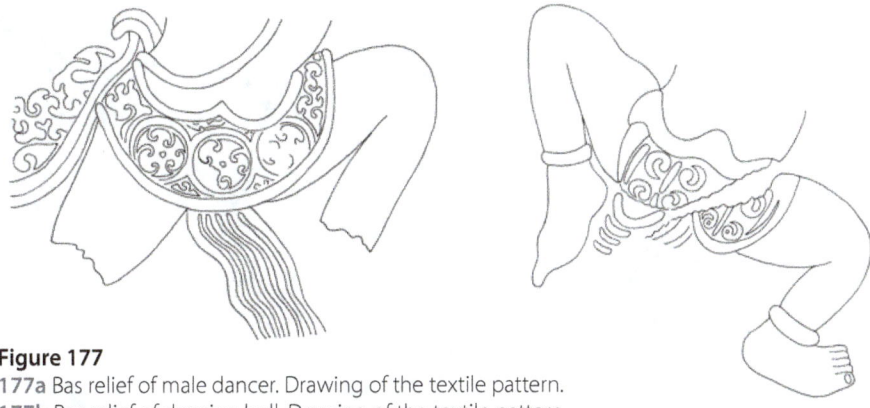

Figure 177
177a Bas relief of male dancer. Drawing of the textile pattern.
177b Bas relief of dancing bull. Drawing of the textile pattern.

Andaya describes the major commercial centre of Panai polity—which is based in central Sumatra around Padang Lawas—as being located in a strategic position of complex trade routes. The conjunction of commercial and religious centres in the ancient world was a common phenomenon, where deities are placed to protect the traders and the royalty. The temples at Padang Lawas reveal they were occupied by priests who followed Esoteric Tantric Buddhism, of Śiva and Buddha together. Among the finds was a rare image of Heruka, a little-seen deity in Java or Sumatra. He wears a necklace of human skulls, has flaring hair and has the bodhisattva Akṣobhya in his headdress. It is apparent that the Javanese influence on the art, language and writing styles of the southern part of Sumatra had gradually increased during the tenth century and expanded as far north as Padang Lawas (Andaya 2008, pp. 87–88).

Figure 178 Masked dancer at a Tshechu, Dzong festival, Bhutan, 2006. Pullen photo.

Summary

Esoteric practices were undeniably a force in East Java, and their impact was considerable, as can be seen in the evidence of a group of Gaṇeśa depicted with skull and *kāla*-head textile patterns. Within this last phase of the Hindu-Buddhist period of the thirteenth and early fourteenth centuries in East Java, there is no longer any evidence of esoteric iconography in the textile patterns (instances in Sumatra for the same period have also ended). By the end of the Majapahit, the production of large statues of deified kings and queens had also ceased. This was followed by a resurgence of ancient Javanese practices, and figures of Bhīma and Kertolo began to appear. Evidence of the *kawung* pattern only re-emerge in the seventeenth and eighteenth centuries in the batik textiles created within the courts of Central Java. Based on a series of circles, the *kawung* motif is essential to the people of the royal court, "as the Central Javanese believe that the circle symbolises the world or universe, the theme was once one of the restricted patterns reserved for the ruler and his immediate family" (Warming and Garwoski 1981, p. 171).

The Majapahit style follows three principal indicators. First, the *sinjang kawung* is always carved in deep relief and depicted at the ankles with a simple pleat at the front of the body. The modelling of the *sinjang* is suggestive of a heavy textile where the cloth appears to drape over rather than to cling to the legs. Second, the exuberant and heavy ornamentation is especially evident in the sizeable jewelled tassels and buckles, along with the five-strand pearl *ratnopavīta*, whereas the *seléndang* is not as apparent as in the previous Singosari style. And third, is the full-frontal upright stance. The wearing of the *sinjang kawung* garment appeared to be imperative to the Majapahit monarchs, and this is the reason this garment is depicted on the important statues of this period.

The Majapahit rulers were powerful and wealthy. They had control over most of the Indonesian archipelago to as far as the Philippines Islands and New Guinea. Textiles and ideas were brought back from these different regions and traded with the many sojourning merchants who poured into the hinterland by travelling along the Brantas River. The local rulers appeared to encourage and legitimize the traders based at the indigenous ports and they subsequently aided their trade for foreign products into the hinterland. These many international traders brought gifts for the king, who amassed over time a significant amount of prestige goods. The king in turn would distribute some of these goods, such as silks and porcelain to his many allies. Each ruler who was acclaimed in his own country could claim unique "universal" sovereignty, which derived from a divine authority (Wolters 1999, p. 27). Wolters suggests that a "person's spiritual identity and capacity for leadership was established when his fellows could recognise his superior endowment and knew that being close to him was to their advantage not only because his entourage could expect to enjoy material rewards" (1999, p. 19). Wealth was also created by the trade in rice, which was critical to the legitimacy of the rulers. The rice was traded to the people of Eastern Indonesia, who in return brought their spices to Java. This two-way trade was the reason Java became such an essential entrepôt in the fourteenth and fifteenth centuries.

Another sign of their significant wealth was the many ceremonies given by the kings to the local community. Depending on the rank or social position of the person in attendance, gold or silver platters were used, and different types of food served. A wide distribution of Chinese ceramic sherds have been found in Majapahit sites, many of which are now in the Trowulen Museum, which attests to the appetite the Javanese had for these luxurious items. Trade in ceramics, textiles, precious metals and rice made the Majapahit royalty exceptionally wealthy. This extreme wealth would seem to be the reason why the rulers chose to portray such luxurious cloth and gems on the stone statues of their monarchs, and to have them appear as divine beings, as a way of demonstrating and legitimizing their power.

An exhaustive study of Majapahit sculpture in its various forms is not possible within the scope of this book. There remain so many more Majapahit sculptures that are not decorated with textile patterns than there are those with designs. It seems evident that these usually large sculptures were carved with textile patterns because they were destined for the important temples associated with the more central figures of Javanese monarchs. There was a need therefore for the statues to be carved wearing a *sinjang kawung*—a pattern that appears to have been symbolically important for the Majapahit. The physiognomy of the royal couple depicted in the statue at the MNI is undoubtedly in the later Majapahit style, with a strong jawline, a profusion of jewellery and a rendering of the hair and crown in an undeniably Javanese style, and with no apparent Pāla influence, except perhaps for the posture itself. Stylistically, however, the two figures do represent a strain of Pāla art from between the tenth and twelfth centuries. In truth though, this sculpture is clearly of Majapahit origin, as demonstrated by the fully frontal nature of the presentation and, of course, in the use of the *kawung* textile pattern.

The rich cloth—which could have been made with imported gold leaf or woven with gold thread with a *kawung* pattern—appeared to hold a deeply symbolic meaning for the Majapahit monarchs, as only a few statues were carved with variations of the same pattern. The minor nobility were evidently not permitted to use the prestigious *sinjang kawung* on their sculptures or have it placed on their own commemorative *caṇḍi*. There remain, unfortunately, no smaller *caṇḍi* with the statues still in situ for us to be able to truly understand this complex period in East Javanese history. The term *songket*, known initially as *songket lungsi*, was a textile that flourished in the port cities of Sumatra—trading centres that were later influenced by Islamic culture. Cross trading between the early maritime kingdoms in Sumatra—such as Palembang, followed by Jambi and those ports on the northeast coast of Java—were perhaps the source of this gold woven textile. The colour gold was a symbol of kingship. As a consequence, the textiles woven for the royalty were produced with silk and gold thread. The silk was introduced by Chinese and Indian traders, and the weaving was conducted locally in Sumatra, or perhaps in Java, using existing traditional weaving tools. Jan Wisseman Christie, in her analysis of the *sīma* tax-transfer charters, indicates that the use of the *cadar* loom must have had a discontinuous warp, and that it was in practice at the time. The practice of *tinulis ing mas* (drawing upon with gold) required an instrument that was the precursor to the present-day *canting* to apply the pattern upon which the gold was attached. The technique was later known as *parada/perada/prada*, from the Sanskrit *parada*, meaning quicksilver. The use of the term *parada* in the court verse signified a form of poetic luxury, indicating romance, and it remained prominent in literature for centuries (Christie 1991b, pp. 14, 16–18).

A recent publication by Arci refers to the many aspects of Bhīma, who shares features with Kāla-Bhairava, known as the demonic aspect of Lord Śiva. The iconography of Bhīma-Bhairava alludes to both figures sharing demonic and gigantic traits and, amongst other elements, a chequered black and white loin cloth (Acri 2017, pp. 117–20). The black and white loincloth is, however, only depicted on the figure of Bhīma: the only known figure of Mahākāla/Bhairava (in the RV) is naked, whilst the Mahākāla/Bhairava in Sumatra (now at the MNI) does not wear a *polèng* chequered cloth.

The island of Sumatra is strategically placed on the Maritime Silk trade route bordering the Straits of Malacca. The numerous ships that traded from China to India and beyond had to pass the shores of Sumatra and through the straits. From January to April, the ships were aided by the northeast monsoon for their journey to the west. Their return voyage was assisted by the southwest monsoon, which carried the Chinese vessels home. The monsoon winds also brought to the waters of Southeast Asia ships belonging to Arab and Indian traders. These merchants had to wait out the time for the monsoon to turn before they could return to their original destinations or to continue on with their journey. As a consequence, the port towns of Sumatra became the place to stock up on supplies, make repairs and trade goods (Keurs and Stuart-Fox 2009, p. 14; Hall 1981, pp. 66–81).

Sanskrit texts from the third century CE mention a land called Suvarnadvipa, or Gold Island. It is not known whether this meant a region in Southeast Asia or just an island, but it certainly would have encompassed Sumatra (Krom 1931, p. 248; Keurs and Stuart-Fox 2009, p. 15). The "Sea of Malayu" is a term known from Arabic documents dated to circa 1000 CE. The term was used by travellers on their way to China. (Further Chinese terms for this region are in the appendices.) But perhaps this sea was in reality a region that stretched from India via Sumatra to Vietnam. The pivotal point was the Straits of Malacca and the Malay people living along its coastline on both sides of the straits. Evidence for this trade has been revealed by recent research into Indo-Pacific trade beads that have been found all across the region. The core of these communities lay along the northern and eastern shores of Sumatra, and they provided the Southeast Asian products that were so greatly desired by China and the Arab world. The network of communities that made up the Sea of Malayu shared many values; from architecture and language to the numerous artefacts they left behind. Numbered among them were the Malays in Funan, the Angkorians on the Isthmus of Kra and the Chams in the Malayu world. They were bound together by shared economic interests, a lingua franca, ideas of religion and statecraft, and above all they thought of themselves as Malayu and "a family of communities". The Nāgarakṛtāgama describes the islands of Java and Sumatra as two separate communities. Java is termed *bhumi* Jawa and Sumatra as *bhumi* Malayu. These two terms go some way to indicate how the two populations differed and were thought of as different at the time by the people in Java (Andaya 2008, pp. 23–49).

On Sumatra, from the eleventh to the thirteenth century, Esoteric Buddhism appeared to be prevalent. Great emphasis was placed on the use of rituals and meditation, and these were the tools used for immediate salvation. Sites that show evidence of Esoteric Buddhism are Muara Takus, Padang Lawas and the Batang Hari region, which includes Muara Jambi (Schnitger 1937, pp. 6–10). The two wildly dancing figures in the stone reliefs from Biaro Pulo in Bahal Village are a testament to the type of Esoteric Buddhism practised at Padang Lawas. These two panels (along with three other dancing figures, two with human masks and one with an elephant head; ibid., plate XXXVI) are not the only figures at Pulo that display any kind of textile patterns. There are two figures, one of a bronze female and one of a stone guardian figure, that appear with a hip wrapper with carved patterns. These two have not been added to the book as they are out of the scope of this research. I have also not been able to make an on site analysis. They have, however, been published in a Dutch Archaeological Report dated to 1930. The dancing figures are reflected in modern Buddhist dancers from Tibet, Bhutan or Mongolia, who demonstrate the same kind of vigorous movements reflected in the Biaro Pulo stone reliefs.

A comparative chart of line drawings is included at the end of this chapter to enable the reader to see at a glance the various textile patterns depicted during this period.

Majapahit – Comparative Chart of Line Drawings

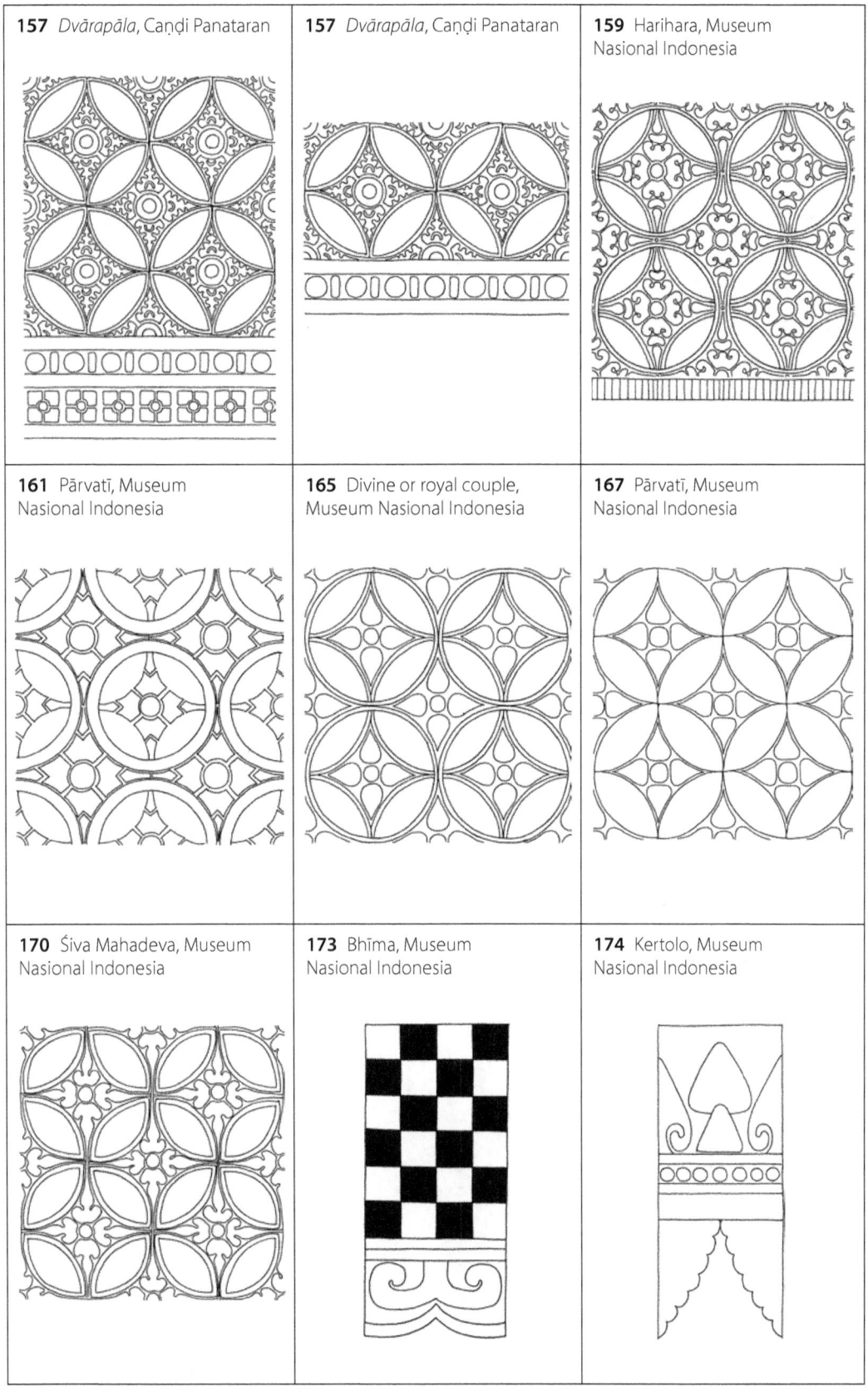

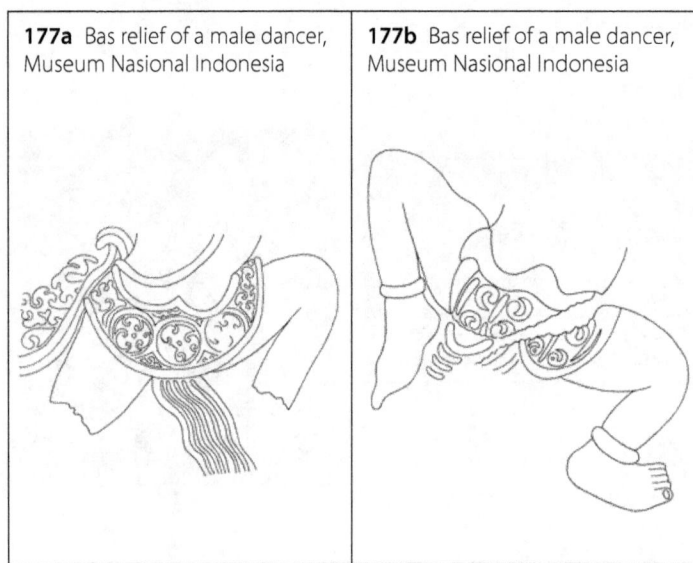

177a Bas relief of a male dancer, Museum Nasional Indonesia

177b Bas relief of a male dancer, Museum Nasional Indonesia

6. Conclusion

The extant sculptures have been divided into three chapters covering three periods. The first from the ninth to the early eleventh century, followed by the thirteenth century, and the last covering the fourteenth to the early fifteenth century. Within these three chapters, sub-groups have been developed that enable the categorization of the many different textile patterns into "style" groups. The data gained from the different pattern groups has enabled the subsequent research into the transmission of patterns from textiles to sculptures. With this additional factor of the textile patterns, the datings of the sculptures, where possible, have been amended from those provided by the existing literature. These patterns have then been used as a basis to propose examples that highlight the relationship between South and Southeast Asia through the interregional textile trade.

The four sculptures originating from Sumatra portray textile patterns that are contiguous with the classical period in Java and which reflect some of the Javanese designs, clearly indicating the close trading links between Java and Sumatra during this period. There is also clear evidence of the transmission of textile patterns from foreign textile sources to sculptures on both the small bronzes and large stone statues. The peak of the variety of textiles on stone sculptures appears to have been between 1269 and 1292 CE during the reign of King Kṛtanāgara, in the last phase of the Singhasāri period. During the Central and early East Java period, many more sculptures were produced with textile patterns—a cross-section of which have been discussed in this volume—but the variety of designs does not match in any way the variation seen in the Singhasāri period. Hiram Woodward has said that "a fabric recreated in stone may tell us more than would actual textile fragments or impressions, for it documents the local response to the imported object" (Woodward 1977, p. 233)—the distinctive artistic traditions can be seen, therefore, as proof of the textile tradition at the time.

I have maintained that the fabrics represented on the dress of most of the bronze, gold and stone sculptures from the classical period in Java appear to document local responses to the successive arrivals of textiles via trade, and to subsequently reflect the local interpretations of these imported items. Throughout, I have made certain proposals as to what the textile patterns on the sculptures represented. To precisely place the material discussed here into context, it is useful to summarize by reiterating that the sculptures created during the rule of King Kṛtanāgara were the most varied and distinctive. As suggested by Heller, the examples from Central Java that relate to the Tang period represent, paradoxically, our only real knowledge of Tang period textiles that are contiguous with the Central Java period. Many examples of Tang fabrics remain, however, in the Japanese depositories of the Hōryūji and the Shōsō-in—materials that have been inventoried and have been stored in perfect condition until now (Heller 1998, p. 764).

Nevertheless, I also conclude that in some instances the whole corpus of material from Java reflects textiles from the Tang to the Yuan periods in Chinese, Central Asian, Indo-Persian and Tibetan histories. The only motif that appears to cross over from ornament to dress pattern in the late thirteenth century is that of the skull, the *kāla*-head and the one-eyed *kāla*-head motif, a motif not depicted in textiles in any of the above countries, and where there are no points of similarity.

Research Contributions

Art historians generally prefer placing "art objects" into neat categories to enable the identification of any given art object by either its iconography, its dress, ornaments, and countenance or by the contrapposto of the body. In the past, however, if patterns were visible on a particular sculpture they were not included in the categorization. It is for this reason that I have aimed to add to this stylistic grammar and classification by expanding the idea and illustrating how in the classical arts of Java there is a distinct and marked difference not only between the three known historical periods but also in five stylistic periods. These have been categorized not only on the basis of the textile patterns but also by employing an evaluation of the "art historical style" of the sculptures, with all five periods differing to varying degrees. The methodological approach taken with this group of sculptures has been holistic. In taking this approach, substantive evidence has indicated the certainty that the ancient East Javanese would have acknowledged the importance of textiles as a political statement, and thus fashioned their sculptures with a vast array of patterns and dress styles. Two factors became evident: first, whether the statue represented a figure of either the Hindu or Buddhist religion appeared to make no difference to the types of patterns used; and second, the gender represented in the sculptures did not affect the dress style or textile patterns except for a few examples from Central Java, such as the gold statues and plaques. The classification of the sculptures was accomplished using the physiognomy, dress, ornaments, posture, lotus plant motif and, in some instances, textile patterns. I was unable, however, to place the textile patterns of the thirteenth century into any clear classification, apart from the statues originating from the Tower Temple at Singosari. By the mid-fourteenth to the early fifteenth century, all the textile patterns manifested as a similar design, and they therefore could be classified as a group.

There were many Śaivite sculptures created during the eleventh and twelfth centuries in the Kediri period that, almost without exception (from the numerous sculptures studied), are not carved with textile patterns, except for the Boro Gaṇeśa. This statue remains an enigma, as P.H. Pott has suggested, and it was probably worked on during two different periods. He describes it as "later reworked ... shows a remarkable clumsiness in the style and certain execution of certain elements, in particular, those having to do with the 'demonic' aspects of this sculpture". The demonic features and the row of skulls upon which the statue is seated do not appear to be related to the conception as a whole (Pott 1962. p. 131). Moreover, the textile pattern appears out of place at this early date of 1239–40 given on the inscription. Despite this date falling into the Singhasāri period of 1222–93, the statue would seem to fit more closely with a Kediri Gaṇeśa. In addition, the *kawung* textile pattern closely resembles those from the Majapahit period. Given that our knowledge of the history of the Kediri period is limited to the *kakawin* and *kidung* texts, and *prasasti*, stone inscriptions constantly being discovered and translated, other than the sculptures there is little evidence upon which to base our knowledge; hence the importance of an analysis of the textiles and the general style and iconographic features of each sculpture.

A compelling and significant aspect to such a study is the presentation of material previously unseen. Art historians of past centuries did not have the benefits of advances in cameras and computers, and the ease and availability of inexpensive travel and access to sculptures worldwide. These have, without doubt, aided me in arriving at the conclusions I have reached. Against this, however, have been the negative aspects of the passage of the last centuries (Pullen 2019). Erosion, theft, destruction by natural calamities in Java, and the increasingly stricter policies of some museums and institutions against photograhy and access to research collections have in some instances made finding and cataloguing the textile patterns and the overall features of the sculptures much harder than for the scholars of the early twentieth century. Having said this, we are fortunate in the twenty-first century of being able to bring to a broader audience the extraordinary breadth of material that has been influenced by many areas across Asia, as can be seen with this range of bronze and stone sculptures and their diverse textile patterns.

Dating

The many different find-spots, along with the dating for each of the figures, has emphasized the different periods of Central and early East Java. The artefacts from these two periods consist mainly of small to medium size bronze and gold statuettes, along with some more prominent stone statues. The diverse statue types have been divided among eight categories of textile patterns. Patterns appeared not only on the figures that have been selected for discussion but also on many more pieces that have not been included. There are two figures in this early group of Prajñāpāramitā and the Goddess Dhupa, both of which clearly show the beginnings of an early East Java style—in the elongation of the body, and with the ornaments being "blobby" and not particularly identifiable—but the textile patterns still follow the Central Java models. The ornamentation, as it appears on the Nganjuk bronzes, seems to predominate over the form. Attempting a classification of these bronzes presents a complex dilemma—a new type of classification has therefore been developed. In 1988, the groundbreaking book at the time, titled *Divine Bronze*, placed the bronzes into five groups (and one for Sumatra, which is not pertinent to this book). The textile patterns added here do not appear to follow the date categories made in this earlier publication, which suggests the Javanese during this short period in history were replicating all manner of different textile patterns. Some of them have been dated as close as possible to the Central and early East Java period. In contrast, the overriding designs on the stone statues appear to be of a large rosette or daisy flower scattered over the textile. This kind of patterning was of course possible because of the large size of the statue, whilst it would not have been practical on the small bronze statuettes—that is, apart from one example of a Nganjuk figure at the NMI. The statues range from the late eighth to the early

Figure 179
Unidentified damaged statue of a deity, the lower right hand in *varadamudrā*. Trowulan Archaeological Museum, Mojokerto, East Java. Pullen photo.

eleventh century. During this period, what appeared to be prevalent and consequently often replicated was a particular type of block-printed or ikat textile, either imported or locally produced.

Apart from these two bronzes of Prajñāpāramitā and the Goddess Dhupa and some of the gold plaques, the features of the remainder of the statuettes appear to be somewhat Indianized. However, there are apparent differences between a Javanese bronze figure and a similar Indian example. In the form of the Indian drapery and jewellery that decorate the early styles, though, there are some examples where the sartorial style is sophisticated and appears Javanese. This Javanese style is apparent not only from the more sophisticated patterning on the *kain* but also the style of dress as a long *kain* that is often folded at the front with a pleat. In some instances the *kain* would appear smooth, which would indicate a tube sarong such as a *tapis* known from the Lampung region in South Sumatra, where often the limbs are not visible beneath the cloth. This style is particularly evident in the small gold standing Pārvatī.

By the thirteenth century, all the textile patterns from the previous period had disappeared and a new classification had become apparent. The extreme differences between this Central and early East Java period to the following Singhasāri become very evident, not only in the types of sculptures produced (now just in stone) but also in the wide variety of patterns that are carved in deep relief on the surface of the andesite stone. This period of sculpting is distinguishable by the lighter colour and the more exceptional quality of the stone compared with that of the Central Java statues, which appear darker and rougher in condition. In addition, the textile patterns changed from small overall repeated designs to more compound ones incorporating horizontal and vertical geometric patterns. Changes are also reflected in the facial features, which no longer follow those of the earlier more Indic features, and nor does the dress reflect Indic styles.

Taking the example of the damaged sculpture shown in figure 179, perhaps it will be possible to date the statue by examining its dress style and carved pattern. The damaged statue remains on the grounds of the Trowulan Museum. Only the lower body, without feet, exists. The only remaining identifying features are the lower right hand, which appears to be in *varadamudrā*, the large belt buckle, the sash across the legs and the *kain*. The plain sash is folded over at the front—a relatively typical Central Java feature. The textile is carved with a pattern of triangles in which an eight-pointed-petal daisy flower is applied to the surface in shallow relief. From this fragment alone, the statue could be dated to a period somewhere between the tenth and twelfth centuries. The figure was probably found in this region; hence the assumed dating is taken from its location in East Java. The earlier date of the tenth century reflects the type of pattern and style of dress.

Meaning of Images – Emphasis of Esoteric Practices

To fully understand the depiction of the skull imagery on the statues originating from the Singhasāri period, and the one figure from Padang Roco in Sumatra, further research is needed into the tantric practices of Kṛtanāgara and his priests who created this group of Śaivite statues. The *kāla*-head textile patterns could be taken as an "iconographic sign" and the esoteric iconography in the patterns as sufficient evidence of esoteric practices. This is compounded by the evidence from the Śaivite and Buddhist sculptures in existence at Caṇḍi Singosari. The uncommon esoteric depictions on some of the textile patterns could also have been a product of Kṛtanāgara's unusually devout religious affiliations. It is stated in the *Nāg.* that during the latter half of the king's life he adopted the name Śiva-Buddha (*Nāg.* 43:5) (Casparis 1983, p. 16). The *Sutasoma* tells us that Kṛtanāgara claimed that the divinity of both Śiva and Buddha was a solution to bind his subjects together (O'Brien and Mpu 2008, p. 239). Hunter describes this union as a complex one:

> Socio-political needs that were played out in the fields of religious symbolism and aesthetics just as much as in the fields of kinship and political organization.... In terms of the study of 'syncretism' of the Singhasāri period we can now speak of a series of initiatives undertaken by Kṛtanāgara with the ultimate aim of forcing a fusion of elements that represented the metaphysical reflection of his pragmatic political policies. (Hunter 2007, p. 52)

This extract of course does not help us to determine why the sculptures displayed skulls and *candrakapāla* motifs on the textile patterns. A head or skull is an esoteric attribute, and a sculpture of Gaṇeśa seated on a base of skulls is indicative of a cremation ground. Another esoteric feature first appeared at Caṇḍi Kidal (fig. 98, p. 154) in 1260, on the upper register where a row of "skull cups", or *kapāla*, act as a small decorative architectural feature. Caṇḍi Kidal was built at the beginning of Kṛtanāgara's reign. The stylized pattern of a *kapāla* is replicated in the textile border pattern of both Singosari Gaṇeśa and on the border of all three forms of textiles on the Durgā Mahiṣāsuramardinī from Singosari. Evidence of this version of a *kapāla* motif represents another iconographical sign of esoteric practices in the latter half of the thirteenth century—symbols that do not appear on any form of architecture, textile pattern or sculpture or on modern day textiles in Java, India or Tibet. If this pattern is not the cross-section of a *kapāla*, then it is hard to determine the reason for its presence in this one *caṇḍi* and only on these statues from the Singhasāri period. There is, however, a depiction of the *kapāla* on an eleventh-century mural painting of Mahākāla at Alchi. Here we see the protective deity Mahākāla, who is treading upon a corpse, placed upon a *kapāla* shape or form.[1] The Singosari statues of Gaṇeśa in contrast hold a cup in each hand in the form of a "brainpan". Both of these are examples of the demonization of deities used as forms of protection.

The practice in Java of using the demonic features of skulls, heads and the *kapāla* in relief architecture and the borders of some of the textile patterns reflects the destructive and demonic nature of some of these statues. The sculpture of Mahākāla originating from Sumatra is dated to the early fourteenth century. This figure also appears with the *candrakapāla* motif carved in low relief on his short *kain*. The sculpture possibly promotes the interests of the king, with explicit references to his esoteric practices characterized in the circle of skulls, representing the cremation ground, depicted around the base. The *kāla*-head belt and the fact he is depicted holding the skull cup are symbolic of Mahākāla as the highest god of his sect. They could also have been seen as aids for the king in repelling his enemies (Reichle 2007, p. 13; Kozok and Reijn 2010, p. 142). This monumental figure appears as one of a kind, in contrast to the remaining Sumatra sculptures carved with textile patterns. The iconography and modelling of the figure appears, however, to fit into the corresponding Singosari style of statues, and not into the Majapahit, which would fit more closely with his dating to the fourteenth century. What is apparent are the stylistic elements of the textile pattern; where the shape of the skull pattern differs slightly from that of the giant standing Gaṇeśa from Karangkates. The unique stylistic and iconographic features of each statue differ, as they have been made on two different islands, but they appear to share a very similar style in the carving of their textile patterns.

Summary

The ultimate shared link between the Singhasāri sculptures and all of the Majapahit statues is a textile design that is part of the *ceplok* group of patterns known as *kawung*. This pattern emerged as the favoured motif on the *sinjang* to indicate that the deities represented were deified monarchs. The concept of 4+4+1=5 was enough to see the protective value of this pattern to dress the gods that represented the Javanese royals. This was a pattern concept that was representative of the outer four points of the compass, with one point in the centre that represented the Supreme Being; together they formed the sacred five. The roots of this concept are pre-Hindu and they date back to the culture of Austro-Asiatic speakers (Velduisen-Djajasoebrata 1979, p. 205). Acri has written of a new paradigm that represents a

> "strong convergence theory", which envisages the diffusion, filiation and localization of cultural and linguistic elements that developed across Monsoon Asia in parallel,... [This refers to the Austro-Asiatic and Austronesian speakers, all of which are in Java and Sumatra, and highlights how the cultural] practices that once existed in the Indian Subcontinent could so easily be revived or connected with those still found in other parts of the Indic world, namely mainland and insular Southeast Asia. (Acri 2017, pp. 130, 132)

This extract from Acri emphasizes the popularity of the 4+4+1=5 theory in East Java, as this paradigm is also reflected in the *navagraha* and *chabadhi bhat* or *jilamprang* pattern, which originated from India. In addition there are a number of examples of variations of this motif originating from China.

While the "convergence" theory proposed by Acri and many before him is entirely possible, this theory perhaps indicates the development of the culture of Java and Sumatra leaning primarily to the Indian subcontinent. The fragmentary and possibly second-hand nature of the relevant Chinese sources such as the *Zhufanzhi* does not help us to understand what the exact textiles were that were traded from China. All that is known of them is that the terms "brocade" and "silks" were used a number of times in different publications. There are reflections of various versions of the Javanese *kawung* pattern and examples of other designs that appear primarily on the Singosari sculptures. The patterns are also reflected on numerous Chinese silk brocade textiles from the Yuan period of the thirteenth to the fourteenth century. The similarity in pattern layout is uncanny. For example, we see small rosettes and a sizeable oval version of the *kawung* motif woven with double lines around each vesica shape; textiles with a supplementary weft motif consisting of small circles of adjoining vesica shapes; and a jacket with lotus flower medallions against a background of cross-hatching infilled with small daisy flowers. These examples from China are just some of the few that show how this pattern—regarded as spiritually powerful by the Javanese—has continued in use over a long span of history up until today, as evident from its earliest depicted roots in Java dating back to the thirteenth century. These patterns did not, however, appear to have the same spiritual meaning to the Chinese.

The theory behind this archaic design probably originated in the Indian subcontinent and was subsequently reinterpreted in Java. By the late fourteenth or early fifteenth century, the *kawung* motif had emerged as the most popular, the most religious and the most spiritually symbolic of the Hindu-Buddhist period. Finally, this led to the widespread use of the pattern in the Islamic period that followed, for batik textiles in the Mataram courts of Surakarta and Jogjakarta, where the *kawung* motif became one of the *larangan*, or forbidden patterns. They were restricted to the princedom of Surakarta, as decreed in 1769, 1784 and 1790, and to the sultanates of Jogjakarta

While recognizing that the Javanese were producing textiles from at least the tenth century in the form of cotton ikats—and that later, by the eleventh-century, silk brocade production was also known—it is clear that the inspiration for many of the patterns was of foreign origin. Even if the techniques were perhaps locally inspired, *songket* textiles made in Java and Sumatra today and on the east coast of the Malay Peninsula do reflect the cultural heritage of these regions in their patterns, and it would be the same case in the layout on a number of the Singosari sculptures.

After the decline of the Majapahit, this weaving technique did not continue in Java, but flourished in the Muslim courts of Minangkabau,

Jambi and Palembang on Sumatra, on the east coast of Malaysia and in East Malaysia and Brunei. The cultural heritage of Java appears reflected in the art of batik textiles, with one pattern group, the *ceplok*, and the *kawung* motif having endured to the present day. One pattern that has completely disappeared from Java and the Malay world is that of the roundels, which leaves the statues of Prajñāpāramitā and of Mañjuśrī Arapacana as the only testaments of a textile type now otherwise lost to the cultural heritage of Javanese textile history.

This book has presented the first comprehensive catalogue of textiles represented on the figurative sculptures that remain as a unique window into the "remnants" of textiles in the Classical Java period. It forms a starting point for the next generation of students to pursue further multidisciplinary research into the origins of these textiles and their implications for the cultural heritage and religious art history of Java. The book sheds fresh light on—and in some instances irrefutable evidence for—the possible inspiration behind some of the intricate textile patterns depicted on the sculptures that have provided a visual vocabulary and a unique inventory of sculptures in Java.

Notes

1. Information gained from Dr Christian Luczanits, SOAS University of London. Dr Luczanits was the supervisor for my doctorate.

Epilogue

It is not unusual with an art history publication of this nature, which analyses a corpus of medieval sculpture, for the sculptures addressed to be found in a single public or private collection, or even one archaeological site. The sculptures addressed in this publication, however, are presently located at numerous locations, both within Indonesia and across the world.

This book has attempted to include as many as possible of the accessible figurative sculptures that exhibit textile patterns on their dress. It does not assume to have located, from amongst all the reserve and private collections worldwide, all such sculptures. Many relevant sculptures identified during the course of the underlying research have also been omitted where they either represent a duplication of others included or where there exists any doubt as to their true provenance.

The sculptures addressed here vary in importance, from some that have become iconic images of their time and place, such as the Prajñāpāramitā in the Museum Nasional Indonesia, to others that are almost unknown and which may not have been published previously.

This book addresses seventy-three stone and metal sculptures originating from Java and Sumatra between the eighth and fifteenth centuries. Of these seventy-three, fifty-one remain in Java and Sumatra to this day, either on site or in museums, whilst twenty-one are now to be

262 Patterned Splendour

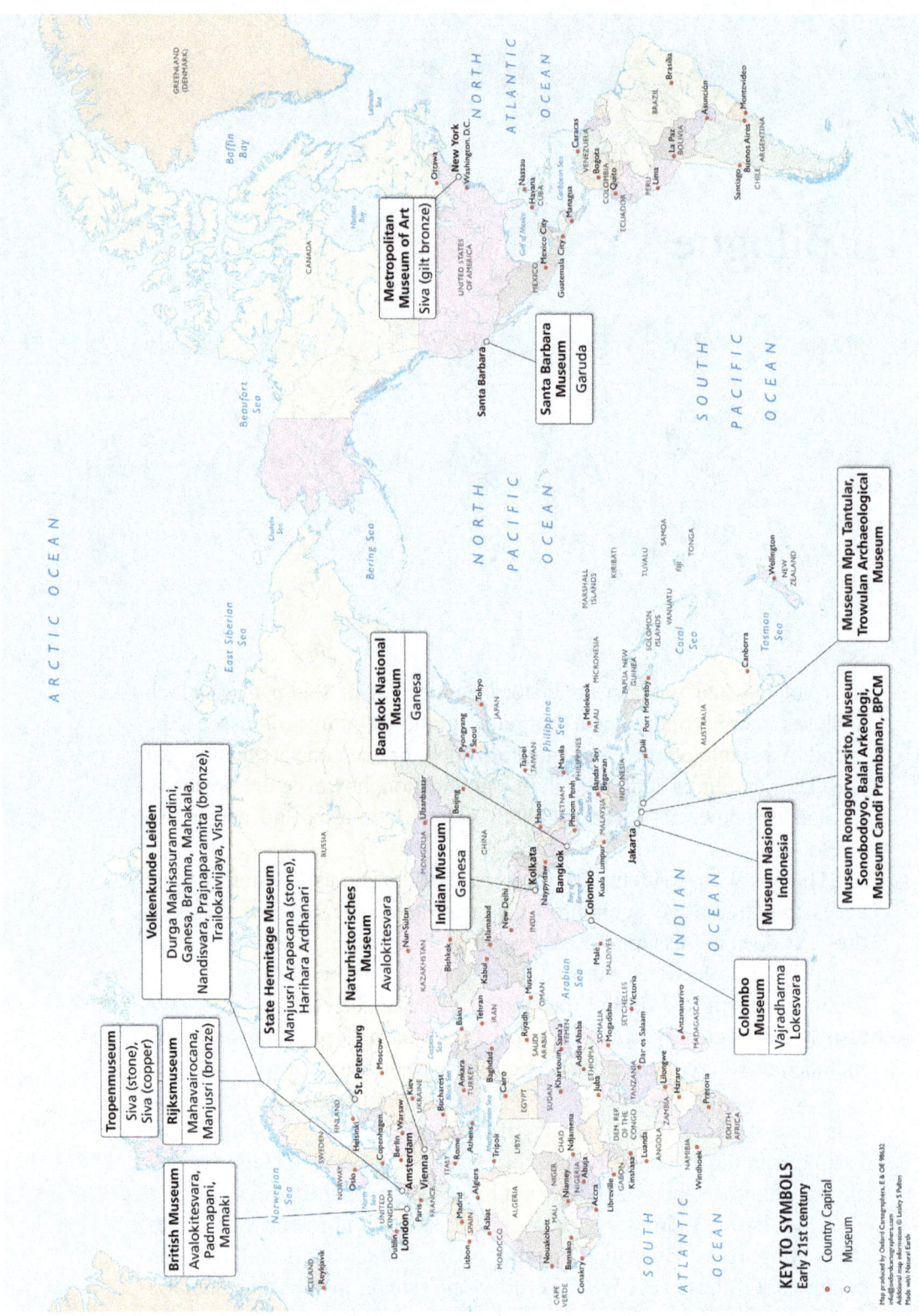

Map 5 Diaspora of Javanese Statues.

found elsewhere in the world. The location of one sculpture is presently unknown.

This diaspora of sculptures is indicated in map 5, which illustrates that over a quarter of these sculptures are to be found across eleven museums in nine countries. Within Indonesia, on the islands of Java and Sumatra, fourteen different museums, institutions and sites hold the remaining sculptures. Not included among this number is the single bronze for which the location is unknown. The most significant number of Central and East Javanese sculptures are to be found in Java, followed by those in three museums in Leiden and Amsterdam in the Netherlands.

A number of the sculptures found within Europe reveal fascinating "object stories". From the early nineteenth to the early twentieth century, Dutch and English authorities were particularly involved in the relocation of several statues that now reside in European museum collections. One administrator in particular was instrumental in the removal of the Durgā Mahiṣāsuramardinī, Nandīśvara, Mahākāla, Brahmā and Gaṇeśa statues from Caṇḍi Singosari in East Java. This was Nicolaus Engelhard, governor general of the north coast of Java (1801–8). Amongst others, these five colossal stone statues were first placed in the garden of his official residence in Semarang, Batavia, now Jakarta, from 1804. They were subsequently shipped to the Netherlands, where he later "relinquished" them to the Dutch government. These sculptures all found their way into what is now the Volkenkunde in Leiden and they form the core of this museum's collection. In the early nineteenth century, Engelhard and Stamford Raffles, lieutenant-governor of Java (1811–16), worked together on various excavations in Java (Hoijtink 2012, pp. 95–101).

The statue of the goddess Prajñāpāramitā from Caṇḍi E in Singosari, East Java was discovered in 1818 by D. Monnereau. In 1820 the statue was given by Monnereau to C.G.C. Reinwardt. Reinwardt represented the kingdom of Holland and the Batavian Republic. In 1820, Reinwardt took the statue to Holland, where it was eventually placed in the Volkenkunde. Here this statue remained until January 1978, when the Government of the Netherlands formally returned the goddess to the Republic of Indonesia, where it was placed in the Museum Nasional Indonesia in Jakarta. She now stands in the Treasures Room on the second floor, placed on a high plinth and behind glass. This statue is often considered one of the national treasures of Indonesia, assuming a near diplomatic status in international relations. A recent journey out of Java in the first quarter of 2020 found her in the "Lost Kingdoms" exhibition in Muzium Negara in Kuala Lumpur.

In 1802, Engelhard was also instrumental in the removal of the stone statue of Mañjuśrī Arapacana that originated from Caṇḍi Jago. In 1823 the statue was taken to Batavia, along with many others, and subsequently shipped to the Netherlands. Since then this statue has enjoyed a complex story around Europe. At first it was placed in the garden of Engelhard's sister in Ziudlaren, and then in 1860 the family sold the statue through the Groote Koninklijke Bazar (Le Bazar Royal) owned by Dirk Boer in The Hague to the new Ethnographical Collection in Berlin. It may have been on display in Berlin sometime after 1864 and in the Museum für Völkerkunde. The museum opened in 1926, where the statue was probably on display in Bay 7 of Room XXVII, although, unfortunately, no photos remain of its exhibition. During World War II, along with several art objects from Berlin museums, this sculpture was moved to safety into a bunker in the "Flaktürme Zoo", one of the flak towers constructed to defend the city. Shortly after the end of hostilities in 1945, the statue was transferred, along with other art objects, to the former Soviet Union and then to Leningrad. According to Bernet Kempers, these statues were placed on trucks heading east, after which their whereabouts are unknown. Following the first convocation of the State Duma (Assembly) of the Russian Federation in 1995, when such art objects were considered the property of Russia, the statue was assigned to the State Hermitage Museum in St Petersburg. In 2002, the Staatliche Museen zu Berlin published a catalogue of their "lost" art objects, *Dokumentation der Verluste, Band III*. The Mañjuśrī statue appears on page 93 as item number 1065. In 2016, Olga Deshpande published *Works of Art from Southeast Asia*, which accompanied the temporary exhibition "Sacral Gift to Deity" at the State Hermitage Museum. This Mañjuśrī and other stone statues from Java—including the Harihara Ardhanari from East Java, which we can assume originated from Sagala (Robson and Prapanca 1995, p. 56), a subsidiary temple to Caṇḍi Singosari (now disappeared)—were placed in this exhibition for three months before being returned to storage.

In the East Indies Room of the Noordeinde Palace in The Hague stands a replica of the statue of Mañjuśrī. The East Indies Room was developed by the Dutch East India Company between 1900 and 1911 as a gift to Queen Wilhelmina to celebrate her marriage to Prince Henry in 1901. The objective of the room was to represent the East Indies and the crafts of its subjects. A craftsman was identified in Java who was engaged to carve a number of replica stone statues of various Hindu-Buddhist deities, and a particularly fine-grained and light-coloured volcanic stone was identified for this. J.L.A. Brandes (chairman for the Commission for Archaeological Research in Java and Madura) suggested to Van Es (the architect of the East Indies Room) that the Mañjuśrī statue, which was located in Berlin at this date, was of the highest quality and the most appropriate for the East Indies Room. Photographs were taken and a plaster cast made and sent to Batavia, where the craftsman carved a replica, which was shipped back to adorn a prominent niche. A high wood platform was constructed, upon which this Mañjuśrī continues to stand, raised on a square stone base beneath an elaborate canopy of *kāla* and *makara*. It is unclear from photographs whether the sculptor attempted to reproduce the intricate textile patterns in any detail. Access to this royal apartment remains difficult, leaving file photographs the only available record.

The National Museum in Bangkok houses the large stone Gaṇeśa from Caṇḍi Singosari in East Java. This seated Gaṇeśa was a gift to King Chulalongkorn (Rama V) of Siam on the occasion of his first visit to Batavia in 1871. Following its arrival in Bangkok, the statue was donated to the National Museum, established by Chulalongkorn in 1874, where it would have been one of the earliest objects in their collections. It remains in a prime position in the Java Sculpture gallery to this day.

Another stone seated Gaṇeśa reveals a very different story. It departed Java far earlier than the Bangkok statue. In 1811, Colonel Colin Mackenzie was ordered from India to the Dutch colony of Java to embark on an extensive survey of the monuments of the island. Stamford Raffles, who was aware of Mackenzie's reputation in India, sent Mackenzie to conduct an accurate survey of the ruins of Prambanan. Mackenzie writes of his surprise at finding Hindu gods on an island inhabited by Muslims. Together with other Brahmanical deities, this Gaṇeśa statue was collected by Mackenzie and, upon his return to India, presented to the Asiatic Society of Bengal in Calcutta, which was to become the Indian Museum in 1814. Unfortunately, no acquisition record remains of this statue or of its donor. The Gaṇeśa also remains on display at the Indian Museum.

The Raffles collection in the British Museum holds the small, seated stone statue of Māmakī that originated from Caṇḍi Jago in East Java. Māmakī was collected by Raffles in the field in 1815. After the statue reached England, it was subsequently donated to the British Museum by the Reverend William Charles Raffles Flint, executor of the estate of Lady Raffles. In 2019 the exhibition of the Raffles collection, "Sir Stamford Raffles: Collecting in Southeast Asia 1811–1824", was held at the Asian Civilisations Museum in Singapore and subsequently at the British Museum in London. The Māmakī was placed on display in both locations, but it is currently held in storage. Also held by the British Museum are two small statues as part of a collection known as the Sambas Treasure: a silver statue of Avalokiteśvara and a small gold Padmapāni. Both are dated to the Central Javanese period, but they were found in Kalimantan. The hoard was found in a large pot in the Sambas region in the 1940s, and was owned by the collector Tan Teok Seong. The collection was subsequently acquired by P.T. Brooke Sewell and donated to the British Museum. The Sambas collection is no longer on display, and remains in storage.

A few other statues have made journeys outside of Java in the last couple of years. For example, the Muara Jambi Prajñāpāramitā travelled to Brussels in 2017 to be displayed in the Europalia Arts Festival Indonesia exhibition. Details were published in *Archipel: Indonesian Kingdoms of the Sea*, along with other objects originating from the Museum Nasional Indonesia: the massive stone seated Gaṇeśa from Caṇḍi Banon, the bronze Tārā with gold inlaid lips, the silver Mañjuśrī Kumārabhūta, and the gold plaque of Śiva from Wonosobo. All of these items originated from Central Java.

Appendices

List of Museums

Ashmolean Museum
Assam State Museum
Bangkok National Museum
British Museum
Chhatrapati Shivaji Maharaj Vastu Sangrahalaya
China National Silk Museum (CNSM)
Cleveland Museum of Art
Colombo National Museum
Indian Museum, Kolkata
Metropolitan Museum of Art
Mpu Tantular Museum
Museum Nasional Indonesia (MNI)
Museum Sonobudoyo
National Museum, New Delhi
Prambanan Museum
Ranggawarsita Museum
Rijksmusem Amsterdam
Santa Barbara Museum
State Hermitage Museum, St Petersberg (SHM)
Tropenmuseum Amsterdam
Trowulan Museum
Volkenkunde – National Museum of Ethnography, Leiden (RV)

Chinese Terms for Geographical Regions

From Yijing, 635–718 CE

Fo-shih: Bhoga is mentioned in Tang history (618–906) as being on the south shore of the Strait of Malacca.

Ho-ling: Java.

Malayu: Seems to have existed for a long time. May also have been called Bhoga (the country). Lay on the southern shore of Malacca. Malayu covered the Southeast side of Sumatra, from the southern shores of Malacca to the city of Palembang.

Mo-lo-yu: Malayu, Shih-li-fo-shih, Srîbhoga.

San-bo-tsai: Land of the southern barbarians, between Cambodia, *Chên-la* and Java, *Shê-p'o*. San-fo-Ch'i, in the History of Sung (960–1279) is probably Shih-li-fo-shih or Srîbhoga. Srîbhoga disappeared and was replaced with the term "Old Port" by the time of the last Chinese conquest in 1379 CE.

Sānfóqí: Was an important trading port where the people had embraced Buddhism but were of Hindu origin. The country was rich in gold. The inhabitants wore *kan-man* (sarongs). *Sānfóqí* was in Malayu Jambi and not in Palembang, thus references to *Sānfóqí* in the tenth and early eleventh centuries could relate to either Palembang or Jambi (Miksic and Goh 2017, p. 396).

Sarbaza: Used by Arab travellers in the ninth century; a corruption of Yavadvîpa.

Srîbhoga: Chin-chou, San-fo-Ch'i, and Golden Isle.

Yuán Shī: The historical works of the Yüan period; also known as Yuanshi. His written records contributed to our knowledge of Śrivijaya and the kingdoms that lay on the route between China and Nālandā (I-Tsing 1998: xli–xlvi).

Chinese Terms for Geographical Regions

From Zhufanzi, Twelfth to the Thirteenth Century

Chön-la: Cambodia

Chu-lién: Coromandel Coast, Chola Domain

Hu-ch'a-la: Gujarat, India

Kién-pi: Kampar, Eastern Sumatra

Ligor: Malay Peninsula

Nan-p'i: Malabar, India

San-fo-ts'i: Palembang, Eastern Sumatra

Shö-p'o: Java

Sin-t'o: Sunda, West Java

Su-ki-tan: Central Java

Tan-ma-ling: Malay Peninsula

Ta-shï: The Arabs

Ta-ts'in: Bagdad

T'ién-chu: India

Source: Hirth and Rockhill 1965.

Old Javanese Literature

Javanese texts throughout the centuries often contained passages describing prominent characters and the dress and costume they wore. Such references occur in Old Javanese literature; namely, *kakawin* and *kidung*.

Kidung: A form of Old Javanese poetry; a style of literary work.

Kakawin: Long narrative poems in Old Javanese derived form Sanskrit literature

Sīma: Tax-transfers charters spanning a period from the early ninth to the late fifteenth century. Preserved on stone and copperplate, they are a corpus of legal documents.

Texts from the Tenth to the Twentieth Century

Deśawarṇana Nāgarakṛtāgama (Nāg.) by Mpu Prapañca (1350–1389), translated by Th. G. Th. Pigeaud (1960–63). Current translation by Stuart Robson (1995).

Kidung Harsawijaya (KH)

Kidung Panji Wijayakrama (KPW)

Kidung Rangga Lawe (KRL)

Kidung Sudamala (KS) – Sri Tanjung, Javanese folk tales

Kidung Sundayana (KS)

Korawacrama Kakwin (KK)

Pararaton – written sometime after 1481 CE

Parthayajna Kakwin (PK)

Serat Bhīma Suci (SBS)

Serat Jayalengkara LOr. 5787 (SJ); Panji Priyembada LOr.8941 (PP) – Panji stories

Serat Pararaton (SP)

Serat Pranacitra (SP) – Rara Mendut is the leading character

Serat Tatatjara (ST) – text on manners and traditional customs

Sumanasantaka Kakawin (SK)

Glossary

Abasana: vendor of clothing

Angunkir*:* the sculptor of deities, known in the Kediri and Singhasāri

Antariya: white cloth draped around the hips and between the legs in the kachcha style

Arcā: stone statue, figure, image or idol

Babayabon: type of silk with a particular design

Baju: Malay upper-body jacket with long sleeves

Batik cap: wax resist textile made with a metal stamp

Batik tulis: wax resist textile drawn with a *canting*

Benang bal: wound ball of threads

Bhumi: capital during the Singhasāri period

Bunga: Malay word for a flower pattern

Bunga kemunting cina: Chinese rose myrtle motif

Cadar or **Acadar**: the cloth weaver; the term *cadar* now refers to a type of gauze

Candrakapāla: the moon now resembles fangs that curl up each side of the skull

Ceplok: pattern group consisting of squares, rhomboids and circles

Channavīra: crossed belts across the chest

Cinde/Cinte: Javanese term for silk double ikat from India

Desa: village

Gĕringsing: double ikat cotton cloth from Bali

Harnas: Dutch word for armour

Ikat: resist process of creating a pattern in either the warp or weft threads

Jilamprang: Indonesian name for the Indian flower-basket motif depicted on *patola* textiles

Kain: cloth used as a hip wrapper

Kain balapak: songket cloth with an all-over gold thread design

Kapas: natural cotton

Kawung: pattern of intersecting circles; part of the ceplok pattern group

Keling: people of the Coromandel Coast, South India

Kemben: cloth to be worn as a breast wrapper

Kraton/Keraton: palace

Krodha: demonic or angry

Kulambi: jacket

Lañciṅan: Old Javanese term for trousers

Larangan: forbidden batik patterns restricted to members of the royal family

Limar: weft ikat in silk

Lurik: striped cotton cloth of Java

Manca-pat: literally, the outer four, with one supreme being

Mordant: chemical that serves to fix a dye to a fabric or threads

Mudrā: hand gestures

Nasīj: gold woven brocade textiles found in China

Negara or **Rājya**: the king's residence

Pacadaran: the loom used by the *cadar* weavers, or *cadar* loom

Pande: skilled worker

Patola: double ikat in silk from Patan, Gujarat

Pending: ornate belt buckle

Perada/prada: gold-leaf glue work known in Bali and Java

Pinggir: border pattern on a batik textile

Poleng: a pattern of black and white alternating squares

Prasasti: stone inscription

Rantai/rante: linked chains enclosing a bunga motif in songket textiles

Sabut/Sabuk: metal or fabric belt tied around the waist

Samit: weft-faced compound twill cloth from China

Sarong: tube skirt in cotton

Seléndang: sash depicted worn across the upper body

Sembagi: Indian trade cotton that replicated the patterns of a *patola*, particularly found in Sumatra

Sinjang kawung: long cloth wrapped around the lower body displaying a *kawung* pattern

Songket: supplementary weft with gold, silver or coloured threads

Tapis: thin or fine cloth tube skirt in Lampung, south Sumatra

Tassel: tassel at the end of a chain or uncal

Tulis mas: drawing with gold

Tulis warna: drawing with colour

Tumpal: triangular-shaped pattern at the border of a textile

Udharabhanda: Indian term for a stomach band

Uncal: long metal or fabric belt

Utpala: blue lily flower

Uttariya: fine cotton scarf draped across the upper body or over the arms

Varman: protective cloth

Warp: vertical threads on a loom

Wayang Kulit: leather shadow puppet

Wayang Wong: theatre with human players

Weft: horizontal threads on a loom

Extended Glossary of Textile Terms

Some of the pattern terms from the *kidung* and sīma texts are reflected on East Javanese sculptures. These are *patola, gĕringsing, ceplok/ kawung* and *prada*. These terms have been selected as they appear to be the only known patterns relating to the sculptures of the thirteenth and fourteenth centuries, thus firmly establishing provenance and making them historically immutable.

Patola

This fine silk cloth was probably brought to Indonesia by Muslim merchants from Gujarat from circa 1500. The silk *patola* was woven in Patan and was known to be exported to Indonesia (Fischer 1980, p. 37; Gittinger 1979, pp. 45–48). The precious textiles appeared to transcend the genre of trade goods, and their suitability for ceremonial use ensured they would be revered as sacred heirlooms. It would often be the case that they would only be displayed on formal occasions. Once outside Patan in Gujarat, where it was produced, *patola* became universally regarded as a high-status, prestige cloth, and its use was confined to those of high social status. In Java, *patola*, and later batik, were used as aspects of royal ceremonial dress. Many of the designs created in Gujarat were solely for Southeast Asian markets, and each country would value a different series of patterns. Guy states that literary references to silk *patola* as we know it date from the fourteenth century. The word *patola/patolu* appears in Indian writings from the seventh century. From the seventeenth century, the Persian word *patolu* (pl. *patola*)—from the Sanskrit *patta*—referred to a double ikat silk cloth. The plural term is widely used in Indonesia to mean both the singular and the plural—I use the plural in this book (Warming and Garwoski 1981, p. 103; Pal 2004, p. 6; Crill 2016, p. 160; Guy 2010, pp. 6–9).

Patola cloth was woven in double ikat, where both the warp and weft are tied and dyed with the same pattern. The fabric was fabricated on an upright fixed loom to create the design. The most iconic design associated with *patola* is the eight-point flower known in Indonesia as *jilamprang* (Warming and Garwoski 1981, p. 171). The word *patola* can refer to both the pattern and the technique; here the word refers to any pattern with the *jilamprang* motif.

The various sections of the cloth may be referred to using the following terms: *badan* is the body of the fabric; *pinggir* are the narrow borders along each long side; and the *tumpal* pattern of inverted triangles appears along each end at the *kepala*, or the head of the cloth (Elliot 1996, pp. 214–23). In most cases, however, the *tumpal* pattern cannot be found, either on the trousers of Javanese princes nor, indeed, on any of the textile patterns on the stone statues of East Java. Paradoxically, these clothes were a critical influence on many types of Indonesian textiles, but the *tumpal* pattern itself is not apparent on any of the sculptures of the thirteenth century. Guy and others have suggested that if *patola* and Indian cotton textiles reached Java and Sumatra by the fourteenth and fifteenth centuries (Guy 1998, pp. 39–42), then many of the textiles depicted on the sculptures of East Java would have a shared visual vocabulary. Whilst this might be the case, what types of textiles may have reached Java and, similarly, which of them may have been represented on the sculptures of the thirteenth century remains unknown. The textile experts Langewis and Wagner have said that "it is almost certain that the influence of *patola* and other imported cloths has contributed to the development of the many *ceplok* patterns" (1964, p. 29).

All things considered, the evidence for textile designs on sculptures representing *patola* appears convincing. But if *patola* did not reach Java and Sumatra until the fifteenth century, then Indian textiles would not have been the primary source of inspiration behind the patterns on the sculptures. Having said this, a small quantity of so-called Indo-Egyptian kinds of cotton similar to the Fustat pieces (Barnes 1997b) have been found in Java. Moreover, it has been attested that they have been replicated on some of the Central Javanese bronze statues. I cannot account for their exact origin, nor is there any record of their being traded to the island. Some of the *patola* patterns are reflected to a degree on the thirteenth-century sculptures, but I do not hold the view these important sculptures were depicting these silk fabrics. As discussed earlier, fine silk *patola* would have been treasured and used for sashes and waist wraps, and not as hip wraps. A close inspection of the thirteenth-century sculptures does not reveal any evidence of the *patola* motif.

Gringsing

Gringsing, or *gĕringsing,* is a double ikat cotton cloth woven in the Tenganan Pegringsingan village of East Bali (Langewis and Wagner 1964, p. 108). The term *gĕringsing* can refer to either the cloth or to the pattern, as is the case with *patola.* Both Gittinger and Fraser-Lu describe Balinese *gĕringsing* cloth as having magical and protective powers (Gittinger 1979, pp. 178–79; Fraser-Lu 1988, p. 71). There are also a number of verses in the KH that mention the term *gĕringsing kawung* and the expression "white cloth with gold" (Berg 1931, p. 57, verse 45b). The *kemben gĕringsing,* or breast cloth, is known as a ritual garment with magical potency. It is described as being used to protect people from threats, defilement and decay (Hauser-Schäublin, Nabholz-Kartaschoff and Ramseyer 1991, p. 120). Perhaps this was how the *gĕringsing* was seen in the thirteenth-century. This description of textile patterns in the KH employs some terms that are still in use today and which could have been reflected on the textile patterns of the thirteenth-century sculptures. For example, Raden Wijaya, a king in the Majapahit period, is described as follows:

> Thus, Raden Wijaya himself to the queen who was dressed in *gĕringsing wayang* and decorated with floral patterns in liquid gold or *prada* and a pink *kampuh*,[1] with gold threads, the upper side made of green silk (Song 1, verse 59b). There he met the two princesses of the king who wore *sinjang gĕringsing kawung* made of selected fine cloth with *tumpal*[2] ornament, red at the bottom and green at the top (Song 1, verse 62a–62b). (Sumaryoto 1993, p. 33)

Given that the term *gĕringsing* has been known since the fourteenth-century texts, it must have had a specific symbolism and ritual power for it to appear in the KH. For example, some *gĕringsing* patterns—such as *gĕringsing cemplong* and *gĕringsing papare*—appear to be very similar in design and layout to some *patola* patterns. Guy has noted that the *papare* pattern has unmistakably been influenced by *patola.* The basic pattern consists of intersecting circles and four-pointed stars, but although the elements are the same as the *patola,* the structure differs (1998, p. 13, fig. 9). In this instance, the terms refer to the pattern; whereas the quote above refers to the cloth itself

The *gĕringsing kawung,* written in Middle Javanese, is the name for the pattern; that is, a double ikat with a *kawung* design. One type of Indian trade cotton is depicted with a *gĕringsing* motif similar to a variation of the *patola* pattern mentioned above. The central section of the cloth has a four-pointed star surrounded by a circular theme in a stylized version of the *jilamprang.* The correct terminology would be *gĕringsing* chintz;

and the suggestion is that textiles such as these were prototype textiles in ancient Indonesia. Precepts set by textile scholars such as Holmgren and Spertus suggest a clear relationship between the similar iconography from the Persian, Chinese and Mediterranean worlds and local products such as this one. Holmgren and Spertus have conducted extensive research into the subject of *gĕringsing* and have questioned whether it is really Balinese. They ask, who influenced whom? And what was the prototype textile for the Balinese *gĕringsing*? It is generally thought that prototype textiles circulated throughout the Indonesian archipelago and Mainland Southeast Asia. What developed out of these so-called prototypes is of course subject to conjecture. Nevertheless, the patterns depicted on historical monuments and stone statues were the result of the local manufacture of these prototypes, perhaps representing locally produced material and techniques. Hence, the designs on the stone sculptures then became the prototypes, and the patterns were copied many times over the following centuries (Holmgren and Spertus 1991, p. 61).

Descriptions taken from the *Nāg.* appear to be the earliest evidence of the *gĕringsing/grinsing* pattern. The term *grinsing*, however, refers to an old motif that is often discussed in relation to batik (note the difference in spelling). The pattern refers to a series of small dots overlapping like fish scales, and which is often used as a filler design for a *ceplok* pattern. In this instance of course the explanation of the *sinjang* refers to a *gĕringsing* cloth with a *kawung* pattern. Another section from the *Nāg.* describes a canopy using the term *grinsing* to refer to a *gĕringsing* cloth with gold as follows: "adorned with canopies of red *lobheng lĕwih grinsing*[3] painted with gold", referring to the King of Majapahit's carriage (*Nāg.* 18:4) (Robson and Prapanca 1995, p. 38).

Many similarities have been pointed out between the patterns on *gĕringsing* and *patola* (Stuart-Fox 1993, p. 92). I have discussed the *patola* and *gĕringsing* patterns with respect to their use in the fourteenth century, as is evident from the KH. However debatable this suggestion might be, the design on the unidentified goddess (fig. 139, p. 191) is the closest in design layout to a *patola jilamprang* motif or the *gĕringsing papare* pattern. I also concur with Holmgren and Spertus that the sculptures themselves became prototypes, and that the models have been copied and replicated over the subsequent centuries.

Tulis Mas (Old Javanese) or Prada/Perada (contemporary)

Tulis mas is the Old Javanese term for *prada*, the term that is used today. This cloth remains in use, particularly in Bali, where it is culturally associated with the island. *Prada* designs are regularly portrayed on the statues of deities outside the *pura*, or temples, of Bali. The term *prada* refers to both the technique and the design. It is a process where the gold leaf or gold dust is applied directly on to the cloth and it adheres to a pre-applied pattern that has been stamped on with glue. *Prada* is a favoured way of decorating textiles, to either enhance the existing design of a batik or to apply *prada* to a plain silk fabric (Warming and Garwoski 1981, p. 141). The most common patterns are large lotus blossoms and other flowers, along with tendrils and leaves (Hauser-Schäublin, Nabholz-Kartaschoff and Ramseyer 1991, p. 53). The Chinese influence is frequently apparent when the design also includes the *banji* patterns, as we see on the border patterns of Harihara Ardhanari (fig. 2, p. 8) in the SHM. In ancient times, *prada* appeared to be a favourite way to create "gold-coloured" textiles or textiles decorated with gold glue-work, as suggested by Christie, "possibly in imitation of Persian gold-decorated cloth" (1998b, p. 25).

The *Smaradhana Kakawin* of the late twelfth century mentions the term *tinulis mas* for a gold cloth. The *Tuhanaru Charter* of 1323 includes the term *tulis ing mas*, meaning drawn upon in gold (Boechari 1986, pp. 77–85), along with the Old Javanese term *tulis warna*, meaning drawing with colour (Christie 1998b, p. 25). These two terms represent types of textiles that were only permitted to be worn by high-ranking members of the community (Christie 1991a, p. 16).

Kawung

The term *kawung* is another historically immutable pattern from among the *ceplok* or geometric group of patterns. The term *kawung* can be traced to a number of different sources over the centuries that offer differing meanings and interpretations. It is quite possible that this ubiquitous Javanese motif originated from within Java itself. Langewis and Wagner have described the *kawung* motif:

> As a simple ellipse in which two focal points are clearly indicated, these ellipses are placed crosswise opposite one another; repetition of this placed at regular intervals forms the decorative filling of the whole area ... the most significant feature is the four-pointed star that appears between the ellipses which in-turn display a plain stylised flower. (1964, p. 30)

I would suggest that the description by Langewis and Wagner of the *kawung* pattern does not use the correct term to describe this shape. I have instead chosen the term *vesica piscis*.[4] The precise origin of the *kawung* pattern is lost to the past, but the earliest visual evidence of the motif in Java is on the Boro Gaṇeśa (fig. 25, p. 59). This textile pattern is often referred to as a batik pattern, but it is more likely to be replicating a known technique as *tulis mas* or *prada* (Langewis and Wagner 1964, p. 30). Even though there appear to be similarities in design, given that we do not know what type of textile is represented on the sculptures, only assumptions can be made. Further reference to the Old Javanese texts leads us to note that while the term *kawung* appears many times as a "pattern" name (Berg 1931, p. 57, verse 45b, p. 60, verse 62a), the technique used is unknown. Thus, following the premise suggested earlier that a *kawung* pattern is a series of vesicae made into circles, the Gaṇeśa is the earliest representation of this motif in Java. Guy, in his book *Woven Cargoes*, describes the pattern: "It's highly probable that the Gaṇeśa was represented wearing a prestigious imported Indian cloth. This design became a critical pattern in the later Javanese repertoire, where it is known as *kawung*" (1998, p. 62).

Another example refers to the now destroyed sculpture of King Sanatruq I, the Persian king of Satra (r. 140–80). His garments of a long tunic and robe are decorated with a pattern, possibly representing stitched pearls, in a motif of interlocking circles. The statue of Sanatruq once stood at the entrance to the Hatra Temple of the Sun—the centre of the sun cult—where it is suggested he was seen as the representative of the cult of sun worship. We could assume therefore that this ancient pattern has a direct relationship with the cult of sun worship (Forman 1998, p. 73). Historically, this figure has had no relationship with Java, but the details are presented here as an example of the popularity of the motif on garments.

Bahasa Terms for Dress

The apparel depicted on the sculptures consist mainly of a long cloth and sashes. These are combined with belts and girdles that could represent a woven material and belts that possibly represent a metal of some sort, perhaps gold. By observing the various structures of the sashes and belts, and by referring to silver belts worn by the Iban in East Malaysia and to silver gilt belts worn by the Peranakan in Peninsular Malaysia, it is possible to deduce how the many belts and girdles might have looked. It is also apparent from the *Zhufanzhi* that gold in Java was the medium of payment for salaries to civil servants, that the king sat on a gold throne and ate off gold dishes, that gold was given in marriage exchange, and that criminals were not given corporal punishment but instead fined in gold.

The sarong, or *kain* or *sarung* in Bahasa Indonesia, and the word *sinjang*, taken from Old Javanese Literature, represent the long cloth wrapped around the lower body. In the present day, the *sarung* or sarong is worn as a tube skirt by women—meaning the fabric is sewn into a tube to be wrapped around the body—whereas the *kain* is a flat sheet to be wrapped around the body and held in place with belts and girdles.

The bronze and gold statuettes of Central Java are depicted as either Śaivite or Buddhist deities. More often than not they are dressed in a *dhotī*, which is an Indian word for a lower-body cloth that is wrapped around the body. In many instances it would be pulled up between the legs, tucked in at the waist behind the body and held up by a girdle. The style is very similar to that depicted on the small bronze figures from India. There are instances, however, where statues are depicted wearing a *kain*. The *antariya* was worn in the *kachcha* style—secured at the waist by a sash or *kayabandh*, often looped at the centre front of the abdomen. In the post-Vedic era, this garment became the predecessor of the *dhotī*, worn pleated at the hips and drawn up between the legs. *Dhotī*, derived from *dhauti* in Sanskrit, is the evolved form of this garment and is the general term used in this book.

The long cloth waist belt is a long fabric belt that is wrapped many times around the waist to secure the *sinjang*, as can be seen in the figure of Mahākāla (fig. 107, p. 161), where it is apparent that the belt is tied up in a knot at the front of the body. The sash is a kind of scarf worn by princesses and female dancers over the ceremonial dress, tied around the waist with the two ends hanging down. This garment appears on virtually every statue in Central and East Java. In East Java, the sash is usually shown in a double layer lying flat over the thighs. In the case of the stone sculptures and bronzes from Central Java, however, more often the narrow sash is depicting as twisted on the front of the thighs.

Cloth belts are frequently shown with the addition of circular plaques, which possibly would have been made of gold. They can also signify a woven or reticulated gold belt with circular plates that could represent *batu* or jewels of some sort. At the end of this long belt is the tassel. The girdles on the late East Javanese sculptures have been carved as a very decorative feature compared with those of the earlier Central Javanese bronzes.

The word *seléndang* is the term used for a shawl or stole that is worn over the left shoulder or across the upper body. The sash, or *uttarīya*, is clearly visible on almost all the Pāla sculptures of the eleventh and twelfth centuries, where the *uttarīya* is shown by a series of undulating lines and is sometimes decorated to replicate the pattern on the *dhotī*. In contrast, in Central Java the sash was often carved with two lines realistically drawn across the body. By the East Javanese period, the *seléndang* came to be depicted as a broad sash in a typical Singosari style, represented as a wide band with a thin line carved in the centre and with the flap rendered realistically over the right shoulder.

Notes

1. *Kampuh* is the Balinese word for a *kendit*, which is the short hip cloth worn over a long *kain* or *sinjang*.
2. *Tumpal* is the name given to the inverted triangular pattern often depicted at the border edges of the silk *patola* and the cotton block printed and mordant dyed replicas from western India. The *tumpal* motif became very popular in almost every aspect of the woven cloth and batik produced across all the Indonesian islands. The *tumpal* motif, however, never once appears on the sculptures of this period in Java.
3. This refers to some sort of pattern. It is also used to describe the pattern on a waist sash.
4. The correct term to describe this shape of a lens—pointed at each end—is *vesica piscis*. In Italian, the name for the shape is *mandorla*, meaning almond. It is also called *aureole*. The word *vesica* is best used when describing the geometrical form of the *kawung* pattern.

Bibliography

Acri, A. 2015. "Revisiting the Cult of Siva-Buddha in Java and Bali". In *Buddhist Dynamics in Premodern and Early Modern Southeast Asia*, edited by D.C. Lammerts, pp. 261–81. Singapore: Institute of Southeast Asian Studies.

———. 2017. "Tantrism 'Seen from the East'". In *Spirits and Ships: Cultural Transfers in Early Monsoon Asia*, edited by A. Acri, R. Blench, and A. Landmann, pp. 71–145. Singapore: ISEAS – Yusof Ishak Institute.

Allsen, T.T. 1997. *Commodity and Exchange in the Mongol Empire: A Cultural History of Islamic Textiles*. Cambridge: Cambridge University Press.

Andaya, B.W. 1994. "Political Development between the Sixteenth and Eighteenth Centuries". In *The Cambridge History of Southeast Asia*, vol. 1, *From Early Times to c.1800*, edited by N. Tarling, pp. 402–60. Cambridge: Cambridge University Press.

Andaya, L.Y. 2008. *Leaves of the Same Tree: Trade and Ethnicity in the Straits of Melaka*. Honolulu: University of Hawai'i Press.

Bade, D. 2002. *Of Palm Wine, Women and War: The Mongol Naval Expedition to Java in the 13th Century*. Singapore: Institute of Southeast Asian Studies.

———. 2016. "(Spi)ritual Warfare in 13th Century Asia? International Relations, the Balance of Powers, and the Tantric Buddhism of Krtanagara and Khubilai Khan". In *Esoteric Buddhism in Mediaeval Asia: Networks of Masters, Texts, Icons*, edited by A. Acri, pp. 141–63. Singapore: ISEAS – Yusof Ishak Institute.

Barnes, R. 1997a. "From India to Egypt: The Newberry Collection and the Indian Ocean". In *Islamische Textilkunst des Mittelalters: Aktuelle Probleme*, edited by M. Abbas Muhammad Salim, pp. 79–95. Riggisberg: Abbeg-Stiftung.

———. 1997b. *Indian Block-Printed Textiles in Egypt*. Oxford: Clarendon Press.

Bart, B. 2016. "Textile Patterns on Stone Sculptures and in Songket Weaving". In *Textiles Asia* (April): 12–20.

Bautze-Picron, C. 1993. "Crying Leaves: Some Remarks on 'The Art of Pala India (8th–12th Centuries) and Its International Legacy'". *East and West* 43: 277–94.

———. 2014a. "Textiles from Bengal in Pagan (Myanmar) from Late Eleventh Century and Onwards". In *Studies in Heritage of South Asia: Essays in Memory of M. Harunur Rashid*, edited by B. Mokammal H., pp. 19–29. Dhaka: Bangla Academy Dhaka.

———. 2014b. "Buddhist Images from Padang Lawas Region and the South Asian Connection". In *History of Padang Lawas, North Sumatra*, edited by D. Perret, pp. 107–28. Paris: Association Archipel.

Berg, C.C. 1931. "Kidung Harsa-Wijaya: Middel-Javaansche Historische Roman". *Journal of the Humanities and Social Sciences* 88: 49–238.

Bernet Kempers, A.J. 1959. *Ancient Indonesian Art*. Amsterdam: C.P.J. van der Peet.

Bielenstein, H. 2005. *Diplomacy and Trade in the Chinese World, 589–1276*. Leiden: Brill.

Blom, J. 1939. *The Antiquities of Singasari*. Leiden: Burgersdijk & Niermans.

Boechari. 1986. *Prasasti Koleksi Museum Nasional*. Jakarta.

Bosch, F.D.K. 1921. "De Inscriptie op het Manjusri beeld van 1265 Saka". *BKI* 77: 194–201.

Brown, R. 1999. *Art from Thailand*. Mumbai: Marg.

Buckley, C.D, and E. Boudot. 2015. *The Roots of Ancient Weaving: The He Haiyan Collection of Textiles and Looms from Southwest China*. Oxford: Oxbow Books.

Canepa, M.P. 2014. "Textiles and Elite Tastes between the Mediterranean, Iran and Asia at the end of Antiquity". In *Global Textile Encounters*, edited by M.L. Nosh, F. Zhao, and L. Varadarajan, pp. 1–15. Oxford: Oxbow Books.

Casparis, J.G. de. 1983. *India and Maritime Southeast Asia: A Lasting Relationship*. Kuala Lumpur: University of Malaya.

Casparis, J.G. de, and I.W. Mabbett. 1994. "Religion and Popular Beliefs of Southeast Asia before c.1500". In *The Cambridge History of Southeast Asia*, vol. 1, *From Early Times to c.1800*, edited by N. Tarling, pp. 276–341. Cambridge: Cambridge University Press.

Chandra, M. 1973. *Costumes Textiles Cosmetics and Coiffure in Ancient and Medieval India*. Delhi: Oriental.

Christie, J. Wisseman. 1993a. "Ikat to Batik? Epigraphic Data on Textiles in Java from the Ninth to the Fifteenth Centuries". In *Weaving Patterns of Life: Indonesia Textile Symposium 1991*, edited by M.L. Nabholz-

Kartaschoff, R. Barnes, and D.J. Stuart-Fox, pp. 11–29. Basel: Museum of Ethnology.

———. 1993b. "Texts and Textiles in Medieval Java". *Bulletin de l'Ecole francais d'Extreme-Orient* 80, no. 1: 181–211.

———. 1998a. "The Medieval Tamil-language Inscriptions in Southeast Asia and China". *Journal of Southeast Asian Studies* 29, no. 2: 239–68.

———. 1998b. *Weaving and Dyeing in Early Java and Bali*. Centre for Southeast Asian Studies, Hull.

———. 1999. "Asian Sea Trade between the Tenth and Thirteenth Centuries and its Impact on the States of Java and Bali". In *Archaeology of Seafaring: The Indian Ocean in the Ancient Period*, edited by H. Prabha Ray, pp. 221–69. Delhi: Pragati.

Clunas, C. 1997. *Art in China*. Oxford: Oxford University Press.

Compareti, M. 2020. "Iranian Composite Creatures between the Caucasus and Western China: The Case of the So-called *Simurgh*". *Iran and the Caucasus* 24, no. 2: 115–38.

Crill, R. 2016. *The Fabric of India*. London: V&A Publishing.

Cutsem-Vanderstraete, A. van. 2012. *Magie Van De Vrouw*. Rotterdam: Stichting Wereldmuseum.

Deshpande, O. 2016. *Works of Art from Southeast Asia*. St Petersburg: The State Hermitage Publishers.

Devare, H. 2009. "Cultural Implications of the Chola Maritime Fabric Trade. In *Nagapattinam to Suvarnadwipa*, edited by H. Kulke, K. Kesavapany, and V. Sakhuja, pp. 178–93. Singapore: Institute of Southeast Asian Studies..

Dode, Z. 2014. "Textile in Art: The Influence in Textile Patterns on Ornaments in the Architecture of Medieval Zirikhgeran". In *Global Textile Encounters*, edited by M.L. Nosh, F. Zhao, and L. Varadarajan, pp. 127–41. Oxford: Oxbow Books.

Duijker, M. 2010. *The Worship of Bhima: The Representation of Bhima on Java during the Majapahit Period*. Amstelveen: EON Pers.

Dumarçay, J. 1986. *Le savoir des maîtres d'œuvre javanais au XIIIe et XIVe siècles*. Paris: Ecole française d'Extrême-Orient.

Elliot, I. McC. 1996. *The Fabric of Enchantment: Batik from the North Coast of Java*. Los Angeles: Los Angeles County Museum.

Fischer, J. 1980. "The Character and Study of Indonesian Textiles". In *Indonesian Textiles: Irene Emery Roundtable on Museum Textiles 1979 Proceedings*, edited by M. Gittinger. Washington DC: The Textile Museum.

Fischer, R.E. 1997. *The Art of Tibet*. London: Thames and Hudson.

Flood, F.B. 2009. *Objects of Translation: Material Culture and Medieval "Hindu-Muslim" Encounter.* Princeton: Princeton University Press.

Fontein, J. 1990. *Sculpture of Indonesia*. New York: Harry N. Abrams.

Fontein, J., R. Soekmono, and S. Suleiman. 1971. *Ancient Indonesian Art of the Central and East Javanese Periods*. New York: The Asia Society.

Forman, B. 1998. *Indonesian Batik and Ikat*. Prague: Hamlyn.

Fraser-Lu, S. 1988. *Handwoven Textiles of Southeast Asia*. Singapore: Oxford University Press.

Gittinger, M. 1979. *Splendid Symbols, Textiles and Tradition in Indonesia*. Washington DC: The Textile Museum.

Gombrich, E. 1998. "Style". In *The Art of Art History: A Critical Anthology*, edited by D. Preziosi, pp. 150–65. Oxford: Oxford University Press.

Groeneveldt, W.P. 1960. *Historical Notes on Indonesia and Malaya Compiled from Chinese Sources*. Jakarta: C.V. Bhratara.

Guy, J. 1998. *Woven Cargoes: Indian Textiles in the East*. Singapore: Thames and Hudson.

———. 2010. "Rare and Strange Goods: International Trade in 9th Century Asia". In *Shipwrecked Tang Treasures and Monsoon Winds*, edited by R. Krahl, J. Guy, J.K. Wilson, and J. Raby, pp. 19–30. Singapore: National Heritage Board.

Guy, J., and K. Thakar. 2015. *Indian Cotton Textiles: Seven Centuries of Chintz from the Karun Thakar Collection*. Suffolk: Antique Collectors Club.

Hall, D.G.E. 1981. *A History of Southeast Asia*. London: Macmillan.

Hardjonagoro, K.R.T. 1979. "The Place of Batik in the History and Philosophy of Javanese Textiles: A Personal View". In *Indonesian Textiles, Irene Emery Roundtable on Museum Textiles 1979 Proceedings*, edited by M. Gittinger. Washington DC: The Textile Museum.

Haulleville, O. de. 2000. *Pilgrimage to Java: An Esoteric History of Buddhism*. Lincoln, NE: iUniverse.

Hauser-Schäublin, B., M.L. Nabholz-Kartaschoff, and U. Ramseyer. 1991. *Textiles in Bali*. Singapore: Periplus Editions.

Heller, A. 1998. "Two Inscribed Fabrics and Their Historical Context: Some Observations on Esthetics and Silk Trade in Tibet, 7th to 9th Century. In *Entlang der Seidenstraße*, edited by K. Otavsky, pp. 95–119. Riggisberg: Abbeg-Stiftung.

———. 2006. "Recent Findings on Textiles from the Tibetan Empire". In *Central Asian Textiles and Their Contexts in the Early Middle Ages*, edited by R. Schorta, pp. 175–88. Riggisberg: Abegg-Stiftung.

Heine-Geldern, R. 1925. *Alt Javanische Bronzen*. Vienna: Stern.

Heng, D. 2009. *Sino-Malay Trade and Diplomacy from the Tenth through the Fourteenth Century*. Athens: Ohio University Press.

Hirth, F., and W.W. Rockhill. 1965. *Chao Ju-kua: His Work on the Chinese and Arab Trade in the Twelfth and Thirteenth Centuries, Entitled 'Chu-fan-chi'*. Taiwan: Literature House.

———. (1911) 1966. *Chao Ju-kua: His Work on the Chinese and Arab Trade in the Twelfth and Thirteenth Centuries, Entitled 'Chu-fan-chi'*. St. Petersburg. Reprint, Paragon.

Hoijtink, M. 2012. *Exhibiting the Past: Casper Reuvens and the Museum of Antiquities in Europe, 1800–1840*. Turnhout, Belgium: Brepols.

Holmgren, R.J., and A.E. Spertus. 1980. "Tampan Pasisir: Pictorial Documents of an Ancient Indonesian Coastal Culture". In *Indonesian Textiles*, edited by M. Gittinger, pp. 157–201. Washington DC: The Textile Museum.

———. 1991. "Is Gerinsing Really Balinese?" In *Indonesian Textiles*, edited by K.v.W. and G. Volger, pp. 59–80. Cologne: Rautenstrauch-Joest-Museum):

Hoop, A.N.J.Th. van der. 1949. *Indonesian Ornamental Design*. Batavia: Koninklijk Bataviaasch Genootschap van Kunsten en Wetenschappen.

Hunter, T.M. 2007. "The Body of the King: Reappraising Singhasari Period Syncretism". *Journal of Southeast Asian Studies* 38: 27–53.

Huntington, S.L. 1994. "Some Connections between Metal Images of Northeast India and Java". In *Ancient Indonesian Art*, edited by P. Lunsingh Scheurleer and M.J. Klokke, pp. 57–76. Leiden: KITLV Press.

Huntington, S.L., and J.C. Huntington. 1993. *The Art of Ancient India*. New York: Weatherhill.

I-Tsing. 1998. *A Record of the Buddhist Religion as Practised in India and the Malaya Archipelago (AD 671–695)*. Manoharlal.

Jákl, J. 2016. "The Loincloth, Trousers, and Horse-riders in Pre-Islamic Java: Notes on the Old Javanese Term *Lañcinan*". *Archipel* 91: 185–202.

Jákl, J., and J.T. Hoogervorst. 2017. "Custom, Combat and Ceremony: Java and Indo-Persian Textile Trade". *EFEO* 103: 209–35.

Jessup, H. 1990. *Court Arts of Indonesia*. New York: Asia Society Galleries.

Jessup, H.I. 2004. *Motif and Meaning in Indonesian Textiles*. Bangkok: River Books.

Kartiwa, S. 1979. "The Kain Songket Minangkabau". In *Indonesian Textiles, Irene Emery Roundtable on Museum Textiles 1979 Proceedings*, edited by M. Gittinger. Washington DC: The Textile Museum.

Keurs, T.P., and D.J. Stuart-Fox. 2009. "History and Culture Dynamics of Sumatra". In *Sumatra Crossroads of Culture*, edited by F. Brinkgreve and R. Sulistianingsih, pp. 13–31. Leiden: KITLV Press.

Kinney, A.R. 2003. *Worshipping Siva and Buddha: The Temple Art of East Java*. Honolulu: University of Hawai'i Press.

Klimburg-Salter, D.E. 1994. "A Decorated Prajnaparamita Manuscript from Poo". *Orientations* (June): 54–69.

Klokke, M.J. 1994. "The So-called Portrait Statues in East Javanese Art". In *Ancient Indonesian Sculpture*, edited by M.J. Klokke and P. Lunsingh Scheurleer, pp. 178–202. Leiden: KITLV.

———. 2000. "The Krsna Reliefs at Panataran: A Visual Version of Old Javanese". In *Narrative Sculpture and Literary Traditions in South and Southeast Asia*, edited by M.J. Klokke, pp. 19–42. Leiden: Brill.

Kozok, U., and E. van Reijn. 2010. "Adityawarman: Three Inscriptions of the Sumatran 'King of all Kings'". *Indonesia and the Malay World* 38: 135–58.

Krom, N.J. 1926. *L'art javanais dans les musées de Hollande et de Java*. Paris: G. van Oest.

———. 1931. *Hindoe-javaansche geschiedenis*. The Hague: M. Nijhoff.

Kuhn, D. 2012. "Chinese Silks". In *Culture & Civilization of China*. New Haven: Yale University Press.

Kulke, H. 1991. "Epigraphical References to the 'City' and the 'State' in Early Indonesia". *Indonesia* 52: 3–22.

———. 2009. "The Naval Expeditions of the Cholas in the Context of Asian History". In *Nagapattinam to Suvarnadwipa*, edited by H. Kulke, K. Kesavapany, and V. Sakhuja, pp. 1–20. Singapore: Institute of Southeast Asian Studies.

Langewis, L., and F.A. Wagner. 1964. *Decorative Art in Indonesian Textiles*. Amsterdam: C.P.J. Van der Peet.

Lee, P. 2015. *Sarong Kebya: Peranakan Fashion in an Interconnected World*. Singapore: ACM.

Lin, L.C. 2006. "Buddhist Textiles in the Chris Hall Collection". In *Powerdressing: Textiles for Rulers and Priests from the Chris Hall Collection*, edited by C. Hall, pp. 62–75. Singapore: Asian Civilisations Museum.

Lunsingh Scheurleer, P. 1998a. "Ganesha van Singosari op Bezoek". *Aziatische Kunst* 28: 2–18.

———. 1998b. "Skulls, Fangs and Serpents: A New Development in East Javanese Iconography". *EurASEAA* 7: 189–204.

———. 2008. "The Well-known Javanese Statue in the Tropenmuseum, Amsterdam, and Its Place in Javanese Sculpture". *Artibus Asiae* 68: 287–332.

———. 2013. *Gold from Java, Goud uit Java*. Gemeentemuseum Den Haag.

Lunsingh Scheurleer, P., and M.J. Klokke. 1988a. *Ancient Indonesian Bronzes: A Catalogue of the Exhibition in the Rijksmuseum Amsterdam with a General Introduction*. Leiden: Brill.

———. 1988b. *Divine Bronze. Ancient Indonesian Bronzes, from A.D. 600 to 1600*. Leiden: Brill.

Mahler, J.G. 1958. "The Art of Medieval Burma in Pagan". *Archives of the Chinese Art Society of America* 12: 30–47.

Maxwell, R. 2003. *Sari to Sarong: Five Hundred Years of Indian and Indonesian Textile Exchange*. London: National Gallery of Australia.

McIntosh, L.S. 2012. *Art of Southeast Asian Textiles: The Tilleke & Gibbins Collection*. Chicago: Serindia.

Miksic, J. 1990. *Borobudur: Golden Tales of the Buddha*. London: Periplus Editions.

———. 2007. *Icons of Art: The Collection of the National Museum of Indonesia*. Jakarta: BAB Publishing Indonesia.

———. 2012. *The Court of Surakarta*. Jakarta: BAB Publishing Indonesia.

———. 2016. "Archaeological Evidence for Esoteric Buddhism in Sumatra, 7th to 13th century". In *Esoteric Buddhism in Medieval Asia: Networks of Masters, Texts and Icons*, edited by A. Acri, pp. 253–75. Singapore: ISEAS – Yusof Ishak Institute.

Miksic, J.N., and G.Y. Goh. 2017. *Ancient Southeast Asia*. London: Routledge.

Munoz, P. 2006. *Early Kingdoms of the Indonesian Archipelago and the Malay Peninsula*. Singapore: Editions Didier Millet.

Nihom, M. 1994. *Studies in Indian and Indo-Indonesian Tantrism: The Kunjarakarnadharmakathanajarakarna and the Yogatantra*. Vienna: Sammlung De Nobili.

O'Brien, K., and T. Mpu. 2008. *Sutasoma: The Ancient Tale of a Buddha-Prince from 14th Century Java by the Poet Mpu Tantular*. Bangkok: Orchid Press.

Otavsky, K. 1998. "Zur Kunsthistorischen Einordnung der Stoffe". In *Entlang der Seidenstraße*, pp. 119–215. Riggisberg: Abbbeg-Stiftung.

Pal, P. 2004. *Art from Sri Lanka and Southeast Asia*. New Haven: Yale University Press.

Perret, D. 2014. "History of Padang Lawas, North Sumatra". In *Cahier d'Archipel*, edited by D. Perret. Paris: Association Archipel.

Pigeaud, T.G. 1962. *Java in the Fourteenth Century: A Study in Cultural History; The Nāgara-Kěrtāgama by Rakawi Prapañca of Majapahit, 1365 A.D.*, vol. 4, *Commentaries and Recapitulation*. The Hague: Martinus Nijhoff.

Pollock, S. 1996. "The Sanskrit Cosmopolis". In *Ideology and Status of Sanskrit*, edited by J.E.M. Houben, pp. 197–249. Leiden: Brill.

Polo, M. 1875. *The Book of Ser Marco Polo, the Venetian, Concerning the Kingdoms and Marvels of the East*. London: John Murray.

Pott, P.H. 1962. "Four Demonic Ganesa from East Java". In *Mededelingen Van Her Rijksmuseum voor Volkenkunde, Leiden*, pp. 123–31. Leiden: Brill.

Pullen, L.S. 2013. "Textile Designs in Stone: The Legacy of Medieval Javanese Sculpture". *TAASA Review* 22 (March).

———. 2019. "Worn Textiles of Singhasari". *Aziatische Kunst* 49, no. 2: 18–27.

———. 2020. "Prajnaparamita in the Thirteenth Century Java and Sumatra: Two Sculptures Disconnected by Textile Designs". In *EurASEAA14*, edited by H. Lewis, pp. 38–52. Dublin: Archaeopress.

Raffles, S. 1817. *The History of Java*. London: Black, Parbury and Allen.

Raspopova, V.I. 2006. Textile Representation in Sogdia Murals. In *Central Asian Textiles and Their Contexts in the Early Middle Ages*, edited by R. Schorta, pp. 61–75. Riggisberg: Abbeg-Stiftung.

Reichle, N. 2007. *Violence and Serenity: Late Buddhist Sculpture from Indonesia*. Hawaii: University of Hawai'i Press.

Reid, A. 2015. *A History of Southeast Asia: Critical Crossroads*. Chichester: Wiley Blackwell.

Robson, S., and M. Prapanca. 1995. *Desawarnana (Nagarakrtagama)*. Leiden: KITLV Press.

Rockhill, W.W. 1915. "Notes on the Relations and Trade of China with the Eastern Archipelago and the Coast of the Indian Ocean during the Fourteenth Century, Part II". *T'oung Pao* 16: 236–71.

Santiko, H. 1995. "Early Research on Sivaitic Hinduism during the Majapahit Era". In *The Legacy of Majapahit*, edited by J. Miksic, pp. 55–73. Singapore: National Museum.

Schnitger, F.M. 1937. *The Archaeology of Hindoo Sumatra*. Leiden: Brill.

Schorta, R. 2007. *Dragons of Silk, Flowers of Gold: A Group of Liao-dynasty Textiles at the Abbeg-Stiftung*. Riggisberg: Abbeg-Stiftung.

Schoterman, J.A. 2016. "Traces of Indonesian Influences in Tibet". In *Esoteric Buddhism in Mediaeval Maritime Asia: Network of Masters, Texts, Icons*, edited by A. Acri, pp. 113–23. Singapore: ISEAS – Yusof Ishak Institute.

Sedyawati, E. 1990. "The Making of Indonesian Art". In *The Sculpture of Indonesia*, edited by J. Fontein, pp. 97–112. Washington DC: National Gallery of Art.

———. 1994. *Ganesa Statuary of the Kediri and Singasari Periods: A Study of Art History* (translation of PhD dissertation, University of Indonesia, Jakarta 1985). Leiden: KITLV Press.

Selvanayagam, G.I. 1990. *Songket: Malaysia's Woven Treasure*. Singapore: Oxford University Press.

Sen, T. 2009. "The Military Campaign of Rajendra Chola and the Chola-Srivijaya-China Triangle". In *Nagapattinam to Suvarnadwipa*, edited by H. Kulke, K. Kesavapany, and V. Sakhuja, pp. 61–76. Singapore: Institute of Southeast Asian Studies.

Sidomulyo, H. 2010. "From Kuta Raja to Singhasari". *Archipel* 80: 1–62.

Singh, M. 1945. *India: Paintings from the Ajanta Caves*. New York.

Soekmono, R. 1969. "Gurah: The Link between Central and the East Javanese Arts". *Bulletin of the Archaeological Institute* 6: 1–20.

———. 1995. *The Javanese Candi: Function and Meaning*. Leiden: Brill.

Stuart-Fox, D.J. 1993. "Textiles in Ancient Bali". In *Weaving Patterns of Life: Indonesia Textile Symposium 1991*, edited by M.L. Nabholz-Kartschoff., R. Barnes, and D.J. Stuart-Fox, pp. 85–93. Basel: Museum of Ethnology.

Stuart-Fox, M. 2003. *A Short History of China and Southeast Asia: Tribute. Trade and Influence*. New South Wales: Allen and Unwin.

Stutterheim, W.F. 1929. "The Meaning of the Kala-Makara Ornament". *Indian Art and Letters* 3: 27–57.

———. 1932. "Eine Statue des Javanischen Königs Krtanagara in Berlin?" *Berliner Museen* 53: 47–50.

———. 1936. "Da dateering van eenige Oost-javaansche beeldengroepen". In *Tijdschrift voor Indische Taal-Land-En Volkenkunde*, pp. 249–320. Leiden: Koninklijk Bataviaasch Genootschap van Kunsten en Wetenschappen.

———. 1989. *Rama-Legends and Rama-Reliefs in Indonesia*. New Delhi: Shakti Malik.

Sumaryoto, W.A. 1993. "Textiles in Javanese Texts". In *Weaving Patterns of Life: Indonesia Textile Symposium 1991*, edited by M.L. Nabholz-Kartaschoff, R. Barnes, and D.J. Stuart-Fox, pp. 31–50. Basel: Museum of Ethnography.

Summerfield, A., and J. Summerfield. 1999. *Walk in Splendor: Ceremonial Dress and the Minangkabau*. Los Angeles: UCLA Fowler Museum of Cultural History.

Tambiah, S.J. 2013. "The Galactic Polity of Southeast Asia". *HAU: Journal of Ethnographic Theory* 3: 503–34.

Tarling, N. 1992. *The Cambridge History of Southeast Asia*. Cambridge University Press.

Totton, M.-L. 2009. *Wearing Wealth and Styling Identity: Tapis from Lamung, South Sumatra*. Hanover, NH: Hood Museum of Art, Dartmouth Art College.

Velduisen-Djajasoebrata, A. 1979. "On the Origin and Nature of Larangan: Forbidden Batik Patterns from the Central Javanese Principalities". In *Indonesian Textiles: Irene Emery Roundtable on Museum Textiles 1979 Proceedings*, edited by M. Gittinger. Washington DC: The Textile Museum.

Wales, H.G.Q. 1977. *The Universe around Them: Cosmology and Cosmic Renewal in Indianized South-east Asia*. London: Probsthain.

Warming, W., and M. Garwoski. 1981. *The World of Indonesian Textiles*. London: Serinda.

Watt, J.C.Y. 1997. *When Silk Was Gold: Central Asian and Chinese Textiles*. New York: Metropolitan Museum of Art in cooperation with the Cleveland Museum of Art, 1997.

———. 2010. *The World of Khubilai Khan: Chinese Art in the Yuan Dynasty*. New York: The Metropolitan Museum of Art.

Wheatley, P. 1961. *The Golden Khersonese*. Kuala Lumpur: University of Malaya Press.

Wit, A. de. 1912. *Java, Facts and Fancies*. Chapman & Hall.

Wolters, O.W. 1999. *History, Culture, and Region in Southeast Asian Perspectives*, Studies on Southeast Asia 26. Ithaca, NY: Southeast Asia Program, Cornell University.

Woodward, H.W. J. 1977. "A Chinese Silk Depicted at Caṇḍi Sèwu". In *Economic Exchange and Social Interaction in Southeast Asia: Perspectives from Prehistory, History and Ethnography*, edited by K.L. Hutterer, pp. 233–45. Michigan: Centre for Southeast Asian Studies.

Yaldiz, M. 2006. "Die Rezeption von Textilmotiven in der indischen Kunst und ihr Einfluß auf die Malarei Xinjiangs". In *Central Asian Textiles and Their Context in Early Middle Ages*, edited by R. Schorta, pp. 81–101. Riggisberg: Abbeg-Stiftung.

Zhao, F. 2015. "Weaving Technology". In *A History of Chinese Science and Technology*, edited by Y. Lu, pp. 379–493. Heidelberg: Springer.

Zoetmulder, P.J. 1974. *Kalangwan: A Survey of Old Javanese Literature*. The Hague: Nijhoff.

———. 1982. *Old Javanese-English dictionary*. The Hague: Nijhoff.

Index

Page references in bold refer to figures. Numbers prefixed by "n" refer to notes.

A

abasana, 26
abaya, 48
acadar, 26
Acri, Andrea
   on 4+4+1 scheme, 258–59
   on Bhīma, 247
   on Newar artists, 207
adat, 138–39
Ādityavarman, 7, 139, 143, 177, 213n2
Agastya
   in BPCB, 1, 9, 87; upper body detail, **10**
   at Caṇḍi Singosari, 41
   near Caṇḍi Ijo, 76–77, **77**
Airlangga Museum, *prasasti batu*, 215n19
Ajanta murals
   haṃsa/goose motifs, 148, 149, **150**
   ikat examples on, 27, 120
   palace scene, **150**
akṣamālā, 104, **106**
Akṣobhya, 164, 244
Allsen, Thomas, on *nasīj*, 34
Amoghapāśa, 137, 144
ancestors, 52, 87, 131, 173, 211, 223. *See also* deification of ancestors
Andaya, Leonard Y., on Panai polity, 244
Angkor Wat, 55
animal patterns
   deer, 37–38, 40–41, 148
   ducks, 37, 38, 40, 148, 149, **150**
   elephants, **144**, 145–46
   lions, 37, 41, 44, 231
   mythical creatures, 39–40, **144**, 146, 213nn3–5
   octopi, 113
   peacocks, 37
antariya, 281
Anuṣapati, commemorative reliefs for, **145**, 214n8
Arcā Dewa/Leluhur
   at Bumiayu, **45**, 47–48, **47**, 114–16; **115**; drawings of *baju* and *kain*, **116**
   in MNI, 116, **117**, 131
"archetype textiles", 54
Archipel: Indonesian Kingdoms of the Sea, 266
architecture, as replica of the cosmos, 55
Ardhanarīśvara, 223, 224
areng palm fruit (*Arenga pinnata*), 57
Argha candrakapāla, 215n21
arrow patterns, **84**
ascetics, 49, 50, 196, 224–25
Ashmolean Museum, Newberry Collection, 64, 65, 70, 110, 149
   fragment imitating *bandhani*, **84**
   Indian cotton fragment, **151**
Asiatic Society of Bengal, 265
Assam Museum, 232
Aṣṭa-Dikpala, 193
Aṣṭasāharsrikā Prajñāpāramitā, 119
Atīśa
   commentary on the *Kālacakratantra*, 15–16
   in Śrivijaya and Sumatra, 11–12, 120, 243
   and transmission of Esoteric ritual, 243
aureole, 282n4
Avadanas, 29
Avalokiteśvara. *See also* Śiva
   in BPCB, 98, **101**
   in British Museum, 65, **66**

293

iconographic classification of, 120
in Museum Sonobudoyo, **96**, 97
in National Museum, New Delhi, 30
Tibetan, 79
in Volkenkunde, 98, **99**
Ayutthaya, 185

B

bad Ʒu, 48
badan, 276
Bade, David, on Kṛtanāgara, 15
bafta, 31, 132
baju, 48, 49, 116
baju surjan lurik, **49**, 50
balah kacang (split peanut) patterns, 137–40, 213n2
Balai Arkeologi, Sita Mañjughoṣa, **68**
Balai Pelestarian Cagar Budaya (BPCB)
  Agastya, **10**, **88**
  Avalokiteśvara, 98, **101**
  Dhupa, **86**
Balinese military, 42
bamboo shoot motif. *See tumpal*
Bameswara, 176
bananten, 25
bandhani, 65, 69, **84**
banji (swastika), 159–60, **163**, 204–5
Barnes, Ruth, on patterns found in Egypt, 110
Bart, Bernhard
  on *balah kacang*, 137–38, 209, 213n2, 215n23
  on *kawung*, 54, 213n2
  and *songket* production, 178, 215n23
batik
  definition, 58
  production of, 58, 260
batik banji, 205
batik kawung, **57**
batik kraton, 154
batik lokcan kemben, **206**
batik prada, 205
batik sakti tulis, **237**
batik tulis ceplok, 214n10
Bautze-Picron, Claudine
  on Ādityavarman, 139
  on classification of Pāla statues, 15
  on *haṃsa* motifs, 148
  on Kubyauk-gyi murals, 199
  on Mahākāla statue, 177
Bazar Royal, 264
Belitung wreck, 6
Bengal, 15, 16, 207
Bhadracari, 29
Bhairava, 164, 177, 213n2
Bhīma, 30–31, 239–40, **240**
  detail and drawing of pattern, **241**
bhūta, 194
Biaro Pulo dancers, 241–43, **243**, 248

Bihar, 11, 16
blah, 25
Blom, Jessy
  on *kotangs*, 163
  on Singhāsari statues, 211
  on unidentified goddess from Caṇḍi Singosari, 191
bodhisattva, 56, 84
bodhyagrīmudrā, **81**
Boer, Dirk, 264
bolus, 104, **106**
Boro Gaṇeśa, 12, 59, 129–31, 132–34, **133**, 253
  detail and drawing of sash, **134**
  detail of lower body, **59**
Borobudur, 3, 29, 55
Bosch, F.D.K.
  on Mañjuśrī Arapacana inscription, 141
  on "recalcitrant spiral", 145
Boudout, Eric, on looms, 144
bows, 69–70, 192
  of sash on divine couple, **234**
BPCB. *See* Balai Pelestarian Cagar Budaya (BPCB)
Brahmā
  gold statuette, 80, **82**
  in Volkenkunde, 196, **197**; *sinjang* detail, **198**; textile pattern, **39**
Brahmins, 3
brainpan. *See kapāla* (brainpan/skull cup)
Brandes, J.L.A.
  Dikpāla photo, **193**
  excavations with J. Knebel, 191
  on statues for Noordeinde Palace, 264
brassier, 163
breast cloth (*kemben gěringsing*), 277
British Museum
  Avalokiteśvara, **66**
  Māmakī, **140**
  Padmapāni, **67**
  Raffles Collection, 265
Bṛkuṭi, 137, **139**
brocade, 34–35, 42, 79, 134
bronzesmiths, 21
Brooke Sewell, P.T., 265
Brown, Robert, on dating Harihara plaque, 106
Buckley, Chris, on looms, 144
Buddha Amoghasiddhi, 159
Buddha Mahāvairocana, 79, **81**
Buddha Vairocana, 216n27
Buddhahood, 94–95
Buddhism. *See also* Esoteric Buddhism
  and Borobudur reliefs, 29
  influences on Javanese art, 1–2, 9–11, 179
  on Java, 7, 16
  Javanese, 225
  Śaivism and, 22
  on Sumatra, 7, 12, 16

transition from Hīnayāna to Mahāyāna, 2
Buddhist sculptures, 30
buffalo demon (Mahiśa), 152, 201
bunga bintang, 154, **155**

C

cadar loom (*pacadaran*), 26, 33, 144, 247
caṇḍi, 3, 16
Caṇḍi Borobudur reliefs, 145–46
Caṇḍi Boyolangyu, 188
Caṇḍi Bumiayu, 47
Caṇḍi E, 179
Caṇḍi Gumpung, 188
Caṇḍi Jago, 22, 136, 141, 216n28
    seated male figure, **48**, 49–50
Caṇḍi Kalasan, 40
Caṇḍi Kidal reliefs
    dedicated to Anuṣapati, **145**
    kapāla (brainpan/skull cup), 153, **154**, 214n8, 257
    lotus plant, 6, 40
Caṇḍi Panataran, 50, 226
    dvārapalā, **226**, **227**
Caṇḍi Sewu, 41
Caṇḍi Simping/Sumberjati, 229
Caṇḍi Singosari
    Dikpāla, 192–93, **193**
    Esoteric Buddhism and, 16, 206, 256
    and Kṛtanāgara, 129, 165
    Nandīśvara, **13**
    Pārvatī, 37, 39, 40, 147–49, **148**, 209; drawing of pattern, **149**; pattern detail, **37**
    sculptors, 22
    stylistic features of, 211
    textile patterns, 15, 16, 163–64, 196, 256
    Tower Temple, 163, 165
    unidentified goddess, 191–92, **191**, 278; detail of leg and drawing of pattern, **192**
candle patterns, 145
candrakapāla, 174–76, **176**, 178, 257
Canepa, Mathew
    on Taq-i-Bustan rock reliefs, 39
    on transfer of patterns, 40
canting, 58, 247
Casparis, J.G. de, on India and Indonesia, 117–18, 225
casting processes, 22
cella, 141
Central Asian design influences, 13, 29, 43, 149, 191, 209
Central Asian patterns, 29, 34, 37, 44, **139**, **150**
Central Java style, 61, 87
ceplok, 45, 53, 188–94, 201, 279
ceremonies/rituals
    Esoteric Buddhist, 7, 53, 242–43, 248
    and *gĕringsing*, 277
    and *kapāla* (brainpan/skull cup), 153

puja, 84
    rites of passage, 3, 53
    and royalty, 131, 164, 224
    śrāddha temple construction, **145**, 214n8
chabadhi bhat, 258
Chandra (statue), 212
Chandra, Moti, on Jain manuscripts, 64
channavīra, 84, 111, 112–13
Charter of Sarwadharma, 12, 131
Chau Ju-Kua, 28
chimera, 213nn4–5. *See also Simurgh/senmurv*
China National Silk Museum, 26
Chinese design influences
    on Caṇḍi Kidal reliefs, 6
    evidence from Song history, 3
    on Patothamya temple, 199
    from textiles, 41, 43, 185, 191
Chinese patterns, 6, 37, 41, 191, 199. *See also karahana* (Chinese flower); Tang rosettes
Chinese terms for geographical regions, 268–69
Chinese textiles, 33–34
Christie, Jan Wisseman
    on *batik*, 58
    on Indian design influences, 53
    on Javanese weaving, 144–45, 247
    on *sīma* charters, 25, 33, 59, 247
    on trade, 26, 132
Chulalongkorn (Rama V), 265
Chunda, Museum Radya Pustaka, 98, **100**
Chutiwong, Nandana, on Caṇḍi Singosari, 211
cinde cloth, 52
circle patterns
    in Central and Early East Java periods, 80–84, **81**, **83**
    with dots, 27, **67**, **68**, 69
    interlocking, 45, 57, **192**, **229**, 230
Cleveland Museum of Art, Green Tara, **118**, 119
cloth of gold (*nasīj*), 34, 54
cloud patterns, 6, 40
cockspur motif, 185
coinage of Song dynasty, 5
Colombo National Museum
    Avalokiteśvara, 120
    Mahapratīsara, 120
    Vajradharma Lokeśvara, **119**
comb (reed), 26, 33, 144
Compareti, Matteo, on *Simurgh/senmurv*, 213n4
complex "brocade" patterns, 151–78
compound patterns, 94–98, 120, 256
Contadini, Anna, on Sasanian influences, 214n6
convergence of art styles, 29, 258–59
cotton fragment, Ashmolean Museum, **151**

court culture, 24, 26, 52, 224, 245, 259
craftsmen, 21–22
cremation grounds, 164, 257
Crill, Rosemary, on Indian textile trade, 214n7
crowns
  on Buddha Mahāvairocana, 79
  on divine couple, 246
  on divine sow and mare, 111
  on Durgā, 202
  on Garuda, 70
  on Harihara, 229
  on Majapahit statues, 223, 224
  on royal couple plaque, 101
  on Śiva, 93, 134
cumi-cumi, **113**
Cundā, 120
cungkub, 3

D

Danar Hadi, 154
dating, 165, 182, 212, 254–56
deer patterns, 37–38, 40–41, 148
deification of ancestors, 22, 87, 214n8, 224
deification of royalty, 30–31, 53, 55–58, 223–25
demonic iconography. *See also kapāla* (brainpan/skull cup)
  of Bhīma-Bhairava, 247
  of Biaro Pulo dancers, 241
  of Boro Gaṇeśa, 253, 257
  on Caṇḍi Singosari statues, 173
  of a Gaṇa, 111
  of Garuda, 70
  of *kāla*-head, 231
  of Mahākāla, 257
Deśawarṇana. *See Nāgarakṛtāgama (Nāg.)*
Deshpande, Olga, on SHM catalogue, 204
Destroyer. *See* Mahākāla
dharma, 56, 143
dharmachakramudrā, 179, 183, 188
Dharmāśraya, 162–63
dhotīs, 31–32, 281
Dhupa, 84, **86**, 254
dhyānamudrā, 147, 196
diamond patterns, **176**, 177
diaspora of Javanese Statues, **262**
Dikpāla, 193–94, **193**
Dikpāla Nairṛti, 194–95, **195**
  textile pattern, **39**
Divine Bronze (Lunsingh Scheurleer), 254
divine couple, 230–32, **232**, 246
  detail of *kāla*-head, **233**
  detail of sash bow, **234**
divine sow and mare, 109–11, **109**
Dode, Zvezdana, on Kubachi reliefs, 37–38
dodot, 87
Dokumentation der Verluste, Band III (Staatliche Museen zu Berlin), 264
dragon patterns, **144**, 146, 213n3
drawloom, 35
dress typologies, 51–59
dualism, 241
duck patterns, 37, 38, 40, 148, 149, **150**
Dukhang temple, 44
Durgā Mahiṣāsuramardinī
  in Museum Mpu Tantular, 201–3, **201**; detail and drawing of pattern, **202**
  in Volkenkunde, 42, 151–54, **152**, 257; drawing of upper body, **153**; jacket pattern, **153**; lower leg detail and pattern, **155**; short cloth and over sash detail and patterns, **155**; *sinjang* detail, **41**
Dutch East India Company, 264
dvārapalā
  at Caṇḍi Pantaran, 226–27, **226**; detail of sash border, **227**; drawings of sash and *sinjang*, **227**
  in Museum Sonobudoyo, 30, **78**, 79; detail of *sinjang*, **227**

E

early East Java style, 61, 70, 84, 111, 225, 254
earthenware, patterns on, 27
East Indies Room, Noordeinde Palace, 264
elephant patterns, **144**, 145–46
embroidered patterns, 112–14, 187
Engelhard, Nicolaus, 263–64
Esoteric Buddhism
  ceremonies/rituals, 7, 53, 242–43, 248
  Gaṇcakra (tantric feasts), 211
  Kālacakra tradition, 15
  and Khubilai Khan, 15
  and Kṛtanāgara, 7, 9, 15, 164, 225, 256–57
  and Magadha (Bihar), 16
  and Nālandā Mahavira, 15
  at Padang Lawas, 244
  patterns, 9, 146–47, 159, 164, 176
  and skull imagery, 16, 164
  on Sumatra, 248
  and Tantric Śaivism, 6–7
  Vajrayāna forms, 3
Ethnographical Collection, Berlin, 264
Europalia Arts Festival Indonesia, 266
"European pose", 50

F

facial realism, 97, 224, 225, 231, 256
farr, 213n4
fashion, 187–88, 199
"Flaktürme Zoo", 264
fleur-de-lis patterns, 95–96, **97**, 98
Flood, Finbarr
  on Dukhang temple, 44
  on gifting of robes, 200

on hybridization, 54
flower patterns. *See also* lotus flower
 patterns
 daisies: on Arcā Dewa, 116, **117**; on Arcā
  Leluhur, 48; on Cundā/Mahāpratisarā,
  98, **100**; on *dvārapāla*, 79; on Gaṇeśa,
  73; large, 194–99; on Nairṛti, **195**; on
  Sita Mañjughosa, **68**, 69; on unidentified
  diety, **254**, 256
 diagonal bands and flowers, 109–11
 eight-petalled, 74
 fleur-de-lis, 94–95, **97**, 98
 four-petalled: on Dikpāla, **193**; on Gaṇeśa,
  173; on Garuda, **72**; on royal couple
  plaque, 101, **102**; on Śiva, **71**; on Umā,
  106, **107**; on Viṣṇu, **80**
 four-petalled in bands, 87–93, **88–91**, 93
 karahana (Chinese flower), 1, 181
 pointed-petalled: on Durgā, **153**; on
  dvārapalā, **78**, 79; on Gaṇeśa, 74, **75**,
  166; on Mahākāla, 158–59, **160**
 rosettes: on Agastya, **77**; on divine sow
  and mare, 109–10, **109**; on Gaṇeśa,
  70, **73**; on Pagan fresco, **200**; on
  Prajñāpāramitā, **180**, 184, **185**; on
  songket textiles, 154, **156**; on Taq-i-
  Bustan harper, **39**, 199; on unidentified
  goddess, **192**
 in squares, **205**
 stylized, 79
 Tang rosettes, 1, 41, 181, **182**
Fontein, Jan
 on art and architecture of Java, 120
 on dating of Harihara plaque, 106
 on dating of Prajñāpāramitā, 182
 on Indian design influences, 64–65
4+4+1 scheme, 57, 258
Franz Joseph I, 99
Fraser-Lu, Sylvia
 on *gĕringsing*, 277
 on *kebaya*, 48–49
 on textiles' significance, 53
full-dress patterns, 114–16
Fustat cotton fragments, 276

G
Galerie Batik Kuno, 154
Gaṇa, **110**, 111
Gaṇcakra (tantric feasts), 211
Gandavyuha, 29
Gaṇeśa. *See also* Boro Gaṇeśa; Karangkates
 Gaṇeśa
 art styles of, 165
 at Caṇḍi Banon, **75**
 and cremation grounds, 164, 257
 esoteric attributes of, 1–2, 16
 in Indian Museum, Kolkata, 74, **76**, 265
 kāla-heads on, **2**, 166–67, **169**
 kapāla (brainpan/skull cup) on, 165, 173

lotus flower patterns on, 74, **75**, **76**, **166**
 in Museum Caṇḍi Prambanan, **73**
 in Museum Sonobudoyo, 70, **74**
 in National Museum, Bangkok, **168**,
  169–74, 265; jacket detail and pattern,
  169; left thigh detail and pattern, **170**;
  right leg detail and pattern, **169**
 in Prambanan Museum, 70, **73**
 and skull imagery, 16, 153, 257
 in Volkenkunde, 165–66, **166**; trouser
  detail and drawing, **167**; upper leg
  garment detail and drawing, **168**
Garuda
 on Harihara plaque, 104, **106**
 in Santa Barbara Museum of Art, 70, **72**
gĕlung, 239
"*ge-man*" silk, 33
geometric patterns, **84**, **92**, 93, 137–40, **138**,
 139
 complex in bands, 98–107, **99–108**
gĕringsing (*gringsing*), 162, 182, 214n14,
 277–78
 gĕringsing cemplong, 277
 gĕringsing kawung, 277
 gĕringsing pepare, 162, **164**, 277
 geringsing wayang kebo, 50
 kemben gĕringsing, 277
gift lists, 26, 27
gifting of textiles, 200
Gittinger, Mattiebelle, on *gĕringsing*, 277
glossary, 271–73
 extended, of textile terms, 275–82
Go Tik Swan. *See* Hardjonagoro, K.R.T.
Gobog, 5
Gold Island, 247
gold-leaf glue work. *See tulis mas* (*prada*)
Gombrich, Ernst, on "style" and "fashion",
 187–88
's-Gravenzande Store, Viṣṇu, 103, **104**
Greek crosses, 41
Green Tara, **118**, 119
griffin patterns, 40, **144**, 146, 213n3
gringsing. *See gĕringsing* (*gringsing*)
Groote Koninklijke Bazar, 264
Gua Selomangleng, 188
guardian figures, 70, 158, 163, 226–27
Gurah, 212
Guy, John
 on Belitung wreck, 6
 on Boro Gaṇeśa, 134
 on *kawung*, 280
 on *patola*, 275, 277
 on Southeast Asian trade, 28
 on Sumtsek chapel, 44

H
habaya, 49
haṃsa (goose) patterns, 148, 149, **150**
haṃsa (*vāhana* of Brahmā), 196

Hardjonagoro, K.R.T., 58
Harihara, Kertarājasa Jayawardhana, 53, 227–29, **229**
　lower limbs detail, **54**
　pattern drawing, **229**
Harihara Ardhanari, **8**, **203**
　banji (swastika) pattern on, 161, 279
　detail and drawing of pattern, **205**
　drawing of lower body, **203**
　and Krtanāgara, 7, 203
　movements of in Europe, 203–7
　original location of, 264
Harihara plaque, 104, **106**
harnas, 41–42
Harper, Taq-i-Bustan, **39**, 199
Hatra Temple of the Sun, 280
Hayagrīva, 137
Hayam Wuruk, 24
"heart medallion", 179
Heller, Amy
　on design influences, 41, 147
　on Tang textiles, 252
Heruka, 244
Hīnayāna Buddhism, 3
Hindu-Buddhism
　design influence of, 52
　fusion under Krtanāgara, 7, 15–16, 164, 206, 256–57
　suppression under Islam, 7
Hindu-Buddhism, and *mandala*, 55–56
Hinduism, 22, 29, 225
hip wrapper. *See also kain*
　dodot, 87
　wdihan, 25
Historical Notes on Indonesia and Malaya, 3
hlai, 25
Holmgren, R.J., on *gĕringsing*, 278
Hoogervorst, Tom, on *kalambi/klambi*, 163
Hoop, A.N.J.Th. van der
　on *kawung*, 57
　on *sulaman*, 36
Hōryūji, 252
Huang, Yiran, on Nairrti pattern, 209
Hunter, Thomas M., on Hindu-Buddhist merger, 164, 257

I
Iban, 280
iconographic classification, 9, 14–16, 252–53, 256–57
ikat
　on Ajanta murals, 27, 120
　ikat *hol*, 185
　production method, 27
import lists, Song dynasty, 35
Indian cotton trade, 31, 132, 185
Indian design influences
　from Bihar and Bengal, 147
　from Chola and Pāla dynasties, 61
　through religion, 2–3, 9, 11
　through textiles, 43, 50–51, 53, 118–19
Indian Ocean, trade, 6, 114
Indo-Javanese art, 64
Indo-Pacific trade beads, 248
Indra's heaven, 224
inscriptions (*prasasti*)
　of Bameswara, 176
　Charter of Sarwadharma, 12, 162
　gap between Kediri and Singhasāri, 129–31
　as historical source, 22–23
　of Krtanāgara, 7, 131
　on Mañjuśrī Arapacana, 141, **143**
　prasasti batu, 215n19
　and Sanskrit, 225
inverted head patterns, 154, **155**
Iranian, patterns, 37, 39
Islam on Java, 30, 225
Islamic influences, on *kawung* pattern, 30

J
jackets
　on Arcā Leluhur, 47–48, 115
　baju surjan lurik, **49**, 50
　on Candi Jago figure, **48**, 49–50
　on Durgā Mahisāsuramardinī, **152**, **153**
　on Ganeśa, 166
　of guardians, 163
　on Mahākāla, 158, 160
　of palace guards, 50, 163
　Singosari style, 13
　on *wayong wong* performers, **52**
Jacquard loom, 35
Jain manuscripts, 64
Jákl, Jiři, on *kalambi/klambi*, 163
Jambi, 176, 183
jangkêp, 24
jatā, 224–25
Jatakas, 29
Javanese court, 24, 26, 52, 224, 245, 259
Javanese deities statuette, 87, **89**
Javanese style, 51, 63, 87, 246, 255
　Central Java, 61, 87
　early East Java, 61, 70, 84, 111, 225, 254
Jayavarman VII, as incarnation of Visnu, 7
Jessup, Helen, on royal couple plaque, 102
jewellery. *See* ornaments
jilamprang, **36**, 59, 215n25, 258, 276, 277
Jinas, **140**, 204–5
jungkit, 27

K
kachcha style, 281
kain
　and ascetics, 50
　in classical Java, 32
　definition, 25, 280
　as Javanese characteristic, 51
　as name of fabric, 31, 132

kain balapak, 27
kain bebali, 240, **242**
kain limar cual, 185, **186**
kain songket, 27, **103**, **157**
kain songket limar, **156**
kain songket seléndang, **178**
kakawin
   definition, 23, 270
   and textile terminology, 17, 50
Kakawin Sumanasāntaka, 224
Kakawin Sutasoma, 7, 164, 256–57
Kāla-Bhairava, 247
Kālacakra cult, 15–16
Kālacakratantra, commentary by Atīśa, 16
Kalacarya Katha, 64
kāla-heads
   on Boro Gaṇeśa, 132
   and *candrakapāla*, 174
   development of, 231, 252
   on divine couple, **233**
   on *dvārapalā*, 226
   as dynastic signifier, 14, 173–74, 211
   and Esoteric Buddhism, 256–58
   on Gaṇeśa, **2**, 166–67, **169**
   on Mahākāla belt, 257–58
   one-eyed, 166, **167**, **171**, 173–74, 175, 252
   on Pārvatī buckle, 147, 149
kalambi/klambi, 163
kalangwan, 22–23, 32
Kalangwan: A Survey of Old Javanese Literature (Zoetmulder), 22
Kalpasutra, 64, 149, **151**
kampuh, 282n1
kanipha, 31, 132
kapāla (brainpan/skull cup)
   on Caṇḍi Kidal walls, 153, **154**, 214n8, 257
   on Durgā Mahiṣāsuramardinī, 153
   on Gaṇeśa, 165, 173
   on Mahākāla, 177, 257
karahana (Chinese flower), 1, 181
Karangkates Gaṇeśa, **171**, 174, 258
   right leg detail and drawing, **172**
Kartiwa, Suwati, on *songket*, 27
katakaamudrā, **93**
kavaca, 41
kavya, 23
kawung
   and *batik*, 58, 237
   contemporary example, **237**
   cosmic symbolism of, 55, 258
   definition, 17, 279–80
   on Dikpāla, 194
   on Durgā Mahiṣāsuramardinī, **202**
   early Kediri and Singhāsari, 132–35
   inspiration for, 5–6, 57, 214n10, 279
   Islamic influences on, 30
   on Khmer temples, 57
   on Nandīśvara, **158**
   navagraha and, 59
   protective properties of, 57, 258
   and sumptuary laws, 259
kayabandh, 281
kebaya, 48
Kediri kings, emblem, 215n21
Kemper, Bernet
   on architecture and cosos, 55
   on art objects post-WWII, 264
   on *kāla*-heads, 173–74
   on Mañjuśrī Kumārabhūta, 95
   on Singhāsari period art, 207
kepala, 276
Kepeng, 5
Keṛtarājasa Jayawardhana
   as Harihara, 53, 227–29, **227**; drawing of patterns, **229**; lower limbs detail, **54**; pattern drawing, **229**
   Rājapatnī (consort), 182
Kertolo, 239–40, **240**
   detail and drawing of pattern, **242**
kesi, 159
Khmer temples, 57
Khmer textiles, 107, **108**
Khubilai Khan, 7, 15
kidung
   definition, 270
   and textile terminology, 17, 50
Kidung Harsawijaya (KH), 23, 58
Kidung Rangga Lawe (KRL), 23
kingship, 164, 176, 216n27
Kinney, Anne, on *wayang* features, 49
kirītamukuta, 151
Klimburg-Salter, Deborah, on Poo manuscript, 44
Klokke, Marijke
   on Caṇḍi Jago figure, 49
   on divine features, 223
   on size of Majapahit statues, 17
   on statue classification, 65
   on statue symbolism, 224
Knebel, J., on unidentified goddess from Caṇḍi B, 191
kotangs, 163
Kozok, on Mañjuśrī Arapacana inscription, 141
kraton padjurits, 163
Krom, N.J.
   on Atīśa in Sumatra, 12
   on weaving as metaphor, 29
Kṛtanāgara
   as Ardhanari, Vairocana and Locana combined, 204–5, 206
   as Buddha Vairocana, 216n27
   and Caṇḍi Jago, 141
   and Caṇḍi Singosari, 129
   death of, 23, 165
   and Esoteric Buddhism, 7, 9, 164, 225, 256–57
   and Gaṇcakra (tantric feasts), 211

as Harihara Ardhanari, 7, **8**, **203**
Hindu-Buddhist fusion under, 7, 15–16, 164, 206, 256–57
inscriptions of, 7, 131, 162
interment of, 163, 165
and Kālacakra cult, 16
and kingship, 164, 176, 216n27
and Kublai Khan, 164–65, 206, 207, 216n28
and Mahāyāna Buddhism, 7
in the *Nāgarakṛtāgama (Nāg.)*, 24, 164, 206–7, 256
and Nālandā Mahavira, 15
as Śiva-Buddha, 7, 164, 206, 256–57
statues commissioned by, 129, 165, 182, 183–84, 210
and Visnuvardhana (father), 141, 176
Kubachi reliefs, 37–38
Kublai Khan, 164–65, 207, 216n28
Kubyauk-gyi, 199
Kumārabhūta (Mañjuśrī Kumārabhūta), 55–56, 87, **91**, 92–93, **94**
kundika, 104, **106**

L

Lakshmi, 224
lalitāsana, 87, **91**
Lalitavistara, 29
Lampung, 114
lañciṅan (lancingan), 49, 165–66
Langewis, Laurens
  on imported cloths, 276
  on *kawung*, 279
Langkasuka, 34
Lao textiles, 107, **108**
lawi ayam, 185
leaf patterns, **69**, 158, **238**, **242**
Lee, Peter, on Ma Huan commentary, 49
Liang dynasty, 34
lion patterns, 37, 41, 44, 231
lion throne, 179
literary sources, list of, 270
"local genius", 64–65
"localization" theory, 43, 118
locations of statues, 263–66
  in Central Java, **62**
  in East Java, **130**
  outside Indonesia, **262**
  in Sumatra and Kalimantan, **46**
Lokanatha, 243
lokcan kemben, **206**
looms, 33, 35, 144
"Lost Kingdoms" exhibition, Muzium Negara, 263
lotus bud, 147, 196
lotus flower patterns
  on Boro Gaṇeśa cushion, 132, **133**
  and Buddhism, 1
  on Chinese silk brocades, 259
  on Durgā: jacket, **152**, 153; *sinjang*, 26, 41, 42, 154, 215n23
  on existing textiles, 26, 259
  on Gaṇeśa: jacket, **166**; trousers, 74, **75**, **76**
  as "heart medallion", 179
  on Mahākāla jacket, **159**
  on Mañjuśrī Kumārabhūta *kain*, 94–95, **94**
  with *prada (tulis mas)*, 279
  on Prajñāpāramitā: pedestal, **179**; sashes and *sinjang*, **186**, **187**
  on Śiva *kain*, **69**, 70, **95**, 97
  on Tārā *kain*, **97**, 98
  on Tibetan silk tapestry, 159
lotus plant
  on Brahmā, 196
  on Caṇḍi Kidal carvings, 6
  as "dynastic emblem", 14, 211
  on Mañjuśrī Arapacana, 40
  on Prajñāpāramitā, 179, 183
  as "recalcitrant spiral", 40, 145
  in Singosari style, 13
  in Transition style, 14
lotus throne, 70
lotus umbrella, 101, 102
Lunsingh Scheurleer, Pauline
  on *caṇḍi* construction, 3
  on *candrakapāla*, 174
  on "demonization" of skull motif, 173
  on location of Mañjuśrī, 141
  on Singosari style, 210
  on skulls as trantric attribute, 16, 164–65
  on statue classification, 65
  on "tantric circle" of statues, 173
lurik, 50

M

Ma Huan, 49
Mackenzie, Colin, 265
macro- and microcosm, 55
Magadha (Bihar), 11, 16
mah, definition, 23
Mahābhārata, 23, 30–31
Mahājanaka Jātaka, 120
Mahākāla
  on Alchi mural, 257
  in MNI, 139, **175**, 176–77, 257–58; left side sash detail and drawing, **177**; right side *kain* detail and drawing, **176**
  in Volkenkunde, 158, **159**, 161–62; jacket detail and drawing, **160**; *kain* detail and drawing, **162**; right leg detail and drawing, **163**; sash detail and drawing, **161**
Mahakarmavibhangga, 29
Mahapratīsara, **158**
  in Colombo National Museuem, 120
  Museum Radya Pustaka, 98, **100**
Mahāyāna Buddhism, 3, 7
Mahiśa (buffalo demon), 152, 201
Mahmūd of Ghanzī, 12
Majapahit, 23, 30, 239, 245, 246
Majapahit style, 16, 200, 225, 245

makara, 40, 146, 204, 213n5
Malay annals, 42
Malay language, 6, 280–81
Malay textile terms, 45–50
Māmakī, 140, **140**, 265
maṇḍala, 109, 159
mandorla, 282n4
Mañjuśrī, Sita Mañjughosa, **68**, 69
Mañjuśrī Arapacana, 141, **142**
  drawing of pattern, **144**
  "foreign" patterns on, 37, **38**, 147
  inscription, **143**
  movements of in Europe, 263–64
  Noordeinde Palace replica, 264–65
  sash detail, **146**
Mañjuśrī Kumārabhūta, 55–56, 87, **91**, 92–93, **94**
mantjapat, 55–56, 57
maps of statue locations. *See* locations of statues
mare, divine, 109–11, **109**
Mataram, 2–3, 52, 57. *See also bandhani*
Maxwell, Robin, on textiles, 138
Mekong River, 25–26
menanun, 25
menyongket, 26
merchants, 26, 34, 35, 36
Metropolitan Museum of Art, Śiva, **96**, 97
micro- and macrocosm, 55
Minangkabau kingdom, 139, 143–44, 177, 259–60
Minangkabau textiles, 27, 137–40, 178, 209, 215n23
MNI. *See* Museum Nasional Indonesia (MNI)
Mon people, 199
Mongol Empire, 38
Mongol envoys to Java, 15
Mongol textiles, 34, 38
Monnereau, D., 263
monsoons, 247
moral law (*dharma*), 56, 143
mother goddess, 106, **107**
Mount Meru, 57
Mount Pěnanggungan, 213n1
mountain temples, 213n1
Mpu Monaguṇa, **202**
Muara Jambi site museum, Prajñāpāramitā, **35**, **183**
Mucukunda, 49
mudrā
  bodhyagrīmudrā, **81**
  dharmachakramudrā, 179, 183, 188
  dhyānamudrā, 147, 196
  katakaamudrā, **93**
  lalitāsana, 87, **91**
  sitasanamudrā, 70
  tarjanīmudrā, 79
  varadamudrā, 256
Mūla-Mulurung charter, 164

Muntok, 216n26
Museum Caṇḍi Prambanan, Gaṇeśa, **73**
Museum Mpu Tantular
  Durgā Mahiṣāsuramardinī, 201–3, **201**; detail and drawing of pattern, **202**
Museum Nasional Indonesia (MNI)
  Arcā Dewa/Leluhur, 116, **117**, 131
  bronze statuettes, 111
  Chandra, 212
  divine couple, 230–32, **232**, 246; detail of *kāla*-head, **233**; detail of sash bow, **234**
  Europalia Arts Festival Indonesia, 266
  Gaṇeśa, 74, **75**
  Harihara plaque, 104, **106**
  Mahākāla, **175**, 176
  Mañjuśrī Kumārabhūta, **94**
  Padmapāni, **68**
  pair of Javanese deities, 87, **89**
  Pārvatī (no. 113a/3625), **230**; detail and drawing of pattern, **231**
  Pārvatī (no. 126), 234–37, **235**; detail and drawing of pattern, **236**
  Prajñāpāramitā, **179**, 237
  royal couple plaque, 100–103, **102**
  Śiva, **31**
  Śiva Mahadeva, **237**; detail and drawing of pattern, **238**
  Surya, 212
  Śyāmatārā, 137, **138**
  Treasure Room, 263
  Umā, 106–7, **107**
  Viṣṇu, 79, **80**
Museum Radya Pustaka, Chunda/Mahapratīśara, 98, **100**
Museum Sonobudoyo
  Baju surjan lurik, **49**
  dvārapalā, 30, **78**, 79
  Gaṇeśa, 70, **74**
  Śiva Mahadeva, **96**
museums, list of, 267
Muslims, 11, 30, 225
Muzium Negara, "Lost Kingdoms" exhibition, 263
Myinkaba, 199
mythical creature patterns, 39–40, **144**, 146, 213nn3–5

N

Nagapattinam, 16
Nāgarakṛtāgama (Nāg.), 24, 164, 206–7, 209–12, 248
Nairṛti, 41, 194–95, **195**
  textile pattern, **39**
Nālandā Mahavira
  cultural exchange with Southeast Asia, 11–12, 15
  and Esoteric Buddhism, 15
  influence on Caṇḍi Singosari, 15
  and Kṛtanāgara, 15
  ruins of, **11**

Nandi, on Harihara plaque, 104, **106**
Nandīśvara, 41, 42, 156, **157**
  jacket detail, **40**
  jacket detail and drawing, **157**
  upper body detail, **13**
Nanhai islands, 5, 16
nasīj (cloth of gold), 34, 54
National Museum, Bangkok
  Gaṇeśa, **168**, 169–74, 265; jacket detail and pattern, **169**; left thigh detail and pattern, **170**; right leg detail and pattern, **169**
navagraha (*nawagrah*), 25, 59, 258
Newar artists, 207, 216n28
Newberry Collection, 64, 65, 70, 110, 149
  fragment imitating *bandhani*, **84**
  Indian cotton fragment, **151**
Nganjuk figures, 51, 254
Nganjuk style, 65, 109
nine preachers (*wali-sanga*), 30
nine-planet pattern (*navagraha*), 25, 59, 258
Noordeinde Palace, East Indies Room, 264

O

"object stories", 263–66
O'Brien, Kate, on the *Sutasoma*, 164
octopus patterns, 113
Old Javanese texts, 23, 51–52
ornaments. See also *channavīra*; crowns; *ratnopavīta*; *upavīta*
  on ascetics, 50
  Majapahit style, 17
  Pāla style, 92
  of peepul leaves, 115–16, 137, 166, 196
  of skulls, 93, 153, 241, 244
  of snakes, 97, 153, 174, 177, 226, 239
  on Tibetan paintings, 237

P

pacadaran (cadar loom), 26, 33, 144, 247
Padang Lawas, 244
padma, 147
Padmapāni
  in British Museum, 65, **67**
  in Museum Nasional Indonesia, **68**, 69
padmāsana, 179
Pagan fresco painting, 199, **200**
Pagan relief architecture, 146–47, **147**, 148
pair of Javanese deities statuette, 87, **89**
Pak Dwi, 51–52
Pāla style, 9, 15, 92, 180, 208
Palembang, 31, 176, 178
Pamelayu expedition, 176–77
Panai polity, 243
pande, 21
pande-mas, 21
Panji stories, 239
Panjikent, 1, 181
Pārvatī
  at Caṇḍi Singosari, 37, 39, 40, 147–49, **148**, 209; drawing of pattern, **149**; pattern detail, **37**
  Gemuruh statuette, 112–13, **112**, 114, 255
  in MNI (no. 113a/3625), **230**; detail and drawing of pattern, **231**
  in MNI (no. 126), 234–37, **235**; detail and drawing of pattern, **236**; *sinjang kawung* detail, **23**
  at Tribhuwana Tunggadewi, 55; lower limbs detail, **56**
patola
  19th-century example, **53**
  definition, 275–76
  Indian, **36**
  and *navagraha*, 59
  on *wayong wong* performers, **52**
Patothamya temple, 199
patterns. See also animal patterns; *candrakapāla*; circle patterns; flower patterns; *kāla*-heads; *kapāla* (brainpan/skull cup); *kawung*; lotus flower patterns; roundels; skull patterns; square patterns; *tumpal*; vesicae patterns
  arrow, **84**
  balah kacang (split-peanut), 137–40, 213n2
  bandhani, 65, 69, **84**
  banji (swastika), 159–60, **163**, 204–5
  batik banji, 205
  on Buddhist paintings, 44
  Buddhist symbology of, 1
  candle, 145
  Central Asian, 37–41
  ceplok, 45, 53, 188–94, 201, 279
  chabadhi bhat, 258
  Chinese, 6, 37, 41, 191, 199
  cloud motif, 6, 40
  complex "brocade", 151–78
  compound, 94–98, 120, 256
  cumi-cumi, 113
  diamond, **176**, 177
  embroidered, 112–14, 187
  esoteric/tantric, 9, 146–47, 159, 164, 176
  fleur-de-lis, 95–96, **97**, 98
  full-dress, 114–16
  geometric, **84**, **92**, 93, 137–40, **138**, **139**; complex in bands, 98–107, **99–108**
  Greek cross, 41
  inspiration for, 1–2
  inverted heads, 154, **155**
  Iranian, 37, 39
  jilamprang, **36**, 59, 215n25, 258, 276, 277
  leaf, **69**, 158, **238**, 242
  mythical creature, 39–40, **144**, 146, 213nn3–5
  navagraha/*Nawagrah* (nine planet), 59, 258
  pearl arch, 145
  Persian, 37, 48
  persimmon, **153**

polèng (chequered), 239–40, **241**, 247
scallop, **140**, **177**, 190
semi-circle and dot, 79, 84, **86**
Singosari style, 9, 11–12, 13, 38, 39
star (*bunga bintang*), **66**, **67**, **155**, **158**
striped, 50, 120
teardrop, 148, **235**
Tibetan, 11, 147, 159
trefoil, 115, 141, 178, 187, 202
triangle, 115, 136, 184, 256
vajra, 9, 87, **88**, 94–95, 242
vegetal, 40, 136, 145, 230
zigzag, **92**, 93
peacock patterns, 37
pearl arch patterns, 145
peepul leaf ornaments, 115–16, 137, 166, 196
pelangi. *See* bandhani
pepper trade, 114
Peranakan, 280
Persian patterns, 37, 48
persimmon motif in *songket*, **153**
persimmon patterns, **153**
phoenix patterns, 213n3
pinggir, 276
Pitalah, 138
plaques
  Harihara, 104, **106**
  royal couple, 100–103, **102**
  Śiva, 102–4, **105**
poetry of ancient Java. *See* kakawin; kidung
polèng (chequered) patterns, 239–40, **241**, 247
Pollock, Sheldon, on "Sanskrit Cosmopolis", 117
Polo, Marco, 28–29
Poo manuscript, 44
"portrait" statue, 97, 224, 225, 231
Pott. P.H., on Boro Gaṇeśa, 253
prada (*tulis mas*), 25, 54, 205, 247, 278–79
Prajñāpāramitā
  at Boyolangyu, 188–91, **189**; *sinjang* detail, **190**
  bronze statuette, 84, **85**, 254
  in MNI, 36–37, 179–82, **179**, 209, 237, 263; *kain* border detail, **35**; sash drawings, **181**; *sinjang* and sash detail and patterns, **181**
  movements of in Europe, 263
  at Muara Jambi, 182–88, **183**, 208, 209, 266; border pattern detail, **185**; *sinjang* detail, **184**; *sinjang* detail and pattern, **186**
Prajñāpāramitā sutra, 141
prajñās, **140**
Prambanan Museum, Gaṇeśa, 70, **73**
Prambanan ruins, 265
Prambanan village, 98
Prapañca, Mpu, 24
prasasti. *See* inscriptions (*prasasti*)

production processes
  batik, 58, 260
  ikat, 27
  songket, 33, 34, 54, 132, 247
  statues, 21–22
  textiles, 5–6, 26
PT Studio Songket Palantaloom, 215n23
pucuk rebung. *See* tumpal
puja, 84

Q
queens, and royal power, 224

R
Raden Wijaya, 23, 277
Raffles, Stamford, 141, 194, 263, 265
Raffles Flint, William Charles, 265
Rājapatnī, 182
Rājasanagara, 24
Ramayana, 23
rantai, 42, 154
Raspopova, Valentina, on *karahana* pattern, 181
ratnopavīta
  on Brahmā, 196, 201
  on divine couple, 237
  on Durgā, 202
  on Harihara, Kertarājasa Jayawardhana, 229
  on Harihara Ardhanari, 204
  Majapahit style, 225, 245
  on Prajñāpāramitā, **180**, 184, 188
  on Śiva Mahadeva, 239
  in Transition style, 210, 211
"recalcitrant spiral", 40, 145, 158
reed (comb), 26, 33, 144
Reichle, Natasha, on Bhairava, 140
Reijn, Eric van
  on dating of Prajñāpāramitā, 182
  on Mañjuśrī Arapacana inscription, 141
Reinwardt, C.G.C., 263
resist-dyed textiles, 27, 44, 63. *See also* batik
Rijksmuseum, 213n5
rites of passage, 3, 53
rituals. *See* ceremonies/rituals
Ronggorworsito Museum, 111
roundels
  with animals, 39–41, 44
  and Chinese cloud designs, 40
  discontinuation of, 260
  of the Kediri and Singhasāri, 140–50
  with mythical creatures, 40
  pearl, 37
  with rosettes, 39, 41
  with triangles, 115
  with vegetal designs, 40, 180–81, **181**
"royal ancestor", 224
royal couple plaque, 100–103, **102**

S

"Sacral Gift to Deity" exhibition, SHM, 264
saddlecloth, **182**
Śaivism, 22
Śaivite statues, 22, 30
Saleh, Raden, 99
Sambas Treasure, 265
    Avalokiteśvara, 65, **66**
    Padmapāni, 65, **67**
sampot hol, **108**
Samuel Eilenberg Collection, 81
Sanatruq I, 280
Sānfóqí. *See* Śrivijaya
Sanskrit, 225
"Sanskrit Cosmopolis", 117
Santa Barbara Museum of Art, Garuda, 70, **72**
sarcenets, 35
sari, 32
sarong (*sarung*), 32, 280
sarpopavīta, 226
Sarwadharma, 12, 162
Sasanian design influences, 37, 38, 40, 41, 199
Sasanian Empire, 37, 39, 40
scallop patterns, **140**, **177**, 190
Schnitger, F.M., on Biaro Pulo, 241
Schorta, Regula, on influences on Liao art, 191
Schoterman, Jan
    on the *Aṣṭasāharsrikā Prajñāpāramitā*, 119
    on Śrivijaya, 12
sculptures. *See* statues
"Sea of Malayu", 248
Sedyawati, Edi
    on Boro Gaṇeśa, 129–31
    on Kṛtanāgara inscriptions, 215n17
    on Singhāsari period art, 165, 207
    on stonemasons, 22
Sejarah Melayu, 42
seléndang
    definition, 281
    kain balapak, 27
    seléndang songket limar, **156**
    Singosari style, 13
    worn by monks, 16
semi-circle and dot patterns, 79, 84, **86**
Serat Tatatjara (ST), 23
's-Gravenzande Store, Viṣṇu, 103, **104**
shilpa-shastras, 9
shipwreck, Belitung, 6
SHM. *See* State Hermitage Museum (SHM)
Shorta, Regula, on "stylised" patterns, 214n6
Shōsō-in, 252
Si Thep, 106–7
Siamese design influences, 185
Sidomulyo, Hadi
    on *candrakapāla*, 215n19
    on mountain temples, 213n1
    on religous change, 164
śikhādhara, 92, 94
silk. *See also nasīj* (cloth of gold); *patola*; *songket*
    bandhini tie-dye, **84**
    batik *lokcan kemben*, **206**
    fabric with embroidered ducks, **150**
    "ge-man, 33
    as gifts, 5, 26, 32, 33, 185
    Indian *patola* double ikat, *jilamprang* pattern, **36**
    Khmer *sampot hol*, **108**
    Lao Thai *sin mii*, **108**
    production of, 5, 32–33, 35
    and sumptuary laws, 37
silk floss, 113
silk trade, 35, 36, 37
sīma ceremonies, 25
sīma charters
    definition, 17, 24, 270
    dye use in, 27
    textile terminology in, 17, 24–25, 59
    trader terminology in, 26
Simurgh/senmurv, 39–40, 146, 213n4
sin mii, **108**
Singhāsari period. *See also* Singosari style
    centralization during, 131
    growth of Kālacakra cult, 16
    statue production in, 12–13
"single ocean", 29
Singosari style
    characteristics of, 12–13, 207–8
    early stage examples, 137
    jackets, 13
    patterns, 9, 11–12, 13, 38, 39
    sash bows, 192
    seléndang, 13
    statue classification, 210–11
sinjang
    definition, 17, 55, 280
    on Majapahit statues, 17
sinjang gĕringsing kawung, 58–59
sinjang kawung
    definition, 54–55
    magical properties of, 53, 58
    on Majapahit statues, 17, 28, 55, 223
    of Raden Wijaya, 23
    and royalty, 53, 55, 59, 223, 246
Sita Mañjughosa, Mañjuśrī, **68**, 69
sitasanamudrā, 70
Site Museum Desa Bumiayu, Arcā Dewa/Leluhur, **45**, 47–48, **47**, 114–16, **115–16**
Śiva
    Ardhanarīśvara, 223, 224
    attendants of, 111
    Gemuruh statuette, 31–32, **31**, **63**, 93, 112, 114; textile pattern, **63**, **93**

gold plaque, 102–4, **105**
on Harihara plaque, 104, 105, **106**
Kṛtanāgara and, 7
in Metropolitan Museum of Art, **95**, 97
in Museum Nasional Indonesia, 70, **71**
state temple to, 226
in Tropenmuseum, 65, **67**, 134–36, **135**; textile pattern, **136**
Śiva Mahadeva
  Loro Jonggrang statue, **69**
  in MNI, **237**; detail and drawing of pattern, **238**
  in Museum Sonobudoyo, **96**
skull cup. *See kapāla* (brainpan/skull cup)
skull patterns
  as dynastic signifier, 14, 211
  and Esoteric Buddhism, 9, 16, 164–65, 211, 256–58
  on Gaṇeśa, 173, 174, **176**, 178
  in Kediri and Singhasāri periods, 151–78, 252
skulls. *See also candrakapāla*; *kāla*-heads; *kapāla* (brainpan/skull cup)
  on bases/cushions, **133**, **166**, **171**, **175**, 226
  garland of on Mahākāla, **177**
  on ornaments, 93, 153, 241, 244
Smaradhana Kakawin, 279
snakes
  on ornaments, 177, 239
  sarpopavīta in the form of, 226
  upavīta in the form of, 97, 153, 174
SOAS, University of London, 177
Soekmono, R.
  on art and architecture of Java, 120
  on Indian design influences, 64–65
  on statue classification, 212
Sogdian design influences, 1, 41
Sogdian Mural textiles, **139**, **182**
Song dynasty
  coinage, 5
  conflict with Śrivijaya, 5
  import lists, 35
  trade, 5–6, 31, 132
songket
  20th-century examples of, **40**, **42**
  definition, 1, 132
  origin of, 27, 42, 247
  production, 33, 34, 54, 132, 247
songket limar, 39
Sonobudoyo Museum. *See* Museum Sonobudoyo
sow, divine, 109–11, **109**
Spertus, A.E., on *gĕringsing*, 278
split-peanut (*balah kacang*) pattern, 137–40, 213n2
square patterns
  on attendants of Amoghapāśa, 137, **138**
  on Durgā, 154, **155**

on Gaṇeśa, **166**, **169**, 173
on Mahākāla, 161, **161**
on Prajñāpāramitā, **190**
śrāddha temple, **145**, 214n8
Śrivijaya, 5, 11–12, 16, 215n22, 243
Ssu Shu (four Shu), 5, 214n10
Staatliche Museen zu Berlin, 264
star (*bunga bintang*) patterns, **66**, **67**, **155**, **158**
State Hermitage Museum (SHM)
  Harihara Ardhanari, 7, **8**, 161, 203–7, **203**; detail and drawings of patterns, **205**; drawing of lower body, **203**
  Mañjuśrī Arapacana, **142**; pattern detail, **38**
  "Sacral Gift to Deity" exhibition, 264
  statue acquisitions, 204, 264
  Vajravārāhī, 237
statues. *See also specific statues*
  acquisition of, 204, 212, 263–66
  as deified ancestors, 22
  identification of, 1–2
  locations of. *See* locations of statues
  of Majapahit period, 17
  of Pāla period, 15
  as "portraits", 97, 224, 225, 231
  of Singhāsari period, 12–13
  uses of, 2
stomach band, 87, 105
stone, 17, 22, 140–41, 196, 256
stonemasons, 21–22
Straits of Malacca, 248
striped patterns, 50, 120
Studio Songket Palantaloom, 215n23
Stutterheim, Willem Frederik
  on Kṛtanāgara statue, 206
  on lotus emblem, 14, 211
stylistic evaluation, 2
Sudhanakumāra, 137, **139**
suicide of queens, 224
Sukhothai kingdom, 185
sulaman, 36
Suleiman, Satyawati
  on art and architecture of Java, 120
  on Indian design influences, 64–65
Sumatran statues
  Arcā Dewa/Leluhur, **114**
  Mahākāla, **175**
  Prajñāpāramitā, **183**
Sumatran trade, 247–48
Summerfield, Ann and John, on Minangkabau way of life, 138–39
sumping, 239
sumptuary laws, 24, 162–63, 259
Sumtsek chapel, 44
sun worship, 280
Sunda Strait, 114
sungkit, 27
Surakarta kingdom, 23

suri, 33, 144
Surocolo statuettes, 109, 111
Surya, 212
Sutasoma, 7, 164, 256–57
Suvarnadvipa, 247
swastika (*banji*), 159–60, **163**, 204–5
swords, 194
Śyāmatārā, 137, **138**, **139**
syncretism, 7, 9, 164, 257

T

Tai Lue, 107
Tambiah, Stanley
  on *maṇḍala*, 55–56
  on *mantjapat*, 57
Tan Teok Seong, 265
Tanah Datar, 143
Tang rosettes, 1, 41, 181, **182**
Tantrayana, 7
Tantric Buddhism. *See* Esoteric Buddhism
Tantu Panggelaran, 151
tapis, 26, 113–14
Tapis Inuh, **113**
Tapis Paminggir, **113**
Taq-i-Bustan harper, **39**, 199
Taq-i-Bustan reliefs, **39**, 149, **150**, **199**
Tārā, **97**, 98, **118**, 119
tarjanīmudrā, 79
Tarling, Nicholas, on protective duty of kings, 57
"Tartar cloths", 34
tax-transfer charters. *See sīma* charters
teardrop patterns, 148, **235**
Tenganan Pegringsingan village, 277
tenun, 25, 50
textile heritage, 50
Textile Museum, Kuala Lumpur, persimmon motif in *songket*, **153**
textile patterns. *See* patterns
textile terminology
  Malay, 45–50
  in *sīma* charters, 17, 24–25
textile trade. *See* trade
textile typologies, 51–59, 212
Thakar, Karun, on Sumtsek chapel, 44
Tibet, Buddhism in, 12
Tibetan patterns, 11, 41, 43, 119, 147, 159
tiger skin, 65, 69, 97, 104, **105**
tiger-claw amulet/necklace, 92, 94
Tilleke and Gibbins Collection, 185
tinulis ing mas, 25, 247
Tirtha, Iwan, on ikat, 120
tortoise, 193
Totton, Mary-Louise, on Boro Gaṇeśa, 134
T'oung Pao, 200
trade
  between China and Java, 3, 5–6, 26, 33–35, 114, 131

  of cotton, 5, 25–26, 31, 35, 132
  between India and Java, 5, 6, 31, 114, 214n6
  of Indian cotton, 31, 132
  international, 29, 247–48
  Java as centre of, 131, 246
  map of trade routes, **4**
  and the Mekong, 25–26
  and the monsoons, 247
  of pepper, 114
  of silk, 36, 37, 132
  during Singhāsari period, 131
  and Śrivijaya as entrepôt, 5, 31, 36
  and Sumatra, 247
  of textiles, 16, 18, 26, 28, 31, 214n6
trade beads, 248
trade routes, 3, **4**
trader terminology, in *sīma* charters, 26
traders, 26
Trailokya-Vijaya, **92**, 93
transculturation, 118–19
Transition style, 14, 201, 208–9, 210–11
Treasure Room, MNI, 263
"tree of life" motif. *See tumpal*
trefoil patterns, 115, 141, 178, 187, 202
triangle patterns, 115, 136, 184, 256
tribhaṅga, 202
Tribhuwana Tunggadewi, 55, 229
  lower limbs detail, **56**
tritik. See bandhani
Tropenmuseum, Śiva, 65, **67**
trousers
  on Caṇḍi Jago figure, **48**, 50
  on Gaṇeśa, 70, 74, **76**
  on pair of Javanese deities, 87, **89**
Trowulan Museum
  Chinese coins, 5
  one-eyed *kāla*, **171**, 173
  unidentified diety, **254**, 256
Tshechu dancer, **244**
Tuhanaru Charter, 279
tulis mas (prada), 25, 54, 205, 247, 278–79
tulis warna, 25, 58, 279
Tumapĕl, 164
tumpal
  definition, 185, 276, 282n2
  on pair of Javanese deities, 87
  on Prajñāpāramitā, 36, 184–85
  on Sita Mañjughosa, Mañjuśrī, 69
  on Trailokya-Vijaya, 93

U

udharabhanda (stomach band), 87, 105, 111, 166, 202
Umā, 106–7, **107**
unidentified diety, in Trowulan Museum, **254**, 256
unidentified goddess, at Caṇḍi Singosari,

191–92, **191**, 278
  detail of leg and drawing of pattern, **192**
upavīta
  on ascetics, 50
  definition, 14
  in the form of a snake, 97, 153, 174
ūrṇā, 98
uttarīya (sash), 281

V

vāhana, 193, 194, **195**, 196
vajra patterns, 9, 87, **88**, 94–95, 242
Vajradharma Lokeśvara, 119
Vajravārāhī, 237
Vajrayāna, 7
Van Es, L.J.C., 264
varadamudrā, 256
vegetal patterns, 40, 136, 145, 230
vesica piscis, 279
vesicae patterns
  on batik wall hanging, **235**
  on Dikpāla, **193**
  on Durgā Mahiṣāsuramardinī, **202**
  on Mahākāla, **161**
  on Pārvatī, **231**
  on Prajñāpāramitā, 189, **190**
  on Śiva Mahadeva, **238**
Vihara Buddhayana
  Nairṛti, 194–95, **195**
  Nairṛti, textile pattern, **39**
Vikramaśīla, 11, 79
Viṣṇu
  on Harihara plaque, 105, **106**
  monarchs as incarnations of, 7
  in Museum Nasional Indonesia, 79, **80**
  in 's-Gravenzande Store, 103, **104**
Visnuvardhana, 141, 176
viśvajra, 95
vlah, 25–26
Volkenkunde, 1, **152**, **157**, 263
  Avalokitéśvara, 98, **99**
  Brahmā, 196, **197**
  Brahmā, *sinjang* detail, **198**
  Durgā Mahiṣāsuramardinī, 42, 151–54; drawing of upper body, **153**; jacket pattern, **153**; lower leg detail and pattern, **155**; short cloth and over sash detail and patterns, **155**; *sinjang* detail, **41**
  Gaṇeśa, 165–66, **166**; trouser detail and drawing, **167**; upper leg garment detail and drawing, **168**
  Nandīśvara, 41, 42, 156; drawing of jacket and detail of pattern, **157**; jacket detail, **40**; upper body detail, **13**, **157**
  Prajñāpāramitā, **85**

W

Wagner, Frits A.
  on imported cloths, 276
  on *kawung*, 279
Wales, Horace Geoffrey Quaritch, on pre-Indianized cultural resurgence, 223
wali-sanga, 30
Wang Duyguan, 5
wayang kulit, 49, 239
Wayang Wong dancers, **52**
wdihan, 25
weavers, 42
weaving, 26, 33, 35, 137, 144
Wilhelmina, Queen, 264
wnang, 25
Wolters, Oliver William
  on foreign influences, 29–30
  on leadership qualities, 245–46
  on Śrivijaya, 215n22
  theory of "localization" of, 43, 118
Woodward, Hiram
  on Caṇḍi Sewu pattern, 41
  on fabrics in stone, 252
Works of Art from Southeast Asia (Deshpande), 264
World War II, 264
Woven Cargoes (Guy), 280
wulu-wulu, 22
wungkudu, 27

Y

yaksha, 111
Yaldiz, Marianne, on design influences, 147
Yama, 243
Yijing, visit to Śrivijaya, 16
yu, 25
Yuan dynasty, trade, 6
Yuán Shī, 15

Z

Zhao Rugua, 3
Zhufanzhi (Zhao Rugua)
  on gold, 280
  on textiles, 3, 34, 132, 178, 259
  on trade, 5, 29, 178, 211
zigzag patterns, **92**, 93
Zoetmulder, Petrus, 22, 174
zoomorphic figures, 109–11, 148

About the Author and Illustrator

Lesley Pullen is an art historian with a focus on medieval South and Southeast Asian material cultures. She completed at SOAS University of London a Postgraduate Diploma in Asian Art in 1998, a Taught Masters in 2008, and a Doctorate in 2017 with a thesis titled "Representation of Textiles on Classical Javanese Sculpture". Her thesis addressed the repeat patterns evident on certain Hindu-Buddhist figurative sculptures from Java, Indonesia in the eighth to fifteenth centuries. Following her doctorate, Lesley was appointed a SOAS Post-Doctoral Research Associate. Her teaching record at SOAS includes tutor of the Southeast Asian Art module of the Postgraduate Diploma programme from 2009 to 2015. Lesley is also tutor of the Southeast Asian Art module for the Victoria & Albert Museum Arts of Asia year course since 2015. She has published articles reflecting her doctoral research in a number of peer-reviewed journals.

Yiran Huang is a freelance illustrator and a lecturer of Visual Communication at the College of Art and Design, Shenzhen University, China. Yiran studies illustration, pattern design and narrative image. Her research concerns storytelling, *maṇḍala* drawing and art therapy. She has a strong interest in traditional pattern design, which started with her first bachelor's degree at Guangzhou Academy of Fine Arts in Decorative Art and Design. She received her basic education in Chinese traditional art and craft at Guangzhou, and studied for her BA (Hons) Illustration course at Camberwell College of Arts, University of the Arts, London.

Yiran met Lesley and started working with her on her doctoral thesis in April 2014 when she was an MA student at the School of Design, Royal College of Art, London. She claims joining Lesley's project was enormously gratifying as it enabled her to use her line drawing skills to analyse the textile patterns on each sculpture, each with a different historical background. Yiran gained significant experience and enjoyment working on this project with Lesley.

www.ingramcontent.com/pod-product-compliance
Lightning Source LLC
Chambersburg PA
CBHW080534300426
44111CB00017B/2724